Choosing Normative Concepts

Choosing Normative Concepts

Matti Eklund

OXFORD
UNIVERSITY PRESS

OXFORD
UNIVERSITY PRESS

Great Clarendon Street, Oxford, OX2 6DP,
United Kingdom

Oxford University Press is a department of the University of Oxford.
It furthers the University's objective of excellence in research, scholarship,
and education by publishing worldwide. Oxford is a registered trade mark of
Oxford University Press in the UK and in certain other countries

Published in the United States of America by Oxford University Press
198 Madison Avenue, New York, NY 10016, United States of America

British Library Cataloguing in Publication Data
Data available

Library of Congress Control Number: 2017934724

ISBN 978–0–19–871782–9

For Helga, Silja, and Kári

Preface

In normative thought and talk, we employ certain concepts—the concepts of goodness, rightness, of what ought to be, etc.—and we talk of certain properties, the properties of being good, being right, being what ought to be the case, etc. But these concepts and properties are only some of the possible concepts and properties that normative thought and talk could employ and be about. (In fact, there arguably is considerable *actual* variation. But it is enough for my purposes that such variation is possible. So I will not be concerned with the empirical question of what variation there is.) This immediately raises some questions.

What if some other concepts than the ones we actually use are the ones we should employ when deciding how to act? Maybe when deciding whether to perform a particular action, I should be guided not by considerations about what I ought to do, but about what I ought* to do, where "ought*" expresses some alternative normative concept.

Now, there is an obvious problem with how this issue is stated. The issue is stated using "should"—the actual "should." And this is problematic. For doesn't use of our concepts in some sense beg the question in favor of them, and stand in the way of a genuinely objective assessment of the situation? Perhaps if instead we asked which considerations we should* be guided by, we would arrive at a different answer. And in fact there are principled problems regarding how the supposed question at issue about what concepts to employ should be framed. But this does not immediately mean that there is not a question there. If there are alternative frameworks of normative concepts, there seems to be a question of, well, which one to employ. Which framework to employ has consequences for action.

That said, one stance one might adopt regarding this issue, perhaps encouraged by the difficulties in stating the question of which conceptual framework to employ, is that there are facts about what ought to be done, what ought* to be done, what ought** to be done, etc.—and that is that. There is no further question of what concepts are in some supposed neutral sense privileged over others. This might in the end be a reasonable stance. But if one hoped that some ways of valuing or acting were somehow privileged from the point of view of reality itself, it is apt to be disappointing. Suppose that what ought* to be done is some act that we find abhorrent. Surely there is a temptation to say, at least if one is attracted to a certain kind of realism, that our negative view on this act is undergirded by the world itself and does not merely represent an in-some-sense arbitrary stance—that one oughtn't to perform this action but one ought* to do it, and there is no further question as to whether it is actions that ought to be performed or actions that ought* to be performed that are privileged.

Issues like the ones just brought up will be the starting point for much of the discussion in the book. I consider the consequences of taking alternative normative concepts into regard for normative realism, for what it is for concepts and properties to be normative, and for the field of metaethics as a whole.

Metaethics as it is currently practiced tends to be very much concerned with how our actual expressions and concepts work. One may well worry that this investigation is in a certain way parochial: some way or other it is a historical accident that we have the expressions and concepts that we do. Lifting one's gaze, one finds that there are lots of other questions to ask.

I have thought about the issues off and on for more than ten years now, starting off by thinking about Marx's puzzling remarks about justice and morality, and by thinking about what seems unsatisfying about popular forms of naturalistic realism. But it is only during the past few years that I have come to see it as a book project, and the focus of my thinking has undergone significant changes through these years. I now barely mention Marx at all. And I have come to see that my concerns about realism generalize far beyond contemporary naturalistic realism.

I do not think of myself as a systematic philosopher, or as a philosopher with an agenda. And there are precious few categorical theses in this book. I am more concerned to trace connections, argue for conditional claims of the kind *if you want to defend this sort of position then you must hold...*, and highlight possible views otherwise easily overlooked. That said, I have been struck myself by the thematic connections between the present work and earlier work I have done on metaontology and on the liar and sorites paradoxes. My work on metaontology concerns the fate of the claim that there are different concepts of existence, none of which is privileged. This is exactly parallel to a view on normative concepts that rears its head repeatedly throughout the book. My work on the liar and sorites paradoxes has largely centered on defense of the view that these paradoxes arise because key concepts used in their formulations—semantic concepts and vague concepts, respectively—are inconsistent. When we are led down the path to absurdity by the paradoxical reasoning, we just rely on our competence with the concepts involved. Much of my thinking about normative concepts revolves around the idea that normative concepts, including central ones like the concept of right and the concept of good, may in some ways be defective or at any rate not ideal for the purposes to which they are put.

Chapter 2 is a much revised version of my article "Alternative Normative Concepts" (*Analytic Philosophy* 53, 2012). Chapters 4 and 5 are revised versions of material originally published as the article "Evaluative Language and Evaluative Reality" (in Simon Kirchin (ed.) *Thick Concepts*, Oxford University Press, 2013). Chapter 9 incorporates revised versions of material published in "What are Thick Concepts?" (*Canadian Journal of Philosophy* 41, 2011) and "Review Essay: Thickness and Evaluation" (critical notice of Pekka Väyrynen's *The Lewd, the Rude, and the Nasty, Journal of Moral Philosophy*, 2016). Related material has also been published in Swedish, in the article "Förkastliga värdebegrepp och Karl Marx antimoralism" (*Filosofisk tidskrift*, 2009).

Given how long I have worked on this, and in how many places I have presented related material, there are many people to thank. Apologies in advance to anyone I happen to omit. Among those I owe thanks for helpful feedback, whether through conversations or written feedback on the manuscript or parts of it, are Andrew Alwood, Annika Boeddeling, Nate Bulthuis, Alexi Burgess, Krister Bykvist, Chris Cowie, Tom Dougherty, Billy Dunaway, Eric Epstein, Daniel Fogal, Nils Franzén, Anandi Hattiangadi, Jens Johansson, Dan Korman, David Kovacs, Brent Kyle, David Liebesman, Øystein Linnebo, Songqing Liu, Tristram McPherson, Victor Moberger, Jonas Olson, Giulia Pravato, Agustín Rayo, Andrew Reisner, Olle Risberg, Debbie Roberts (who also gave useful feedback as a commentator when I gave part of this material as a talk), Eric Rowe, Henrik Rydéhn, Bernhard Salow, Kevin Scharp, Bart Streumer, Folke Tersman, Pekka Väyrynen, and Tobias Wilsch. Reading groups at Cambridge University, Stockholm University, and Uppsala University have worked through parts of the material and special thanks is due to members of these reading groups. Material directly related to the book has been presented at Ca' Foscari University of Venice, Central European University, Cornell University, the University of Helsinki, the University of Leeds, the University of Oslo, the University of St Andrews, Stockholm University, Uppsala University, Åbo Akademi, and a workshop at the Inter University Centre in Dubrovnik. Work on this book has been funded by a generous grant from Vetenskapsrådet (the Swedish Research Council), for the project *Varieties of Normativity*.

The book is dedicated, with love, to my wife Helga and to my children, Silja and Kári.

Contents

1

Ardent Realism

One issue that has animated much metanormative discussion concerns whether, so to speak, reality itself favors certain ways of valuing and acting, or whether reality does not have a view on this. Often "realists" have favored the first sort of view and "antirealists" the latter. What the realist in question holds is that certain ways of going about things have objective backing; and others are objectively disfavored.

There are different motivations for being a "realist." What I have presented is just one natural sort of motivation, the one stemming from a desire to defend what may be called the objective authority of normativity.[1] (Not to be confused with the specific question about the authority of *morality*. That question concerns whether morality engenders reasons and genuine oughts. What I am concerned with is the status of supposed reasons-facts and supposed ought-facts to begin with.)

Let me illustrate this type of motivation by using the (tired but useful) device of a certain kind of paradigmatic *bad guy* (henceforth: Bad Guy). If you are a realist of the kind I want to consider, you want to say that Bad Guy—someone who does bad things and is motivated by bad desires—is somehow objectively out of sync with how to conduct one's life: in no way are our differences with Bad Guy *merely* a disagreement in taste, or a matter of having different desires. Introducing a label, you are an *ardent realist* if you are a realist and this is part of your motivation. You think any acceptable normative realism should deliver the result that your difference with Bad Guy comes out as something more than a mere disagreement in taste. You think any acceptable normative realism should deliver the result that there is something important that one of you (presumably you) objectively gets right and the other (presumably Bad Guy) objectively gets wrong. There are some facts that Bad Guy fails to properly appreciate.

I will not attempt to characterize ardent realism more precisely, but only rely on remarks like these. The above remarks are somewhat table thumping and impressionistic. Despite this, I believe they suffice well enough for present purposes to indicate what sort of character the ardent realist is supposed to be. What is more, the

---

[1] Here and throughout I will use "normative" *broadly*, to encompass also what is sometimes called evaluative. Sometimes a distinction is drawn between what is normative in the sense of prescriptive or action-guiding, and what is evaluative in the sense of related to approval and disapproval. This may be a reasonable distinction for some purposes, but it will not matter to the purposes at hand.

problems I go on to discuss—regarding exactly what would satisfy the ardent realist—are also problems for how to characterize the outlook more properly, and these problems will occupy center stage in the discussion to follow.

I stress that the character I am talking about is an ardent realist, not a realist simpliciter. The label "realism" is used in importantly different ways in the literature, and I won't spend much effort getting clear on it. But it is common to take it to be sufficient for normative realism that normative statements are apt for mind-independent truth, and that some atomic normative statements also are mind-independently true. When without any qualification I speak of realism, this is the kind of view I will have in mind—sometimes I will speak of this as *broad* realism, to emphasize that this is different from ardent realism. One can, as the discussion will illustrate, be a realist in the sense just characterized without being an ardent realist.

"Ardent realist" is my label, and I will not pause to discuss which theorists in the literature are ardent realists. But I am confident both that many realists are in fact ardent realists, and that even many theorists who are not ardent realists find ardent realism attractive at an intuitive level.

If you are an ardent realist, then you will for obvious reasons be unhappy with traditional antirealist alternatives to realism such as traditional *non-cognitivism* and *error theory*. Traditional non-cognitivism has it that normative sentences express attitudes and not beliefs about facts.[2] Your difference with Bad Guy comes down to a disagreement in attitude. Error theory says that all (atomic) normative statements are untrue.[3] An error theory about the moral or the normative has the consequence that you and Bad Guy are in the same boat in that neither you nor he values things in accordance with the objective values: for there are no objective values. Given the error theorist's view on the world, again the difference between you and Bad Guy is in a sense just a matter of attitude. There are no facts by virtue of which one of you has the right attitudes and one has the wrong attitudes.

Moreover, if you are an ardent realist, you won't be happy with a *quasirealist* view that simply weds deflationism about truth to traditional non-cognitivism.[4] The non-cognitivist view says, in brief, that normative judgments function to express attitudes, and, for example, it is semantically appropriate for you to say that something is right just in case you approve of this something. Deflationism about truth says that "P" and "it is true that P" are in some strong sense equivalent, so that, for example, whenever it is semantically appropriate for you to utter declarative sentence "P," it is equally appropriate for you to utter "It is true that P." A quasirealist view, combining both, allows one to say that it is true that such-and-such things are bad whenever one has the right attitude, and that when Bad Guy believes something to the contrary, he believes something false. But it is clear that Bad Guy can with equal propriety say the

---

[2] For some main defenses of non-cognitivism, see Ayer (1936), Blackburn (1993, 1998), Gibbard (1990, 2003), Hare (1952), and Stevenson (1944).

[3] See Mackie (1977), and also Olson (2014).   [4] See especially Blackburn (1993).

corresponding things about us. Given his attitudes, it is semantically appropriate for him to assert that (say) torturing babies for fun is right, and it is then, on the quasirealist view, equally appropriate for him to assert that it is true that torturing babies for fun is right; and there are no genuine facts about which he is mistaken.[5]

If you are an ardent realist, you should also find various forms of *relativism* unsatisfactory, where relativism is the view that normative propositions cannot be absolutely true but are only true relative to a judge or a standard. You don't want merely to say that your normative views are the right ones relative to you or your framework and Bad Guy's are the right ones relative to him or his framework. You want to say that Bad Guy is mistaken, full stop.

Of course, relativism is consistent with there being some kind of Bad Guy that gets some things wrong. Maybe Bad Guy shares fundamental values with you even though there are particular normative claims about which he is tragically wrong. A relativist can say about this Bad Guy that his views on these particular matters are not the right ones even relative to his framework. A friend of relativism might say, in an attempt to defuse an ardent realist's concerns, that actual disagreements with Bad Guys often or always are like this. But regardless of whether actual disagreements are like this, an ardent realist will want to say that even a Bad Guy whose values are consistently and fundamentally different from ours in some way gets things objectively wrong. Similar remarks apply to other kinds of views I consider in this chapter and later in the book where I refer to Bad Guy. The views might allow that some, many, or even all actual Bad Guys get something objectively wrong, but the ardent realist's concern will remain so long as some possible Bad Guys are let off the hook. I will let context indicate what sort of Bad Guy I focus on in individual cases.

What I have said so far about what you would and should think if you are an ardent realist should, I believe, be totally unsurprising. And I believe that also the next few things I will go on to say are unsurprising. But I will go on to consider what exactly would and should satisfy the ardent realist's demands—and it is then that things get more interesting.

Some philosophers are *Humeans* about reasons. A Humean about reasons thinks that for something to be a reason for an agent, this must be explained by some psychological state of the agent, such as what the agent desires. For present purposes let us consider a simple Humean view according to which an agent has a reason to ϕ only if ϕ-ing would help satisfy one of the agent's desires. If you are an ardent realist, you may be unhappy with this Humean view, for the Humean view has the consequence that if Bad Guy's desires are sufficiently warped, Bad Guy indeed has no reason to do what we would regard as the right thing. Reality in and of itself does not, given the Humean view, favor our way of valuing, unless there are some desires such

---

[5] Quasirealism, incidentally, is one type of view that problematizes the general characterization of realism offered above. For the quasirealist seems to satisfy the characterization without being a genuine realist. But again, I won't be much concerned about "realism."

that an agent would necessarily have to have these desires, for what reasons there are depends on what desires agents happen to have. (There is more to say about this. I am more concerned to give the flavor of what my ardent realist can be expected to hold than to defend any particular claim about ardent realism and the Humean view on reasons.)

Consider next the view that although it is objectively true that doing so-and-so is *morally* right and it is objectively the case that so-and-so *morally* ought to be done, in no way is there such a thing as an *all-things-considered ought*. Various oughts that in different ways are relativized to different ends or standards are all there are. There's what one morally ought to do, what one prudentially ought to do, and what one ought to do to promote such-and-such a goal, etc., *and that's it*. And when one asks "I ought to φ relative to R but to ψ relative to R*, but what *ought* I to do?", that last, italicized "ought" is itself, insofar as it has any meaning at all, to be understood as somehow implicitly relativized; context supplies a relevant parameter. You may well be unhappy also with this view, if you are an ardent realist. For given this view, Bad Guy can respond to the fact that he doesn't do what he morally ought to do by noting that what he does is what he ought to do to further some cause of his—and there is nothing that in any way privileges the moral ought over his ought.

When talking about what you would and should hold if you are an ardent realist, I am not talking about what one would and should hold simpliciter. Perhaps there is no otherwise defensible way of making good on the ardent realist's motivation. Perhaps, some way or other, our differences with Bad Guy always in some way do come down to a mere disagreement in attitude. Perhaps one of the alternative views mentioned is the best one. But what I am primarily concerned with is not the defensibility of realism motivated in the way indicated, but with the question of what exactly would satisfy the relevant sort of realist. It is here that there are some good and instructive questions to ask.

Suppose that normative discourse doesn't function the way the non-cognitivist or error theorist or relativist believes. Suppose, that is, that normative discourse is truth-apt (and not merely in a deflationary sense but in the sense of truth as correspondence[6]), that some atomic normative sentences are true, and that the truth of normative statements is mind-independent. Suppose, moreover, as against the Humean view on reasons, that it is true that Bad Guy has reason to (say) treat all people as equals, even if doing so furthers no desire of his. Suppose too that in addition to relativized ought-facts, there are facts about what plainly, or all things considered, ought to be done. Generally, there are many debates that come up in the

---

[6] I don't wish to suggest that ardent realism is incompatible with deflationary truth. Assuming truth to be correspondence simply goes with granting the ardent realist everything that tends to be at issue in metaethical debates over realism. (Above I talked about a quasirealist view that simply weds deflationism to traditional expressivism. That view should not satisfy the ardent realist. But that does not mean that the ardent realist cannot be a deflationist.)

literature, such that it is natural to think that the ardent realist's sympathies would have to lie on one side or the other. Let us stipulate that in each case the side the ardent realist's sympathies can be expected to be on actually does win (without in any case taking a stand on whether the ardent realist actually needs to be committed one way or another in all these cases). Would this be sufficient for the ardent realist?

Not without further ado. And this is where things start getting interesting—and more controversial. What follows is aimed to describe my idea in general terms. I will produce more proper arguments pertaining to this in Chapters 2 and 3.

Suppose that all the above is true, but it is true because, for example, *analytic descriptivism* is true: all normative expressions are systematically analytically equivalent to descriptive expressions. For example, some sentences of the form "S has reason to φ, independently of her desires and interests" may be true, but because "has reason to" is analyzable in suitable descriptive terms. It expresses a relation between agents and actions that holds independently of the agent's desires and interests.

But suppose then further that Bad Guy speaks a different language from us, and employs different normative concepts. And he uses, for action-guiding purposes, expressions that are not analytically equivalent to the descriptive expressions that our corresponding expressions are equivalent to, but are instead analytically equivalent to other descriptive expressions. Where what our "good" and "ought" are equivalent to are—say—expressions about happiness-maximization, his "good" and "ought" are equivalent to something that strikes us as more sinister. We can still say that Bad Guy doesn't do what he all-things-considered ought to do or has reason to do. But using his language, Bad Guy can say the corresponding things about us. Using his counterpart of "wrong"—the word in his vocabulary that has the role for him that "wrong" has for us—he can say that we do "wrong" things. And he is as correct in his verdict about us as we are in our verdict about him. The same would go for all other normative vocabulary, including, for example, "reason." Bad Guy can be envisaged as having his counterpart notion of "reason." Despite all the realist trappings that our normative language is supposed to have, there may still for all that has been said be *parity* between us and Bad Guy that the ardent realist would want to avoid. For all that has been said, Bad Guy is not objectively mistaken about anything; he just does not employ our notion of reason or our notion of what ought to be done but instead employs alternative normative notions. To be sure, he does things that are "wrong," in our sense, but equally, we do things that are "wrong*" in his sense. (I will keep using asterisks to indicate alternative normative notions.) He may not pay attention to things he "ought to pay attention to," but equally, we may not pay attention to what we "ought* to pay attention to." For all that is said, there is nothing that undergirds our stance of favoring our way of doing things—e.g. seeking to do what is right—over Bad Guy's way of doing things—e.g. seeking instead to do what is right*. We can say that it is *right* to seek to do what is right; but Bad Guy can equally congratulate himself by saying that it is *right** to seek to do what is right*. This should trouble the ardent realist, who wants reality to undergird some ways of valuing over others.

If what I have said above about the situation is not immediately persuasive, let me approach this sort of scenario from another perspective. Still operating under the assumption of analytic descriptivism, suppose we study a foreign language and find that the words of that language that correspond in normative role to our "right," "wrong," etc. are systematically analytically equivalent to different purely descriptive expressions, and suppose further that this community's words are not coextensive with our corresponding normative words. Without further ado, this hardly puts any pressure on *us* to think that *we* should act and think differently. But by analogy, why would *Bad Guy* feel any pressure to change his ways when confronted with how we reason about how we "should" act and think?

I am putting the point in epistemic terms, as concerning what puts pressure on someone to act and think differently. But the point is metaphysical: what could possibly be at issue between us and Bad Guy? The ardent realist wants to find an objective difference. We are better than him. *Really*. But what might that difference consist in? Sure, we can say that we do the "right" things and he does "wrong" things. But Bad Guy can say the corresponding thing about us. Is there anything that warrants our concern for rightness and goodness over rightness* and goodness*?

When giving voice to these concerns I am running up against inexpressibility problems. How can we even express, using our conceptual resources, the sorts of doubts I am gesturing toward? We *may in fact be* "better" than Bad Guy, in the sense of *our* "better," even if he is "better*" than us. We may have reason to do things our way rather than his, in the sense of our "reason," even though he has reason* to do things his way rather than ours. Philosophers of a certain bent of mind may wish to use these inexpressibility problems to dismiss the problem. Call dismissing the problem on this ground *the complacent reaction*. Real though the inexpressibility problems may be, I think that this reaction is clearly unwarranted. Consider the matter from a third-party perspective. Imagine there are two linguistic communities. Members of one community use "good1," "right1," etc.; members of another use "good2," "right2," etc. After initially not having been in contact, the communities come into contact and start interacting. The complacent reaction is to stick with the normative concepts one has got. Members of the first community can think they are "better1" than the members of the second; members of the second can think they are "better2" than the members of the first. From the outside it is clear that there may well be parity despite how members of each community can pat themselves on the back: there may be nothing objectively favoring one set of normative concepts over another. A similar reaction may be appropriate when it comes to us: we may be one of the communities. (None of this *gets around* the inexpressibility problem.)

"Ardent realism" is, again to stress, my label. Theorists do not call themselves ardent realists. I will not enter into any discussion about which normative theorists actually deserve the label ardent realist—such a discussion would only distract from the general points I am concerned to make. But I do think that ardent realist intuitions and motivations are widely shared: that many would think that in the situation just described, where analytic descriptivism is true but Bad Guy simply has different normative concepts, there still is some way in which Bad Guy somehow gets things wrong—there is something *off* about his stance toward reality.

The truth of analytic descriptivism of the kind described would not be sufficient for the purposes of the ardent realist. Analytic descriptivism of this kind could be true while there is nothing about the world itself that favors our way of going about things over Bad Guy's. Even if our normative terms are analytically equivalent to such-and-such descriptions, there could easily be other terms of the kind indicated, equivalent to other descriptions. And for all that analytic descriptivism itself yields, there is, or can well be, something arbitrary about what descriptions the normative terms one employs are equivalent to.

Nothing discussed so far—objective truth of some atomic normative statements, there being categorical reasons, there being an all-things-considered ought, etc.— goes to what would be sufficient for the truth of ardent realism. This is illustrated by the example of analytic descriptivism. All this serves to raise the question: what would actually be sufficient for ardent realism?

It is not sufficient simply to add that analytic descriptivism is false. Suppose instead that some causal theory of reference-determination of the kind that since the work of Kripke and Putnam is popular at least in the case of natural kind terms and ordinary proper names is true of normative terms.[7] Normative terms refer to what their use is appropriately causally linked to, in the way that natural kind terms are regularly said to refer to what their use is appropriately causally linked to. The problem remains. Even if all our normative terms have their reference determined to be such-and-such worldly items, Bad Guy's corresponding terms are determined to be true of such-and-such *other* worldly items. Although he does not do what he "ought" to do or has "reason" to do, in our sense of "ought" and "reason," it can still be that he does what he "ought" to do or has "reason" to do, in *his* sense of "ought" and "reason." Still there is parity.

Some readers may perhaps suspect that the general lesson of the discussions of analytic descriptivism and the causal theory is that no form of *naturalist* realism is sufficient for the purposes of the ardent realist. These are theories of reference-determination associated with naturalist theories in metaethics, and it may be natural to suspect that what ardent realism requires is that there are properties that somehow differ fundamentally from the ordinary properties found in the natural world.[8] Whichever natural properties our normative terms ascribe,[9] we can imagine a Bad

---

[7] See Kripke (1980) and Putnam (1975) and, for the application to normative expressions, Boyd (1988) and Brink (1989).

[8] See Moore (1903), Shafer-Landau (2003), Dworkin (2011), Enoch (2011), Parfit (2011), and Scanlon (2014).

[9] When careful, I will use "ascribes" for the relation between a predicate and the property it stands for. One reason is that a question I will keep returning to has to do with whether a normative property can be ascribed using a non-normative predicate—and one might think it trivial that one can *refer* to a normative

Guy language where the normative terms ascribe other natural properties—and for all that is shown, there will remain the sort of parity between us and Bad Guy that we sought to avoid. But maybe all that shows is that we need *non-natural* properties to do the job?

The issue of how to characterize the relevant notion of (non-)naturalness is vexed.[10] But very roughly, natural properties are those of the same general kind as the properties countenanced in the sciences; non-natural properties are of a different kind. Needless to say, this brief gloss on the distinction is not extremely helpful. Even unclarity aside, it is doubtful that appeal to non-natural properties by itself can help. Suppose our normative terms ascribe non-natural properties, but Bad Guy's corresponding terms ascribe different properties, perhaps different non-natural properties. For all that is said, there may still be parity of the same kind as before. It still is the case that our normative terms ascribe some properties and his terms ascribe some others. We focus on some properties in our normative deliberations; he focuses on some others in his normative deliberations. For all that has been said, that is all there is to it, even if the properties we ascribe are non-natural. Nothing objectively warrants our way of doing things over Bad Guy's way of doing things. Whereas naturalists in metaethics have devoted considerable attention to the question of how the reference of normative terms is determined, non-naturalists have not focused as much on that issue. A non-naturalist metaphysics of normativity, invoking non-natural normative properties, is fully compatible with each of the theories of reference-determination mentioned thus far, and does nothing to get around the problems mentioned. Analytic descriptivism can be true even given the non-naturalist metaphysics, and what normative expressions are synonymous with may be different for different expressions, and the same problem as before arises. And at least if the non-natural properties can be causally efficacious, the non-naturalist metaphysics is perfectly compatible with a causal theory of reference for normative terms—and as before, the normative expressions of different communities may be appropriately causally linked to different properties.[11] A non-naturalist metaphysics might help get around these problems if, but only if, it is combined with an alternative theory of reference-determination which avoids the problems noted.

So what else might the ardent realist say is sufficient for her view to be vindicated? What we have mentioned already is not sufficient, but might there be some other feature, not mentioned so far, such that if we add this feature we get something sufficient for ardent realism?

---

property using a non-normative expression. (Consider "the referent of 'right'.") Jackson (1998), p. 119fn10, uses this terminology for the same purpose.

[10] See for example Ridge (2014b) for discussion. Already G.E. Moore, who introduced the notion of a non-natural property into the debate, himself admitted that the notion is unclear. See Moore (1942), p. 582.

[11] Oddie (2005) defends a non-naturalist view according to which the non-natural normative properties are causally efficacious.

One suggestion is that the ardent realist should appeal to the distinction some theorists are happy to draw between properties that are *elite* (natural, fundamental, make for genuine similarity ...) and properties that are not elite, and characterize her view as the one that some properties ascribed by some normative predicates are elite.[12] There are many different, non-equivalent characterizations of the sort of feature of properties that I have in mind, and I will use *elite* to mark the independence of what I have to say from any specific conception of eliteness.[13] The idea would be that even if we and Bad Guy ascribe different properties by our normative terms, our way of going about things could be relevantly privileged over his way of going about things for the reason that the properties our terms ascribe are elite. In the end I will reject this suggestion. Briefly, my criticism of the suggestion will be that on any adequately informative and otherwise reasonable conception of being elite, there are counterexamples to the claim that eliteness could supply what is needed: because for all that is said, there can be normative predicates ascribing elite properties that are in no way normatively privileged. (Bad Guy's alternative normative concepts can ascribe elite properties as well: only ones that, intuitively, are not normatively significant in the way Bad Guy takes them to be.) But the suggestion is in the same spirit as that which I find more plausible, and I will also be concerned to, in a more constructive spirit, draw out some of its consequences.

A different suggestion is that the ardent realist should hold that what is at issue between us and Bad Guy is whether it is the property ascribed by *our* "right" that is a *normative property*, or whether it instead is the property that is ascribed by *his* "right" that is a normative property, or neither. The feature we have so far omitted to bring up as required for ardent realism is simply *normativity*. Indeed, this idea might underlie the temptation to think non-naturalism gets around the problem: for it may surreptitiously be assumed that the non-natural properties ascribed by normative predicates would be normative, and natural properties cannot be. Again this is a suggestion I find unsatisfactory. To my mind, the appeal to normativity, even if acceptable as far as it goes, just cannot be the end of it: for it immediately simply prompts the follow-up question of what it is for a property to be normative. As it stands, the appeal to normativity is just a promissory note. And if it is suggested that normativity is a primitive feature of properties, not capable of being further elucidated in independent terms, then questions arise about why having this primitive feature matters. For example, Bad Guy can insist that even if the property ascribed by his notion of what is right does not have this primitive feature of normativity, it is still *normative**—and what privileges normativity over normativity*?

---

[12] For prominent general uses of the notion of eliteness, see Lewis (1983, 1984) and Sider (2011). For different appeals to eliteness in metaethics, see Wasserman (2012), Schoenfield (2016), van Roojen (2006), Dunaway and McPherson (2016), and Edwards (2013).

[13] Lewis (1984) does speak of being "elite" in this connection and some theorists have picked up on this usage, but since this label has been used less often than other labels, it carries less baggage than other labels used in the literature.

Putting things in terms of what Bad Guy can insist can suggest that the issue is dialectical; it may sound as if it concerns what can reasonably convince Bad Guy. But what I am primarily concerned with is a metaphysical question: what could there be about normativity, as opposed to, for example, schmormativity, that makes it special in the requisite way?

Even if, for the reasons given, I find the appeal to normativity, or primitive normativity, unhelpful, this suggestion, like the one of appealing to eliteness, has some important structural features in common with what I will eventually favor, and I will occasionally be concerned with drawing out consequences of the view.

There are also other possible ways around the problem for the ardent realist. In Chapter 2, the—admittedly very radical—possibility that what is at stake between us and Bad Guy simply is *ineffable* will come up. But rather than go through further suggestions I think we in the end have reason to reject, let me turn to the positive suggestion I am the most optimistic about.

The source of the problem that I have been concerned with is that it can be that some possible normative terms can have their reference determined in such a way that what the terms ascribe is not anything one really ought to focus on in normative thought. The reason why what we have focused on is not actually sufficient for ardent realism is that the suppositions made have been compatible with normative terms having their reference determined in such a way that what they ascribe is normatively irrelevant. Once the problem is stated this way, the outline of a possible solution would seem to have to be this: what would suffice for ardent realism would have to involve normative expressions getting their reference determined in the right sort of way. This is just an outline, for nothing is as yet said about what the right way might be.

Here is what I more specifically would suggest on the ardent realist's behalf. The discussion of this suggestion will be a major theme in this book. If we spot ourselves the (perhaps objectionably obscure? I will keep getting back to this) notion of the *normative role* of a predicate or concept—the action-guiding role, perhaps motivational role, which is associated with the predicate or concept and is that by virtue of which the predicate or concept counts as normative—one can propose the view that normative role can be *reference-determining*, in such a way that two predicates or concepts conventionally associated with the same normative role are thereby determined to have the same reference. Let us say that predicates or concepts whose reference is determined by the normative roles that they are associated with are *referentially normative*, and they are *non-defectively* so if they are not empty, or wildly semantically indeterminate, or in some other way only have some kind of trivial extension.[14] If some possible central normative predicates and concepts are non-defectively referentially normative, then the sorts of scenarios I have described in the last few paragraphs, starting with the discussion of analytic descriptivism,

---

[14] This characterization of non-defectiveness is rough and disjunctive. There may for all I say here be other relevant ways in which a term may be defective.

cannot arise with respect to them.[15] (Note that with "referentially normative" understood this way, it is an open question whether all, or even any, *normative* predicates are *referentially normative*.)

The idea is that something about properties picked out by non-defective referentially normative predicates renders them apt to be picked out by these predicates. Compare the case of logic. It is standardly held that logical expressions are characterized by their *conceptual roles*, which in turn are given by the associated inference rules.[16] A logical expression characterized by some associated inference rules has as its semantic value an operation that makes the inference rules correct. Consider conjunction. The inference rules are *from p, q to infer p&q*, and *from p&q to infer p and q*, respectively. The operation that "&" is determined to stand for, on the standard story, is such as to validate these inferences. The operation is apt to be picked out by an expression with this role. Mutatis mutandis—the present suggestion on the ardent realist's behalf is—for normative concepts. The difference is just that for the normative concepts, the roles are distinctly normative, and concern the roles of concepts in practical reasoning.

Return to Bad Guy. The idea is that if normative role can determine reference as suggested, then we have ruled out the situation where Bad Guy's normative terms simply refer to different things and there is parity between us and Bad Guy. If Bad Guy's terms have the same normative roles as ours, then they cannot fail to corefer with our terms. And if Bad Guy's terms don't have the same normative roles as ours, then in no way, shape, or form does he address the questions about what to do that we ask. Under the assumption of, e.g., analytical descriptivism, a Bad Guy like the one there discussed seems relevant: he could have terms that are normative in the way that ours are, while still his terms are true of things different from what our terms are true of. But—the guiding thought is—given referential normativity, if normative role determines reference then if Bad Guy's terms have the same normative role as ours, his terms will be coextensional with ours; and if his terms do not have the same normative role as ours, then he does not address the same normative issue that we address.

I think it is natural for the ardent realist to appeal to the idea of non-defective referentially normative predicates; indeed, I think she has no other reasonable choice

---

[15] Two remarks by way of clarification: (a) A note on the talk of "possible" predicates, here and later in the discussion. Suppose there is no actually used non-defective, for example non-empty, predicate true of exactly the Fs. What does it take for there to be a non-defective *possible* predicate true of exactly Fs? One may think there is such a predicate so long as Fs exist in some possible world: just take a predicate in that world true of exactly Fs. However, that is not how I use talk of possible predicates. In the relevant sense, for there to be a possible predicate true of exactly Fs, there must be Fs. It must be possible for there to be such a representational device *given how the world is in other ways*. One way to avoid the complications here is to think of predicates and other linguistic expressions as abstract entities existing independently of being used. Given that conception, one can simply strike the talk of what is "possible." (b) There are many different kinds of normative concepts. As I will discuss properly only later, it is the referential normativity of suitably "thin" concepts that is of importance.

[16] See e.g. Prawitz (1979), Harman (1986), and Peacocke (1987).

but to appeal to this idea. Later in the discussion I will attempt to be more careful regarding this notion of referential normativity. I will also problematize, in Chapter 3, whether this appeal to referential normativity actually does suffice for the ardent realist's purposes.

What I have just presented is what I think is the only possibly viable way out for the ardent realist. Saying that this is the only possibly viable way out is not to say that I in the end favor this. Some problems regarding the viability of this route will be prominently discussed later, primarily in Chapter 3. But let me for now emphasize some consequences of this suggestion on the ardent realist's behalf.

One consequence is that the possibility of a new kind of normative skepticism opens up. Even if I have found that our normative predicates are objectively true of some things, I can wonder: are these normative predicates referentially normative? If they are not referentially normative, then what I have found is less significant than I might otherwise have taken it to be. Similarly, we get new kinds of normative skepticism if we adopt the strategy of appealing to eliteness, or if we adopt the strategy of appealing to normativity of properties. Maybe the properties our normative predicates ascribe are not elite? Maybe the properties our normative predicates ascribe are not among the normative ones?

I will let considerations about ardent realism animate much of the discussion. But just as one can be a broad realist without being an ardent realist, one can in principle embrace certain aspects of the ardency of ardent realism without being a realist. One can wish to say that there is something *objective* that privileges us over Bad Guy without this having the sort of metaphysical explanation that a realist would advert to. One can, for example, adopt the expressivist's view on normative thought and language but still seek to preserve normative objectivity. A reasonable question to ask is whether problems similar to those I present for the ardent realist arise also for the, so to speak, ardent expressivist. Briefly, I think the answer is yes. But consideration of this sort of issue will only come up in Chapter 8. Until then all discussion will take place in a broadly realist setting.

I have just introduced at some length one of the themes with which I will be concerned in this book. Attention to the possibility of alternative normative concepts presents problems that tend to get unnoticed. Even if the character I called the ardent realist is spotted victory in every even potentially relevant specific debate found in the present literature, some Bad Guy can use an alternative set of normative concepts, and nothing that has been said serves to avoid the conclusion that there is parity between us and this Bad Guy. I also briefly indicated what I think is the best way around the problem for ardent realism that this presents.

Let me now present two other themes that will come up. I will be briefer about them.

First, there is the question of what it is for there to be normative properties and facts as opposed to merely normative linguistic and conceptual representations. Distinguish between the question of what it is for *representations of the world* (words and sentences, concepts and contents) to be normative, and what it is for the kinds of *things in the world we represent* using normative language and thought (e.g. properties, facts) to be normative. Once this distinction is clearly drawn, one can start to worry about how well normative representations and normativity in the world line up. For example, there is the possibility that while we of course talk about the world in normative ways, the world itself is not normative. While the word "right" is normative and stands for a property, rightness, that property is not normative. Compare how many people find it natural to talk about pejoratives, such as, for example, racial slurs. There are pejorative expressions and some of them stand for properties, but there are no *pejorative properties*. (Indeed, the very locution "pejorative property" sounds odd: it sounds like a category mistake.) Might the normative be like the pejorative in that regard? And there are, I think, natural connections to the discussion of ardent realism with which I began. One can think that what the ardent realist seeks, and is not immediately afforded by, e.g., analytical descriptivism, is normativity in the world. What I will eventually suggest (Chapter 5) is that the normative properties are exactly the ones that can be ascribed by referentially normative predicates.

Second, let *ideological conservativeness* in normative theorizing be the attitude of simply employing and studying the normative concepts we find ourselves with, and not in any way adopting a critical stance toward the question of whether these are indeed appropriate concepts for normative theory. I doubt that anyone is completely ideologically conservative. For example, I don't think many philosophers would cheerfully reason as follows:

If someone satisfies descriptive conditions so-and-so, then she is behaving *sluttily*—this is revealed by my philosophical analysis of "slutty" (or sluttiness)—and since *slutty* is a negative normative concept, any behavior which is slutty is bad, so what satisfies descriptive conditions so-and-so is bad.

It is recognized, more or less explicitly, that some normative concepts, like the concept *slutty*, are somehow or other *objectionable* concepts, and one does not reasonably arrive at normative conclusions by studying them or the properties they stand for in this straightforward way. However, I do think that some degree of ideological conservativeness still is rather widespread. For example, it is natural for many to reason as follows: By my philosophical analysis of justice, a society that satisfies such-and-such conditions is just, and since *justice* is a positive normative concept, it follows that we should favor a society that satisfies these conditions. But might it not be that analogously to how *slutty* is objectionable, *justice* is objectionable? There are three different theoretical questions suggested by these considerations. First, I have spoken intuitively about concepts being objectionable, but what exactly should we take objectionableness to be? The question is all the more pressing since some may wish to take issue with a feature of how I talked about the example of *slutty*. My description of the example presupposed that *slutty* indeed is true of some behaviors (the ones fitting the conception associated with the concept), despite there being something objectionable about the normative views with which it is associated. Some might take issue with this description, saying that the correct account is rather that nothing falls under the concept *slutty*. Is my preferred description best, or is this alternative view more reasonable? Second, assuming some normative concepts of some kinds can be objectionable, does that go for all kinds of normative concepts, or are only some kinds of normative concepts amenable to this sort of defect? In particular, the natural examples of objectionable concepts are all so-called thick concepts. But can also so-called thin concepts like those expressed by "right" or "ought" (in their most general, thinnest uses) be objectionable? Third, what is the proper methodology, if any, for judging which normative concepts are objectionable? If one could presuppose that the thinnest concepts are not objectionable, one could simply use these concepts when framing the relevant questions: one could ask what concepts *ought* to be used, or what concepts are associated with values that *ought* to be embraced. But if one cannot presuppose that—if "ought" itself might reasonably be thought to be a source of trouble—then what can be done?

These questions just brought up, about ideological conservativeness and objectionable concepts, are different from the other themes I will talk about, but there are connections. Our normative concepts appear to present the properties they ascribe as meriting certain kinds of responses. But the properties ascribed may not objectively merit these responses. The possibility of ardent realism being false and there being no normativity in the world is a grand-scale hypothesis on which it is so. Alternatively—and this is where the issue of some concepts being objectionable comes in—one may think that some but not all of our normative concepts are such that the properties they ascribe do not merit the responses they seem presented as meriting. A different sort of possibility, a kind of hybrid version of the two brought up, is that ardent realism is true and there is genuine normativity in the world—but the normative concepts we actually find ourselves with all suffer from some general defect.

To dramatize the possibilities mentioned, it may be useful to consider what I will call the Tragic community. This Tragic community has normative vocabulary like we do. The members of the Tragic community, perhaps unlike us, are deeply concerned to do what is "right" and "good," in their sense. And the members of the Tragic community are good at coming to know what is "right" and "good," in their sense. But what is *tragic* about the Tragic community is that their "right" and "good" do not ascribe normative properties; the efforts of the members of this community are to this extent misdirected. Considering the possibility of this Tragic community, one can ask: might we be Tragic? How can we know? To stress, this is not run-of-the-mill normative skepticism about whether we can know what is right and good. We might know very well what is right and good, but still wonder whether the properties of being right and good—the properties ascribed by our "right" and "good"—are normative.

The Tragic community can be Tragic for different reasons. It may be Tragic because although there are properties objectively meriting the attention they bestow upon some properties, they don't focus their attention on those properties but on others. Or it may be Tragic because there are no properties objectively meriting this kind of attention.

Calling the community in question "Tragic" is of course contentious. It can be objected, and perhaps reasonably so, that our concerns don't need the sort of metaphysical backing that calling the predicament of these communities "Tragic" suggests. But from an ardent realist's point of view, the predicament really is tragic.

Given my positive suggestion on the ardent realist's behalf, what matters is what possible expressions there can be, not how our actual expressions work. According to the suggestion presented, ardent realism escapes the threat so long as some possible normative expressions are referentially normative. The suggestion is in accordance with a general metaphilosophical perspective I find attractive. Whereas philosophers often have been concerned to understand our actual expressions and concepts, and what these expressions and concepts stand for, I think we should be more concerned with the space of possible expressions and concepts pertaining to a given subject, and with questions about what the most apt expressions and concepts are. The latter is what some theorists talk about under the heading of *conceptual engineering*, or *conceptual ethics*.[17] I will discuss these metaphilosophical issues in their own right in Chapter 10.

A different, but again related, theme concerns *antimoralism*—or more generally, *antinormativism*. From time to time, philosophers bring up the supposed possibility that one can adopt the view that one can be against what is right, seeing that which "right" stands for as not being of any particular merit. This kind of view may sound self-contradictory, and as just stated perhaps it is: doesn't being right conceptually entail being of some merit? There are, however, different ways that one can make theoretical room for an antimoralist or antinormativist view, and the present discussion will highlight a number of them. For example, one can think that some other possible notion of "right" and not the actual "right" is normatively privileged. In Chapter 7 I will turn to these questions explicitly.

The above summarizes the main themes I will be concerned with. The following will be the structure of the discussion to come.

First, in Chapter 2, I will expound on the kinds of scenarios briefly described here, purportedly possible scenarios where different communities of speakers use normative terms that have the same normative roles but are not coextensive. I describe the sorts of theoretical issues and problems that arise from allowing that these scenarios are indeed possible. The discussion should serve to display what is prima facie attractive about a view that disallows such scenarios—a view that takes normative terms, or some important subset of them, to be referentially normative. (Although the fact that such a view is attractive of course does not mean that it is in the end

---

[17] See Burgess and Plunkett (2013a, 2013b) for an overview.

defensible.) While I believe that the best suggestion on the ardent realist's behalf is the one already introduced, appeal to referential normativity, I am not wedded to this idea actually working out in the end. Chapter 3 will among other things discuss some objections to the idea that ardent realism can be salvaged by appeal to the idea of normative role determining reference. What the present chapter together with the more substantive discussion of Chapters 2 and 3 provide is a discussion of a new kind of challenge to ideas related to normative realism, together with exploration of the best way out and its consequences. The chapters thereafter in different ways discuss various applications, extensions, and comparisons of the ideas brought up. Chapters 4 and 5 are devoted to the general questions of what makes a linguistic expression or concept normative, and of what makes a property or fact normative. In Chapter 6, I continue to bring home the point that some realist views—even ones that don't involve Humeanism about reasons or skepticism about the all-things-considered ought—are not sufficient for the ardent realist. I will do so by considering what I will call *presentationalism*: a view according to which the only normativity there is resides in how properties and facts are presented, and no properties or facts are themselves normative. In Chapter 7, I will relate to the antimoralism and antinormativism. Chapter 8 explores connections to various debates elsewhere in the literature. Chapter 9 focuses on thick normative concepts. Chapter 10 is devoted to broader, metaphilosophical considerations. Chapter 11 contains brief concluding remarks.

It is of course customary in an introduction to spell out exactly what one will argue for in the book. Here I run into trouble, for relatively straightforward claims that I will plainly endorse will be few and far between. However, one claim I endorse is that *ardent realism is true only if there are some possible non-defective referentially normative predicates*. Another claim I happily endorse is that *there are normative properties only if there are some possible non-defective referentially normative predicates*. I will argue for this latter claim in Chapter 5. However, as there are different ways of using locutions like "normative property," debates over that claim are more likely to degenerate into mere verbal disputes. If someone wishes to use "normative property" differently, I will not protest very loudly. What I do think, more cautiously put, is that emphasis on what gets picked out by non-defective referentially normative predicates promises to get at a crucial metaphysical distinction in a way that other construals of what it is to be a normative property do not.

I am also *attracted to* some related theses. One is that appeal to there being possible non-defective referentially normative predicates of a suitable kind would be sufficient for the ardent realist to get around the problems I am here concerned with. But for reasons that will emerge (Chapter 3), I am not in a position actually to assert this, and it is far from easy to see what would be a satisfactory alternative statement of what would be sufficient for the ardent realist's purposes.

I see much of the interest in the present discussion as having to do with which choice points and theses are rendered salient. In particular, as highlighted by the statements of the claims with which I will be concerned, I think questions about what sorts of possible predicates there can be deserve center stage in metaethical discussions. The claims are all about necessary or sufficient conditions for something to be the case. I won't be at all concerned to defend any more categorical claim. However, the discussion will *highlight* some categorical claims. One (obviously) is that *there are possible non-defective referentially normative predicates (of the right kind) and hence ardent realism is vindicated.* A related claim is the presentationalist claim that *although there are non-empty normative predicates and some atomic statements made employing these predicates are objectively and robustly true, there are no normative properties and facts—normativity resides only in the representations, and never in the represented.* More generally, another categorical claim is that ardent realism is false—not because the world is some way that is incompatible with ardent realism, but because *there is no way for the world to be that vindicates ardent realism.* The claim would not be merely that ardent realism is false as a matter of *metaphysical* necessity. The ardent realist couldn't even informatively describe a way for the world to be—whether metaphysically possible or not—such that if the world were that way, ardent realism would be vindicated.[18]

Faced with these categorical claims, one will naturally be interested in deciding which claim is correct. In my discussion, I will occasionally relate to what may be seen as possible ways to decide the issue. But the conclusions will tend to be negative. I will express skepticism about deciding the issue in any of the ways I go on to consider.

[18] The "informatively," vague as it is, is important: without it, the stated claim would be false since "ardent realism is true" does describe a way for the world to be that vindicates ardent realism.

2
Alternative Normative Concepts

In Chapter 1, I outlined some of the main themes of the book. Now I will turn to the details, and provide more by way of argument. I will expand on the challenge to ardent realism that I described, and on the most attractive way out that I can see.

Consider the following scenario:

> *Alternative*. There is a linguistic community speaking a language much like English, except for the following differences (and whatever differences are directly entailed). While their words "good," "right," and "ought" are associated with the same normative roles as our words "good," "right," and "ought," their words aren't coextensive with our "good," "right," and "ought." So even if they are exactly right about what is "good" and "right" and what "ought" to be done, in their sense, and they seek to promote and to do what is "good" and "right" and what "ought" to be done in their sense, they do not seek to promote what is good and right and what ought to be done.

Scenarios of this kind were in effect introduced already in Chapter 1. In this chapter, I will use Alternative to describe a problem that arises for a certain class of realist theories, theories I will call *Alternative-friendly*. These are the theories given which Alternative is possible. *Alternative-unfriendly* theories are ones on which Alternative is impossible.

I will argue that Alternative-friendly theories face a dilemma, and that on the more easily occupiable horn of this dilemma the theories in this class end up seeming rather *deflationary*—while they can accommodate that normative sentences express truths, they deflate the status of these truths, in a way I will illustrate. On the other horn, there are *ineffable* questions about normativity.

Let me relate this to how I framed the issues in Chapter 1. Spotting the ardent realist victory with respect to the debates that tend to come up in the literature—about the objective truth-values of normative sentences, etc.—still leaves open the possibility of Alternative-friendliness. Given Alternative-friendliness, the dilemma arises, and the deflationary theories are not fit for the ardent realist's purposes: ardent realists must then occupy the ineffability horn.

Sometimes one distinguishes between *moral* terms and *all-things-considered* normative terms, by appeal to the seeming non-triviality of worries like: I know that I morally ought to φ, but ought I (all things considered) really to φ? Given such a distinction, which I think is reasonable, what I am talking about when describing

Alternative are the all-things-considered terms rather than the moral terms. Using the fashionable terminology of "thin" and "thick," the terms should be understood in the *thinnest* possible way.

Saying that the terms should be understood in the thinnest possible way isn't yet to say whether these terms are supposed to express the thinnest concepts we employ or instead the thinnest concepts there can be (assuming these things can come apart). My eventual focus will be on the behavior of the thinnest concepts there *can be*. I have stated Alternative as concerning the thinnest concepts *we employ*, but that is just because it is easier to introduce the theoretical problem that way.[1]

Is a different community like the one described in Alternative possible? That is, are alternative normative terms like these possible? Instead of addressing this question directly, I will explore the consequences of the different answers. In sections 2.1 and 2.2, I will make the following points. First, if Alternative is in fact *impossible*, then an important class of popular and otherwise attractive metaethical theories, or, better, theories of the semantics of normative terms—all theories that are Alternative-friendly—are false.[2] Theories of reference-determination central to popular contemporary versions of naturalistic normative realism are Alternative-friendly. Second, if Alternative is in fact *possible*, then, as we will see, a number of novel thorny problems about normative realism and knowledge of the normative can be raised, and we face an uncomfortable choice between different things to say. The Alternative-friendly theorist must either accept that there are ineffable questions about normativity, or else accept that the importance of normative questions is deflated. Neither choice is a happy one.

The kind of problem I will discuss is structurally similar to the well-known Moral Twin Earth argument due to Terence Horgan and Mark Timmons.[3] Later in this chapter I will explicitly compare how this type of argument has been used in the literature, and note the ways in which the challenge that I present differs.

2.1 What if Alternative is Impossible?

If Alternative is impossible, that is because what the thinnest normative words are true of is bound up with their normative roles in such a way that there is no way that words with the same normative role could fail to be coextensive. One can attempt to support the claim that Alternative is impossible by appeal to intuition. It can be said

---

[1] The words considered are of course context-sensitive. I will in effect be focusing on a particular class of *uses* of these words, the "thinnest" uses. For some purposes it would of course be terrible to be cavalier about this context-sensitivity. But as I will be concerned with abstract questions about what possible languages there can be (as opposed to the details of actual normative language), the simplified formulations are all right in the context.

[2] I will keep talking of "semantics" even where properly I should occasionally rather speak of *metasemantics*, since I will speak of theories of how semantic features are determined rather than theories of what the semantic features are.

[3] See e.g. their (1992) and (2009).

that when we imagine a situation of the kind described in Alternative, our reaction is that we and the members of the alternative community actually do mean the same things by "good," "right," and "ought." But however the case may be as regards such intuition-based arguments, several different kinds of popular theories of the semantics of normative terms are Alternative-friendly and demand that Alternative is possible.

Take first causal normative semantics of the kind associated with so-called *Cornell moral realism*: normative predicates have their reference determined by what their use is appropriately *causally linked to*, analogously to how natural kind terms standardly are held to have their reference determined.[4] Causal links are a different matter from normative role, and it would appear that terms can be causally linked to different properties even while they have the same normative role. Two communities could use predicates with the same normative role, even while tokenings of the two predicates stand in relevant causal relations to different things. (Let me call non-coextensive predicates with the same normative role *normative counterparts* of each other. To be Alternative-friendly is to say that there are normative counterparts of our thinnest terms.) Even if the normative role can *help explain* what the use of the predicate is appropriately causally linked to, in the sense that it is relevant to a causal explanation of why the predicate is causally linked to the property it is thus linked to, the causal link is not a function of normative role alone, and that is sufficient for Alternative to be possible. Causal normative semantics is Alternative-friendly.

In his (1988), Richard Boyd, one of the Cornell realists, considers an issue related to the one brought up here:

> The moral realist—in the guise of the homeostatic consequentialist [the specific view Boyd assumes in his article], say—holds that what regulate the use of moral terms are facts about human well-being. But this is simply not so. Consider, for example, sixteenth-century discussions of rights. One widely acknowledged "right" was the divine right of kings. Something surely regulated the use of the language of rights in the sixteenth century, but it clearly wasn't human well-being construed in the way the moral realist intends. Instead, it was the well-being of kings and the aristocratic class of which they were part.[5]

Boyd's reply to the objection is essentially to say that although the belief in the divine right of kings was widespread, the use of moral terms was anyway, at bottom, causally regulated by facts about human well-being generally.[6] This amounts to a piece of—perhaps reasonable—empirical speculation. But even if Boyd's speculation is correct, there is still a question of whether something like what is alleged in the objection is *possible*—is a causal normative semantics like Boyd's Alternative-friendly? Boyd does not even attempt to provide a reason to think it is not.

---

[4] For applications of causal theories of reference-determination to the case of normative terms, see Boyd (1988) and Brink (1989).

[5] Boyd (1988), p. 211.   [6] Ibid., p. 211f.

The Cornell realists tend to discuss specifically *moral* terms. When I present the theory of how reference is determined as concerning normative terms more broadly, a step is taken. One could in principle adopt the proposed theory when it comes to the reference of the *moral* "right," while—if one acknowledges a separate "all things considered" use—rejecting the theory as a theory of the *all things considered* "right." For now, I will slide over such details. Similar remarks will apply to other theories I bring up in this section. In Chapter 3 I will address skepticism about the "all things considered."

Second, compare descriptivist normative semantics of the kind defended in Frank Jackson's (1998). According to Jackson's general descriptivist outlook, the reference of expressions is often determined by associated theories. The referent of the expression is what makes the theory true. In the case of scientific terms, the associated theories are the scientific theories within which the terms are introduced. In the case of ordinary expressions, the theories are folk theories, comprising widely held and firmly entrenched beliefs. In the specific case of moral terms, the view is that the reference of moral terms is determined by *folk morality*, our folk theory of matters moral. Parts of this folk theory only specify how normative terms relate to each other. This alone would, however, be insufficient to pin down the reference of normative terms. So also claims relating normative terms to descriptive terms are part of the folk theory. But then Alternative should be possible: the specifically normative roles of two different normative terms could be the same but the links to the descriptive different, and thus the terms are determined by their corresponding folk theories to refer to different things despite having the same normative role. The important thing is that since, on Jackson's view, beliefs linking the normative to the descriptive play a crucial reference-determining role, Jackson's view is Alternative-friendly.

An apparent complication when it comes to Jackson is that he does not speak of the reference of moral terms as determined by *current* folk morality but as determined by *mature* folk morality, which is an idealized version of current folk morality.[7] But the complication is ultimately irrelevant. If "mature folk morality" was whichever folk morality got the moral facts right, then there couldn't be two differing folk moralities of different communities determining different referents for moral terms. But such a conception of mature folk morality would trivialize Jackson's outlook. "Mature folk morality" is more reasonably understood as simply an idealized version of current folk morality: folk morality purged of, for example, inconsistency. But then different communities can have different mature folk moralities, for they start from different beginnings and the process of maturation does not ensure convergence. If it is retorted that there can be only one mature folk morality

---

[7] Jackson (1998), p. 133.

for there is, so to speak, only one way for a language game constrained by the normative roles associated with our normative expressions to mature, the response is that then the rhetoric of folk theory doing the reference-determination is precisely only rhetoric.

The theories I have brought up as examples are all of the naturalist variety. But Alternative-friendliness and naturalism are not the same thing. Nothing immediately rules out that different communities could use their thinnest normative predicates to ascribe different non-naturalistic properties. And it could in principle be that an Alternative-unfriendly view allows that the thinnest normative predicates stand for naturalistic properties.

To sum up the main lesson of this section: some prominent and potentially attractive theories of how normative language works require that Alternative is possible. I now turn to explore that alternative. It is here that things get more interesting.

2.2 What if Alternative is Possible?

A first thought one might have is that if Alternative is possible, then there is some sort of live issue as to whether we or the alternative community *get things right*. They do what they do based on considerations about what is "good" and "right" in *their* sense; we do what we do based on considerations about what is "good" and "right" in *our* sense. Since our normative terms and their normative counterparts aren't coextensive, we then act differently. But whose normative terms is it that, as it were, limn the normative structure of reality?[8] What set of normative terms ought to be used when we ask ourselves what to do? It could be ours; it could be theirs.[9]

This thought would in turn encourage a novel kind of skeptical challenge concerning the normative: even if indeed we can come to know what is *good* and what is *right*, there would remain the question of whether it is our terms or their normative counterparts that limn the normative structure of reality—and how could we figure out the answer to *that* question? (And is there even an objective answer to that question, even if there are objective answers to questions about what "ought" to be done in our sense and about what "ought" to be done in their sense?)

However, this first thought is prima facie problematic, whatever in the end we should say about it. For exactly how should we conceive of what is supposed to be at issue between us and this other community? To see the problem here, consider the

---

[8] The formulation is intended to echo Quine's talk of attempting "to limn the true and ultimate structure of reality" (1960, p. 221). I use the impressionistic "as it were, limn the normative structure of reality" in part because of the ineffability problems soon to be discussed. Use of the locution does not avoid these problems; it serves only to signal them.

[9] Complications regarding how to talk about this come from special considerations favoring the use of a particular set of terms: for example, suppose someone were to threaten to annihilate humanity if we were to use a particular set of normative terms. That is—of course!—a reason not to use these terms. But I will abstract away from complications of this kind.

following simple suggestion: the issue concerns *which actions it really is right to perform*, those falling under our "right" or those falling under its normative counterpart. That would be a silly way to conceive of the supposed *further question* (the Further Question, as I will keep referring to it), for—*obviously!*—the *right* actions are the ones that fall under our "right." That is just an instance of the general point that the things that are F are the ones that fall under the predicate "F" as it is actually used (in this context).[10]

In the introductory section of this chapter I briefly indicated that my real focus is on possible thin terms and concepts and not merely the thin terms and concepts we happen to have. This is a genuine complication. If our actual normative terms have normative counterparts as characterized but some *possible* thin normative terms do not, perhaps what is at issue between us and the members of the other community can be expressed using these possible terms. Alternative-friendliness as I ultimately wish to conceive of it has to do with what possible normative terms there can be. Given Alternative-friendliness thus conceived, the escape route of considering possible terms as described is foreclosed.

This is obviously relevant also to the discussion of the Alternative-friendly theories in section 2.1. A friend of a causal or descriptivist theory of reference-determination for our actual normative terms can in principle say that there are *possible* terms that work differently, and do not allow for normative counterparts. But to the extent that she focuses on the metaethical significance of there being these possible thin terms differing in important ways from the actual ones, her investigations into the semantic and metasemantic features of actual terms lose much of their purported significance.

Presumably the proposed way of stating what is at issue between us and the alternative community from a few paragraphs ago—in terms of which actions it is "right to perform"—is needlessly crude. But there is a general problem that would appear to afflict all statements of what is at issue: in any statement of ours about what is at issue, our normative terms are employed, and in such a way that the question as framed threatens to be trivially settled in favor of *our* terms, while in any statement of theirs about what is at issue, their normative terms are employed and in such a way that the question as framed threatens to be trivially settled in favor of their terms.[11] Below I will discuss whether one might get around this problem. But for now, let us suppose—what I also think is the case—that the problem cannot be avoided. What then?

There are two things one might say. One is that there is something at issue between us and the other community, along the lines gestured at: it is only that the problems pointed to show that it is *ineffable* what the issue is. Even when it has been

---

[10] Setting aside obviously orthogonal complications related to the liar paradox.

[11] One could imagine normative vocabularies that are not in this way *self-verifying*. But it is enough for the problem to arise if some different normative vocabularies are self-verifying in the way indicated in the text. I assume that it is so, and in the main text I will continue to slide over this type of complication.

determined what falls under our "right," "ought," etc., and what falls under their "right," "ought," etc., there is a Further Question, even if our attempts at stating that supposed Further Question fail, and for principled reasons. While it may be that we have true beliefs about what ought to be done and they have true beliefs about what ought* to be done, either they are wrong in letting their actions be guided by considerations about what ought* to be done or we are wrong in letting our actions be guided by considerations about what ought to be done.[12] I want to discuss the issue in the abstract and not tie the discussion to any particular type of hypothesis about the extensions of the alternative normative concepts, but for illustrative purposes, suppose a deontological theory is true of what ought to be done, but the "ought*" of the other community is consequentialist. Suppose further that they are about to perform some action—say, sacrifice an innocent child for the greater good—that is consequentialistically but not deontologically sanctioned.[13] "Wait," we say, "you ought not to do that!". "We know," they reply, "that we 'ought' not to do this. But we ought* to do it." We persist: "But what you ought* to do is not what you really ought to do." They say: "Yes again—but it is also true that what one ought to do is not what one really ought* to do." Everything they say in reply to us is true, but as the child is killed we may still feel that there is something there that they missed—there is a Further Question there, one about which they are tragically mistaken. (Of course, if we feel that there is a Further Question we might also have a nagging suspicion that it is we who are tragically mistaken about it. As we do what we ought to do and don't always maximize happiness, we may worry: maybe it is instead we who are tragically mistaken? ... Even if, of course, we *ought* to do what we *ought* to do.)

Not that it is of immediate relevance to anything I wish to argue, but it may still be interesting to note that Wittgenstein says things which suggest the ineffability idea floated:

I at once see clearly, as it were in a flash of light, not only that no description that I can think of would do to describe what I mean by absolute value, but that I would reject every significant description that anybody could possibly suggest, ab initio, on the ground of its significance. That is to say: I see now that these nonsensical expressions were not nonsensical because I had not yet found the correct expressions, but that their nonsensicality was their very essence. For all I wanted to do with them was just to go beyond the world and that is to say beyond significant language. My whole tendency and I believe the tendency of all men who ever tried to

---

[12] Of course not even the most conscientious among us are always concerned with what ought to be done; and even when we are so concerned, we can be wrong, and even radically so, about what ought to be done. And if the members of the alternative community are like us, the same will hold of them, mutatis mutandis. In the main text I slide over this, as it doesn't affect the main points.

[13] I choose the illustration because it is familiar and serves to present the problem in stark terms. But there is a way in which it might be misleading to put the issue in terms of consequentialism versus deontology. These are moral theories, whereas what I am concerned with is not the specifically moral, but with the normative more broadly.

write or talk Ethics or Religion was to run against the boundaries of language. This running against the walls of our cage is perfectly, absolutely hopeless.[14]

However, I certainly would not mean to claim that what I am talking about when describing the option of saying that there is an ineffable Further Question is what Wittgenstein talked about in his lectures on ethics. Where I discuss the possibility that normative language may go wrong in that what is expressed by our normative expressions fails to be of normative significance, Wittgenstein instead speaks of the relevant expressions as nonsensical.

Instead of embracing the idea of an ineffable Further Question, we might hold that once it is settled what falls under our "right," etc., and what falls under their "right," etc., all the relevant questions in the vicinity have been settled. There's what's "right" in our sense and what's "right" in their sense, *and that is that*. The idea that there is any Further Question there, whether expressible or not, is mistaken. I will not attempt here to decide which reaction is the most reasonable—although needless to say one may be uneasy about the idea of ineffable questions. Instead I will discuss the upshot of each suggestion.

It is fairly obvious what the upshot is of saying that there is a Further Question. The skepticism mentioned above is then a live issue. Even if we are perfectly successful in figuring out what is right, good, etc., there remains the fact that there are other possible words with the same normative roles as ours but with different extensions, and maybe we should care instead about what falls under those words. (Of course the ineffability issue rears its head as I try to state the upshot. I use the "should" of my language when discussing this. But please don't begrudge me a pinch of salt when I discuss the possibility of embracing the idea of a Further Question— even if, by the end of the day, that idea should be rejected.[15]) And no matter how successful our methodology for figuring out what is good, right, etc. may be, what reason is there to think that we are also right in thinking that this is what we *should* care about? (Again, don't begrudge me that pinch of salt.)

I must confess that at an intuitive level I don't find this entirely unattractive. I do find it somewhat intuitive to hold that what ethics is concerned with is something in some sense transcendent that does not lend itself to being captured in language. But let me stress the serious immediate problems about embracing ineffability, even apart from the attendant threat of skepticism. One question regarding this option is: can that which cannot be expressed in language still be *thought*, and hence understood, or not? If the friend of the ineffability line says *not*, she embraces the idea that we cannot even think, or, I take it, understand, the relevant thoughts, and that seems problematic. What then are we supposed to be debating when we are making up our minds

---

[14] Wittgenstein (1929/65), p. 11f.
[15] The phrase 'pinch of salt' was famously used by Frege, when he saw himself as, in a very different context, having to deem certain things ineffable. See Frege (1892).

regarding something normative? The friend of the ineffability line insists that there is a particular question there, but if she takes this line then by her own lights she does not even understand what she proposes. If instead she insists that we can think these things, then it is incumbent on her to provide a theory of thought which explains how what cannot be expressed in language can still be expressed in thought.

I suspect that, for example, for reasons like this, most would find it more reasonable simply to deny that there is an ineffable Further Question. But also such a denial has important, and potentially problematic, consequences. It is what I alluded to when early in this chapter I spoke of a deflationary view. Consider again a situation like that of the sacrifice of the innocent child, above. Suppose it is right to ϕ but right* to ψ and ϕ-ing and ψ-ing are incompatible. Suppose further that from our perspective, ψ-ing in this situation would be abhorrent (we might continue thinking about it as the sacrifice of an innocent child). Surely we would *want* to say that they—the others—are just mistaken. *What one really ought to do* in this situation is to ϕ. And of course we *can* say this latter thing, and say so truly; it is not as if, on the option we are now exploring, this is untrue. The problem is that *they* can say, equally correctly, that *what one really ought* to do* in this situation is to ψ. We may care more about what one ought to do, but they care more about what one ought* to do. We can say that one *ought* to be concerned with what one ought to do rather than with what one ought* to do, and presumably we can say so truly; but *they* can similarly say that one ought* to be concerned with what one ought* to do rather than with what one ought to do. And so on. If there is no Further Question, this is *all there is to it*.

Return to the ardent realist. The ardent realist should not be happy about a deflationary Alternative-friendly view, on which there is no Further Question. For given such a view, there need be nothing more to it, in a dispute between us and a paradigmatic Bad Guy, than that we use one "ought" with and (often) (strive to) do what "ought" to be done in that sense, and Bad Guy uses another, non-coextensive "ought," but with the same normative role, and (often) (strives to) do what "ought" to be done in that sense. What the ardent realist would be happy with, at least for all that has been said, is an Alternative-unfriendly view, or an Alternative-friendly view on which there is a Further Question.

The considerations presented so far in this chapter function as an extended argument against Alternative-friendly theories. Suppose you are an Alternative-friendly theorist. If Alternative is impossible, you are wrong. So suppose Alternative is possible. Is there then a Further Question of the kind indicated? You might say there is, but then you are committed to the idea of ineffable questions. In addition, even if you can make plausible that sentences about what is good and right and ought to be done are capable of objective truth and falsity, that still does not warrant any claim to the effect that the ineffable question has an objective answer. Suppose then that you instead reject the idea of a Further Question. Then you are stuck with the deflationary attitude; you have ended up deflating the significance of facts about what is good and right and what ought to be done. We might still focus on what is right over what is right*, but it would appear that there is no objective basis for this.[16]

I say that there is no "objective basis" for our focus on what is right when describing the upshot of saying that there is no Further Question. One needs to tread carefully here. Of course it is still objectively the case that it is right to focus on what is right when deciding how to act. The problem is just that, equally, it is objectively right* to focus on what is right*. For every pat on the back we can give ourselves, they can give themselves a similar pat on the back.

One thing that might stand out regarding the problems I have pressed for Alternative-friendly theories is that one can in principle apply the same recipe to try to present problems for theories of all sorts. I have been concerned with normative role and with whether normative role determines reference, but for *any* feature or mechanism that might in principle be held to determine the reference of normative

---

[16] In his (2006), Seiriol Morgan presses an objection against "synthetic naturalism"—the view also called Cornell realism, associated with theorists like Boyd, Sturgeon, Brink, and Railton—somewhat similar to the objection I am here raising against Alternative-friendly theories generally. Morgan calls what is valued from a certain Nietzschean perspective *nobility*—where the point is that nobility is hardly something the rest of us think should be valued—and argues that the Cornell realist's reasons for believing in moral facts generalize to the case of "noble facts." More generally, Morgan argues that the Cornell realist must accept a great variety of "value facts." But why exactly is this a problem? Morgan is clear that there is no "metaphysical embarrassment" as such (p. 332). Rather, the supposed problem is that what has been pointed to makes "painfully clear the arbitrariness at the heart of this kind of externalist value realism, an arbitrariness incompatible with the essence of moral realism as we usually understand it"; "since there are (or even could be) agents with quite different desires, *nobility is normative as well*" (p. 333). Later, Morgan sums up his case: "naturalism might on the face of it appear to establish something called 'moral realism,' but only under a definition which fails to preserve what everyone thought was important about it." Moral discourse is objective and some properties denoted by moral predicates are exemplified, but naturalism anyway does not deliver what realism might be expected to deliver.

Morgan's concerns are evidently closely related in spirit to those brought up here. But Morgan slides over the difficulties that were encountered in section 2.1, where the dilemma was presented. Morgan says, stating his case against naturalism:

> The reality of natural moral properties could not tell us what to value, since noble realism is established by the same considerations and nobility is normatively incompatible with morality. And if their reality cannot tell us what to value, it is hard to see how the truth of moral realism could enable us to "discover what sorts of things are valuable." (p. 334; the quoted phrase is from Brink (1989))

But this way of stating the case against the naturalist is too simple. The naturalist either treats "x is valuable" as she treats the moral predicates she primarily focuses on, e.g. "good" and "right," or she reserves "x is valuable" and its cognates for special treatment. In the latter case, she does seem rather unprincipled. So focus on the former case, where she, e.g., takes "x is valuable" to have its reference determined by a folk theory, along the lines of Jackson, or takes its reference to be causally determined, along the lines of Cornell realism: there is no reason why she should not be able to say that we discover what sorts of things are valuable. To present the naturalist who does treat "x is valuable" and cognates as she treats the moral predicates she primarily focuses on with a problem, what Morgan would have to do is to suppose that those who care about what is noble rather than what is moral correspondingly care about what is *"naluable"* rather than with what is valuable, and argue that the naturalist does not really vindicate realism for she does not show why considerations about what is valuable are objectively privileged over considerations about what is naluable. But that argument is messier. It is exactly that messier argument I seek to make in this chapter.

terms, one can describe a scenario where two communities use normative terms in such ways that they are alike in the relevant respect but differ in other ways, so that if some other conception of what determines the reference of normative terms is correct then the terms used by the different communities do not corefer. The same sorts of concerns arise, in principle.

But there are good reasons for singling out normative role for special consideration. Terms with the same normative role are in a clear and obvious intuitive sense counterparts of each other when it comes to normative matters. By contrast, if some other community used a term "right*" not associated with the same normative role as my "right" but associated with, for example, the same folk theory as my "right," and the associated folk theory does not determine reference so "right*" is not coextensive with "right," why should that in any way give me normative angst?

In sections 2.3–2.7, I will fill in some details and respond to some envisaged objections. Some objections will, however, be left for later chapters. For example, I will only later properly discuss the possible concern that problems of broadly the same kind I have discussed might arise also for Alternative-unfriendly theories.

2.3 Expressing the Further Question?

As earlier indicated, one may think there are ways of expressing what I have called the Further Question, so that this supposed Further Question would not have to be ineffable.

There is, as mentioned in Chapter 1, the possibility of saying that the supposed Further Question concerns which properties are normative: the ones picked out by our terms or the ones picked out by the other community's terms. I don't find this satisfactory as it stands: it just invites the follow-up question of what it takes for a property to be normative. Unexplained talk of normativity here does not solve any problem but just labels it.

If one does not want to rest content with appeal to the notion of a normative property, how else can one express the supposed Further Question? One possible model, broached in Chapter 1, is provided by a suggestion that Ted Sider (2009) discusses favorably: that debates over aesthetic realism should be recast so they are no longer conceived of as being over whether aesthetic sentences have objective truth-values, but over whether some aesthetic predicates, or what they correspond to in the world, are, so to speak, joint-carving—as before, I will use *elite* for the feature in question.[17] Sider's idea is that the would-be aesthetic antirealist fights a losing battle if

---

[17] Sider (2009), p. 401. I will speak as if entities are what are elite; this slides over Sider's preferred nominalism. Moreover, Sider does not speak of antirealism generally but of how best to understand *projection* and *projectivism* in this context. What he says is:

> acknowledging the notion of distinguished structure lets us make sense of claims that this or that feature is merely "projected" onto the world, rather than being "really there". Many want to say that aesthetic features are projections of our standards of evaluation, rather than

she insists that aesthetic sentences lack truth-values. Instead she should insist that there are no most elite possible aesthetic predicates—different counterparts of, say, "beautiful" used in different communities. Correspondingly, the aesthetic realist is to be seen as affirming that there are some unique most elite aesthetic predicates.

Notice the similarity between Sider's proposal concerning aesthetic realism and the themes here brought up. In the dispute over aesthetic realism as Sider conceives of it as being conducted, both the realist and her opponent agree that the aesthetic sentences of the different languages have objective truth-values: they disagree over whether there is an objective answer to the Further Question of which aesthetic notions are elite. Applied to the general issue at hand here: it can be agreed on all hands that claims about what ought to be done, what ought* to be done, etc., have objective truth-values, but—the idea would be—there is a Further Question of whether "ought" or one of its counterparts is elite, and, if so, which one is so.

Sometimes eliteness is held to carry in its wake what is often called *reference magnetism*. The thought is that what is elite is more intrinsically eligible to be meant. One could in principle try to appeal to reference magnetism to argue that Alternative is impossible. The idea would be that because of reference magnetism, all predicates associated with the same normative role of "right" have the same reference. One of the relevant properties is endowed with a reference magnetism that trumps that of other candidates. However, arguing for this would be a tall order: already Lewis, who first made the idea popular, cautioned that use can trump eligibility and it is not absolutely impossible to mean the less elite. (Witness the possibility of using a word that means *grue*.) At any rate, what I am currently concerned with is independent of reference magnetism. The suggestion I am currently concerned with is that of, assuming Alternative-friendliness, seeing if there is any way of stating the supposed Further Question.

Sider's idea might seem attractive to a friend of the idea of a Further Question who wants nothing to do with absolute ineffability. Attempts at asking the Further Question that crucially make use of normative terms fail, for reasons indicated. But, the thought is, we can non-trivially raise the question of which normative terms are the most elite. Thus we can ask the Further Question after all. The Further Question at issue between us and the alternative community concerns what properties are the most elite. When we have the sense that they go wrong when using the *-terms for evaluation, and that they had better use our terms, what that amounts to is our holding that our terms are elite.

---

being "really out there". This should not be taken to require mind-dependence of aesthetic qualities, in the sense that the mountain would not be beautiful if no one ever saw it. It should rather be taken to deny that there is any distinguished aesthetic structure. A language omitting aesthetic predicates would not thereby be worse, in the sense described in the previous section (though of course it might be worse in other respects.) A society employing aesthetic predicates with very different meanings from our own would not thereby carve the world at its joints less well than we do.

But exactly what should we take the talk of eliteness to amount to here? Different things might be meant. But Sider's proposal is unsatisfactory on any extant way to understand eliteness. Suppose first that by eliteness one means something like what is sometimes called *Lewisian* eliteness: the perfectly elite properties are the fundamental physical properties, and something is more elite than something else the closer to this ideal it is.[18] Then the proposal seems unworkable. The following example should help make the point. Consider two different communities with different aesthetic predicates—for example, they may have different, non-coextensive predicates "tasty." Suppose further that the tastes of one community are such that the extension of "tasty" in their mouths is more metaphysically elite, for example because there is one particular chemical element, say *sodium*, such that they like—*gustatorily* like—food and drink that contains this chemical in sufficient quantities, so the referent of their "tasty" is more elite. To take this to be relevant to which community objectively has the aesthetically better taste would clearly be unwarranted. The issues are simply different. Correspondingly, the same goes for other normative disputes, including, for example, moral disputes, even if in other cases it is harder to come up with even prima facie compelling examples of greater eliteness in the Lewisian sense. The general take-home message is this: *even if what is more elite in the Lewisian sense may in some way be metaphysically privileged, it is not relevantly so as far as normativity or aesthetic evaluation is concerned.*

In response to this consideration, the friend of Sider's proposal can say that the specific understanding of eliteness we have operated with so far is not the right understanding to operate with anyway. But then think of what other understanding of eliteness might fare better. Here is one quite different conception: what is elite is whatever is objectively most worthy of consideration for some theoretical enterprise or other, where "theoretical enterprise" is understood broadly so as to include normative theorizing. If eliteness is understood that way, the kind of argument just given falls by the wayside. But on the other hand, to understand eliteness so broadly is in the context to cheat. No longer does talk about eliteness provide the sought-for handle on the Further Question. Compare the stance of treating eliteness as primitive, not susceptible to any informative elucidation. Then one cannot present counterexamples to the idea that the supposed Further Question concerns which property ascribed by "right" or some normative counterpart is more elite. But the claim that the same property of eliteness is what is at issue in this metaethical discussion is the same as what is at issue in a more purely metaphysical discussion becomes a matter of faith.

Let me stress just what it is that I think will become a matter of faith. The skepticism does not target the idea that the notion of eliteness is as applicable to

---

[18] Lewis introduced his notion of eliteness in Lewis (1983). His conception of eliteness underwent changes but what I discuss in the text is one conception prominently associated with Lewis. See e.g. Schaffer (2004), Williams (2007), and Hawthorne (2007) for useful discussion of Lewis' notion of eliteness.

the properties we use normative expressions to ascribe as to other properties. What I am doubtful about is whether the practical or normative question of which concept of rightness to employ when engaged in practical decision-making can really be decided by considerations about which notion of eliteness ascribes a more elite property. For more purely metaphysical purposes—limning the fundamental metaphysical structure of reality, or writing the book of the world—it may matter which property is more elite.

How else might one understand eliteness? There is what I myself would take to be the most reasonable conception of eliteness, where something's being elite is linked to its being *objectively explanatory*, where this is not understood the original Lewisian way, but higher-level properties, for example the ones that are under the purview of various special sciences, can in principle count as perfectly elite.[19] The idea would be to allow higher-level properties to be elite in the relevant sense while still avoiding a too liberal view by tying eliteness to some suitable notion of scientific explanation.

This proposal faces the same problems as the Lewisian eliteness proposal, as far as present purposes are concerned. (Of course none of the present considerations need point to a problem with the idea of eliteness per se; I am only concerned with its usefulness in the present context.) For suppose that we compare two concepts of "right," as earlier in the discussion, and find that one concept ascribes a property that is more explanatory than the property that the other concept ascribes. I don't think that immediately addresses the question of which concept is normatively preferable. Compare Seiriol Morgan's example of an alternative Nietzschean morality, with positive Nietzschean concepts true of the sorts of things Nietzsche deems valuable in relevant respects, and negative Nietzschean concepts being true of what he finds objectionable in relevant respects.[20] The empirical facts could be such that the properties these Nietzschean concepts stand for are more explanatory than the properties ordinary moral concepts stand for: for example, it is the former and not the latter that occur in law-like psychological and sociological generalizations about us and how we behave. This would not be a good reason to conclude that the Nietzschean concepts are preferable for normative purposes. It is only a matter of our psychologies, as they actually are, being best theorized about using these Nietzschean concepts.

The example is of course purely hypothetical. And I suppose I could see how someone could argue that the explanatoriness of the properties ascribed by some normative concepts could provide *some evidence* that we should use these concepts rather than some non-coextensive ones for normative purposes. But what is presently at issue is whether we can use talk of eliteness to express the supposed Further Question, and that is what I am denying. In other words: granted the assumption that there indeed is a Further Question of the kind we are concerned with here,

---

[19] See again Schaffer (2004), Williams (2007), and Hawthorne (2007).
[20] See footnote 16.

I allow that considerations of explanatoriness of properties might be relevant to how to answer it, but what we are concerned with is the more fundamental issue of whether there is such a Further Question to begin with.

Some theorists would stress that ethics is a science among others, and thus apt to point us to which properties are the most explanatory in just the way that other sciences are. Even if they are right, and I am happy to grant for argument's sake that they are, that does not ward off the present concern. For even so, it can be that some property ascribed by some normative concept is deemed objectively explanatory by virtue of its role in some other science than ethics, as illustrated by the Nietzschean example.[21]

2.4 Moral Twin Earth

It may be useful to compare the line of reasoning I have been pursuing in Chapter 1 to the Moral Twin Earth argument of Horgan and Timmons. That argument is a prominent one brought against the causal theory of reference for moral terms, and more recently against descriptivism.[22] Here is one of Horgan and Timmons' presentations of the Moral Twin Earth argument:

Now for Moral Twin Earth. Its inhabitants have a vocabulary that works very much like human moral vocabulary: they use the terms "good" and "bad", "right" and "wrong", to evaluate actions, persons, institutions, and so forth.... But on Moral Twin Earth, people's uses of twin-moral terms are causally regulated by certain natural properties distinct from those that (as we are already supposing) regulate English moral discourse. The properties tracked by twin English moral terms are also functional properties, whose essence is characterizable by means of a normative moral theory. But these are non-consequentialist moral properties, whose functional essence is captured by some specific deontological theory; call this theory Td. These functional properties are similar enough to those characterizable via Tc to account for the fact that twin-moral discourse operates in Twin Earth society and culture in much the manner that moral discourse operates on Earth.... In addition, suppose that if Twin

---

[21] Mark van Roojen's (2006) appeal to eliteness is somewhat different: on his conception, eliteness is discipline-relative, so that something which is elite relative to one discipline may fail to be elite relative to another. As both Schroeter and Schroeter (2013) and Williams (forthcoming) note, this is in tension with letting eliteness play the metasemantic role it is often enlisted to play. Even so, however, appeal to discipline-relative eliteness might be of use in the present context. The privileged concept of rightness might be one that is elite relative to ethics. This promises to get around the wrong-sort-of-consideration concern I have been pushing. One question may be how to individuate disciplines (might the alternative community be concerned with ethics*?), but let me set this aside. A different, more obviously serious concern is this. The appeal to an absolute notion of eliteness is an appeal to a feature that theorists take to be in independent good standing and shed light on what normative privilege might be (although some theorists are of course skeptical of this notion). When instead one speaks of eliteness relative to ethics, this seems like a fancy way of simply saying: normatively privileged.

[22] See e.g. Horgan and Timmons (1992a) for their argument against causal theories, and their (2009) for the argument directed against neo-descriptivism.

Earthlings were to employ in a proper and thorough manner the same reliable method of moral inquiry which (as we are already supposing) would lead Earthlings to discover that Earthling uses of moral terms are causally regulated by functional properties whose essence is captured by the consequentialist normative theory Tc, then this method would lead the Twin Earthlings to discover that their own uses of twin-moral terms are causally regulated by functional properties whose essence is captured by the deontological theory Td.[23]

Horgan and Timmons speak specifically about the *moral*. In the present context, it is more relevant to consider a more general form of their argument focusing on the normative—thus not on what is, for example, morally right and wrong but on what is all-things-considered right and wrong. I will assume it to be straightforward to extend their argument to the all-things-considered case.

In the quoted passage, Horgan and Timmons only say that the Moral Twin Earthlings' words "good," "bad," etc. are used to evaluate. This is insufficient to yield what Horgan and Timmons want: that it is intuitive that their words are coextensional with our same-sounding words. There are many different normative words, with different extensions. But elsewhere they elaborate, saying, e.g.:

Moral Twin Earthlings are normally disposed to act in certain ways corresponding to judgments about what is "good" and "right"; they normally take considerations about what is "good" and "right" to be especially important, even of overriding importance in most cases, in deciding what to do, and so on.[24]

This too is sketchy, but makes clear what the idea is: the Moral Twin Earthlings use "good," "right," etc. in normatively the same ways as we use "good," "right," etc.

As it is typically discussed, Horgan and Timmons' argument is, first, that the theories they target allow that there should be terms of other possible languages corresponding to our terms in normative role but differing in extension, and, second, by appeal to a thought experiment—the Moral Twin Earth scenario—that this consequence is counterintuitive, for intuitively our terms and these possible terms would have the same meaning and reference. The first claim in the argument from Horgan and Timmons is exactly what I am noting here. But the present challenge is independent of the truth of the second claim. Dialectically, this is important. It is not clear to me how persuasive these intuition-based arguments should be taken to be. I feel the intuitive force of the considerations myself but would be hesitant to rely on them. First, there is a point that David Merli (2002) stresses, that the examples relied on in these intuitive arguments tend to be underdescribed, and it is far from clear what our intuitions would be if the examples were more fleshed out.[25] Second, in connection with the idea that some entities are more elite than others, it is often maintained that the things that are thus elite are also reference-magnetic—intrinsically

---

[23] Horgan and Timmons (1992b), p. 245f.   [24] Horgan and Timmons (1992a), p. 188.
[25] Merli (2002), pp. 214ff.

more eligible to be referred to.[26] As, for example, Billy Dunaway and Tristram McPherson (2016), Mark van Roojen (2006), and Douglas Edwards (2013) bring up, reference magnetism might be relevant in the present context. Facts about reference magnetism can help determine the reference of normative terms. And one can think that in cases where such carving facts play a significant role in determining reference, our intuitions are not a reliable guide to reference facts. Third, Janice Dowell (2016) argues that the intuitions drawn upon in Moral Twin Earth cases aren't plausibly directly related to what makes for linguistic competence. On this basis she denies that the intuitions about Moral Twin Earth cases have "probative value."

The arguments of this chapter, concerning what to say if Alternative is possible, illustrate the problems that Alternative-friendly theories face even if the second claim of the Moral Twin Earth argument is false. Hence, it does not rely on intuitions about what to say about a scenario of the kind introduced, and criticisms of such intuition-based arguments are irrelevant to its fate. Later, in Chapter 5, I will return to the use of intuition-based arguments in this context.

As Horgan and Timmons make clear, their Moral Twin Earth argument relates to similar thought experiments in Hare. What Hare (e.g. 1952, 1997) prominently argued was that naturalism in ethics leads to "relativism." One reason it is relevant to bring up this claim of Hare's is that Hare can be seen as attempting, as I am, to investigate the consequences if Horgan and Timmons' second claim is false.

Hare's charge of relativism is *clearly* false on the most straightforward understandings of what relativism is. First, sometimes (I think misleadingly) views on which the semantics of the normative is contextualist—so that, to take a simple case, when I say "this is right," what proposition I express depends on the context, and is something like *this is right relative to standard S*—are described as relativist. But it is hard to see why naturalism would be especially likely to suggest this sort of view, whatever in the end its fate. And again, Alternative-friendliness does not entail a contextualist semantics. Second, relativism can (I think more properly) be held to involve the claim that *proposition truth* is somehow interestingly relative to an assessor, or a point of view, or . . . .[27] The idea is that, say, the proposition that lying is always wrong is not apt for absolute truth but can only be assessed for truth relative to one of these things. This contrasts with the contextualist view that the sentence "lying is wrong" expresses different propositions in different contexts: the proposition *that lying is wrong relative to ___*, for various possibilities as to what goes in for

[26] The idea was introduced into the literature by Lewis (1983, 1984). The label "reference magnetism" was first used by Hodes (1984), for a related view. There is some discussion in the literature casting doubt on whether Lewis himself actually made the kind of appeal to reference magnetism that he is often seen as making. See Pautz (2013), Schwarz (2014), and Weatherson (2012).

[27] Of course, relativism is not just the view that proposition truth is relative in some way or other: saying that a proposition's truth is relative to a world, or even to a time, does not entail relativism in the sense in which it is typically discussed.

the blank. Naturalism does not entail anything about proposition truth being relative. Nor is there anything about Alternative-friendliness that suggests this. (I would myself prefer it if the label "relativism" was reserved for a view of this first kind.)

Anyway, what Hare was really after is that naturalism yields that different communities can have words with the same normative role but with different extensions. (In this connection he also makes the further point that this consequence is implausible.) In his (1997), he says,

There are in most languages words which we translate "wrong". These words are...rough equivalents to one another. But the cultures that use these words call quite different things wrong. In one culture, for example, it may be thought wrong not to fight for one's country, in another more pacific culture it may be thought wrong to fight. The important thing to get hold of is that...the people in these different cultures...may be using the word "wrong", or its equivalents, in the same sense. Otherwise they would not be contradicting one another, which they clearly are. The people in one culture are saying that fighting is wrong and the people in the other are saying that it is not wrong, *in the same sense of "wrong"*, so far as its evaluative meaning goes. But if we follow the naturalists, we shall have to say that the senses of the word in the two cultures are entirely different. This will have the consequence that they are not contradicting one another.... If we distinguish the senses by using different subscripts, we can say that one of the cultures thinks fighting is wrong$_1$, but that the other thinks it is not wrong$_2$. But these two opinions may be mutually consistent, if the two senses of "wrong" are different.[28]

Hare describes the consequence as "relativism."[29]

One may well quarrel with Hare's reasoning as it stands. The fact that the two cultures are calling different things "wrong" does not immediately entail that they use "wrong" with different senses, on any reasonable descriptivist view. (If this is not immediately clear, note that for any descriptive predicate "F" it would seem that two cultures can call different things "F" and yet use "F" with the same sense: all that would be going on is that they have different *beliefs* about what is F.) Perhaps one can interpret Hare as, rhetorically, making the point that any naturalist theory will entail that some two cultures that intuitively use "wrong" with the same sense are using it with different senses. But there is no proper argument for that claim here.

Even assuming that Hare is right about what naturalism entails, I find it somewhat misleading to call the entailed claim "relativism." The consequence that I can truly say "φ-ing is wrong" while an interlocutor can truly say "φ-ing is not wrong" can sound relativist. But if all that is going on is that we use "wrong" in different senses, this is no more relativist than the point that a Brit and an American can point to the same thing and say "that is chips" and "that is not chips," respectively, and yet each

---

[28]   Hare (1997), pp. 68ff. In early writings the target of Hare's criticism was naturalist theories according to which normative terms could be exhaustively analyzed in descriptive terms. But in his (1997), he explicitly also includes Cornell realism. However, he does not indicate exactly how the argument is supposed to work against that view.

[29]   Hare (1997), p. 65.

speak the truth. Hare may be getting at a real problem here, but calling the supposed consequence "relativism" is a bit too quick. And I think Hare is much too quick when claiming that all versions of naturalism need have the consequence in question. It is true that if the reference of normative terms is determined the way a causal theory or descriptivism says it is, then we are faced with this consequence. But is it obvious that a naturalist cannot embrace an Alternative-unfriendly semantics?

Part of what is going on is that Hare is making the point made in the Moral Twin Earth argument. He clearly thinks that the conclusion that the different communities mean different things by "wrong" is false. But when he calls the consequence *relativistic*, another theme seems to be brought in. Elaborating on what he says in the passage quoted, he says:

> There would be no harm in this if all they were doing were *describing* the act of fighting. ... The trouble starts when we begin using "wrong" for the purpose for which it actually is used in language, namely for *condemning* acts. [I]t is very natural, since this *is* actually [the use of "wrong"], to think that the people in the two cultures are, respectively, condemning and refusing to condemn the act of fighting. Then they *are* contradicting each other. But according to the naturalist they may both be right in what they say. There is no contradiction. The naturalist seems to be led to the conclusion that it is both right for one culture to condemn fighting, and right for the other culture not to condemn it. And this is a relativist position.[30]

As Hare actually states his worry, he appears to misdescribe his opponent's position. The opponent's view isn't necessarily that it is "both right for one culture to condemn fighting, and right for the other culture not to condemn it." It is rather that it is, say, right to condemn fighting and *right** not to condemn it. It can be tempting to just dismiss Hare as being unfair to his opponent. But there is a real concern underlying what Hare says. This concern appears similar to one I stressed in connection with what I have called the deflationary view. If one holds that some action can fall under one "wrong" but fail to fall under another expression associated with the same normative role *and that is all there is to it*, then there is a central motivation behind (ardent) realism that one fails to vindicate. Hare brings this up using the label relativism. I describe it by saying that ardent realism is not vindicated.[31]

---

[30] Hare (1997), p. 69.

[31] Brink (2001, p. 166) calls the kind of relativism that would be at issue "semantic relativism" and brings up the question of why it would be incompatible with realism. His answer is that in the case we are dealing with, the reason our words and those of the Twin Earthlings have different referents has to do with our having different *beliefs* and is not explained by differences in the physical environment alone. This is unconvincing. Why should this matter? For example, on some views, like general neo-descriptivist views on language, beliefs generally have a reference-fixing role. Does that mean that such theories entail a rampant realism-incompatible relativism? If I hold that different communities of scientists refer to different things by "electron" because the members of these communities have different beliefs associated with the word, am I then committing myself to a realism-incompatible relativism about electrons? Hardly—all I hold is that they refer to different things by "electron."

Horgan and Timmons sometimes use the label "relativism" when discussing their Moral Twin Earth argument (see e.g. their (1996) and (2000))—but one must be careful about what they mean by it. Consider

Toward the end of his (1988), Boyd brings up something like the relativist worry. He notes that there may be differences in moral beliefs, and that given his own preferred theory of reference-determination, these differences may result in differences in the extensions of moral expressions. But after having brought up this objection under the heading of "relativism," Boyd says that the scenario envisaged

is nevertheless only in a relatively uninteresting sense non-realistic. The dependence of the truth of moral propositions upon moral beliefs envisioned [in the sketch of the relevant type of scenario] would be...an ordinary case of causal dependence and not the sort of logical dependence required by a constructivist conception of morals analogous to a Kuhnian neo-Kantian conception of the dependence of scientific truth on the adoption of theories or paradigms. The subject matter of moral inquiry in each of the relevant communities would be theory-and-belief-independent in the sense relevant to the dispute between realists and social constructionists.[32]

Boyd is certainly right to distinguish the possibility brought up from traditional antirealism or relativism. But even if traditional antirealism or relativism isn't what is at issue, there remains the issue I have described. If the thin terms employed by different communities can have different referents, and there is no proper sense to be made out of the idea that one vocabulary is privileged, then realism does not achieve all one might have hoped it should achieve.

If there is a real threat to Boyd's type of theory in the vicinity, it is not relativism properly so called but the sorts of problems I have focused on here. Specifically, any proponent of an Alternative-friendly theory must either embrace the idea of a Further Question, one that would appear to have to be ineffable, or face up to the consequences of denying that there is such a Further Question.

The point that we are not dealing with anything properly called relativism may seem merely terminological, and not worth belaboring. But the point is important. Calling the consequence we are concerned with—the possibility of Alternative—"relativism" is to attach a label to it which immediately and misleadingly suggests a certain compromise with what is usually called realism. I myself do think the possibility of Alternative does present real problems for standard realist outlooks. But if indeed it does, it does so via the somewhat more laborious route here presented: via the discussion of the threat of ineffable questions and the threat of having to accept a deflationary view.

---

their (2000). There they distinguish two kinds of "relativism." First, they introduce "chauvinistic conceptual relativism" as a *label* for the upshot of the argument. I find the use of the relativist label unfortunate, but be that as it may. One is free to adopt labels as one wishes. Second, they note that one way for the target of their argument to *respond* is to say that even if we and the Twin Earthians refer to different things by our moral words, still the words *mean* the same. This may amount to a genuinely relativist view. But even so, what they are considering under this heading is clearly an *optional move* for their opponent, and not anything that immediately falls out of Alternative-friendly views.

[32] Boyd (1988), p. 225f.

2.5 Sameness of Normative Role

Throughout this chapter I have talked of predicates having the same *normative role*. I have used such talk earlier too, and such talk will be used throughout this book. This may well be a source of considerable, and reasonable, uneasiness. What is it for two predicates—two non-coextensive predicates, at that—to have the same normative role? I find the idea of normative role rather intuitive myself. It is characteristic of normative predicates that they are fit to be used in practical deliberation relating to what to do; it is characteristic of such predicates that their application has, so to speak, practical consequences in addition to merely theoretical ones. They have normative roles. And I think that it is likewise intuitive that different kinds of normative predicates are used differently, as far as such normative roles are concerned. For example, the normative use of "thin" predicates is different from that of the various "thick" ones, and evaluating morally is different from evaluating aesthetically. Different kinds of normative predi-cates have different normative roles. But if one can compare normative roles, one can also judge when two predicates have the same normative role. Even if one cannot state in very informative terms what the normative role of a predicate is, one can intelligibly speak of sameness of normative role.

What I am talking about under the heading of normative role is what Horgan and Timmons (1992a) are talking about in different terms when describing their Moral Twin Earth scenario. When describing the case, they say, as quoted earlier,

Moral Twin Earthlings are normally disposed to act in certain ways corresponding to judgments about what is "good" and "right"; they normally take considerations about what is "good" and "right" to be especially important, even of overriding importance in most cases, in deciding what to do, and so on.[33]

Horgan and Timmons' characterization is so vague that it does not *solve* any *problems* anyone might have with the notion of sameness of normative role. But it does illustrate that the idea of such sameness is found in the literature. Sameness of normative role is also what Hare, from his non-descriptivist perspective, in the passage quoted above discusses under the heading of evaluative meaning, and what he alludes to when calling the different words which we translate as "wrong" "rough equivalents." What justifies calling the words "equivalents" (even rough equivalents) is that they have the same normative role; the (rough) equivalence is not a matter of extension or descriptive content. Generally, anyone who uses Moral Twin Earth-style scenarios to draw general conclusions about the fate of normative realist theories relies on a notion like what I am calling normative role, for she relies on the idea that despite the differences between the communities, the distinctly normative aspects of the use of the terms in question are the same.

Suppose, however, that I should not be granted a notion of sameness of normative role. After all, just because some theorists use the notion, that does not mean it is in

---

[33] Horgan and Timmons (1992a), p. 188.

good standing. Would this mean that the present discussion is somehow completely misbegotten?

No—for even if the notion of normative role is not in good standing, the kinds of *problems* I have been concerned with here do arise, as follows. Consider some different linguistic communities, each with its own set of normative terms, including its own set of "thin" terms, such that the normative terms of the different communities all fail to be coextensive with each other. Suppose further—along the lines of the doubts just brought up—that it is at best unclear whether any of these terms used by the different communities have the same normative role. It cannot be said that any alternative "ought" determinately has the same role as ours does. And suppose lastly that *which* of these normative terms you employ matters for action-guiding purposes. The positive thin terms of one language apply to different things from what the positive thin terms of another language apply to. Again the concern arises: how should you react, knowing that while you ought to φ, you ought* to ψ, where *ought** is what is expressed by one of these alternative normative terms and φ and ψ are incompatible courses of action? The same puzzles as before arise with respect to *this* question.

So the notion of sameness of normative role need not be in good standing for the problems with which I am concerned to arise. However, it is important for the possible *way out* that I have suggested—embracing Alternative-unfriendliness—that the notion of normative role be in good standing. What I have been suggesting is that the problems discussed arise only for a certain class of theories, the Alternative-friendly ones. Alternative-unfriendly ones, ones allowing for normative role to be reference-determining, avoid the problems. The problems are all the more pressing if what seemed like it might have been a reasonable way out does not work.

The same considerations apply in the case of a theorist who not only rejects talk of sameness of normative role but who moreover rejects the very idea that there is an intelligible notion of normative role. One can still state the puzzles I have been concerned with, albeit perhaps more cautiously. One can speak of non-coextensive predicates such that where members of one community take the application of one predicate to speak to what to do, the members of another take the application of another to speak to this issue. The different positive normative predicates they use apply to different things, and the use of the different vocabularies in this way guide action in different ways. Which of these predicates, someone might try to ask herself, is the one that *ought* to be used to guide actions? The same problems arise as before. The skepticism about the very notion of normative role only blocks a certain way out: that of appeal to how normative role can determine reference. (The new version of the scenario brought up, where it is not stipulated that the normative terms have the same normative roles, can be suspected to problematize the suggested way out, even if talk of sameness of normative role is allowed and normative role can determine reference. Our predicates can be determined by normative role to ascribe some properties, and their predicates can be determined by normative role to ascribe some other properties. Still, one can try to ask the problematic question: which predicates ought we to use? This—serious—objection I will return to in Chapter 3.)

My own view is that the notion of normative role, and of sameness of normative role, is in good standing. In section 2.6, I turn to one "model" from the literature. But I do not see the import of the discussion as hinging on the assumption that the notion of sameness of normative role is in good standing. Some of what I discuss assumes that it is; but again, if it is not in good standing then so much the worse for the ardent realist.

2.6 Wedgwood's View

The model alluded to is the kind of theory found in Ralph Wedgwood's (2001, 2007) view, according to which it is a normative predicate's normative role that determines its reference—so every predicate with the same normative role has the same reference. Wedgwood thinks that certain thin normative concepts are such that for a thinker to have such, the concept is for the thinker to have a concept that plays the right normative role in the thinker's cognitive economy. In what follows, I follow Wedgwood's (2001) presentation, which I find somewhat simpler. It is the overall structure of Wedgwood's view that is of relevance for present purposes.

Wedgwood proposes a certain form of conceptual-role semantics for normative terms. When presenting his view, he focuses on a particular predicate, intuitively meaning something like "ought all things considered to prefer," whose semantic value is conceived of as completely determined by its *action-guiding role* or role in *practical reasoning*—what I have kept calling its normative role. More precisely, what Wedgwood proposes is that the predicate is governed by the following basic rule:

Acceptance of "B(x, y, me, t)" commits one to having a preference for doing x over doing y at time t.[34]

Whether or not our actual language contains any expression with the meaning this predicate is supposed to have, a Wedgwoodian claim is that we could employ a predicate with this as the basic rule governing it.

Appeal to the basic rule only goes to the question of what it is to be competent with the predicate: it is to be disposed to employ it in accordance with this rule—to be disposed to prefer doing x over doing y at t when accepting "B(x, y, me, t)," to correct oneself when one notices exceptions to this pattern, etc.

This account of competence is in principle compatible with any number of accounts of the reference, or semantic value, of the predicate. For example, one can consistently adopt a causal theory of reference-determination for the predicate. Wedgwood has a separate story about how the semantic value is determined by the normative role with which the predicate is associated. He holds that the reference, or semantic value, of this predicate is the relation, if any, such that

---

[34] Wedgwood (2001), p. 15.

it is correct for z to prefer doing x over doing y at t and a mistake for z to prefer doing y over doing x at t if, and only if, x, y, z, and t stand in that relation.[35]

The preference is correct if and only if it is in accordance with the goal of practical reasoning. It is a substantive question if there is such a goal and, if so, what the goal is. Wedgwood takes there to be such a goal.[36]

Wedgwood's theory is—or, more cautiously, is meant to be—Alternative-unfriendly, since the basic rule states what the normative role of the predicate "B(x, y, me, t)" is, and this basic rule is then further held to determine reference. All predicates governed by that basic rule have the same reference. It does not follow already from the fact that the predicate is governed by this basic rule that the theory is Alternative-unfriendly. This only follows given the theory of how reference is determined.[37]

When describing how the semantic value is determined by the conceptual role, Wedgwood usefully compares conceptual-role semantics for the logical connectives. If "&" is given a conceptual-role semantics, and its meaning is characterized by the standard introduction and elimination rules, its semantic value is determined to be the operation—conjunction—that best fits these rules (makes them valid, etc.). By analogy, if "B(x, y, z, t)" is characterized by the above rule, its semantic value is determined to be what fits this rule. (And in each case there is a question of whether the world cooperates and there is such a semantic value.)

Modulo some important qualifications, which I will get to in Chapter 3, Wedgwood's theory is Alternative-unfriendly. The reference of the predicate that Wedgwood considers is determined by the normative role associated with the predicate. In this way, Wedgwood's theory differs importantly from Cornell realism and Jackson's descriptivism.[38] I have described only what Wedgwood says about one possible normative predicate, but the example is supposed to indicate a general conception of how normative terms can get their reference determined.

---

[35] Wedgwood (2001), p. 18. What if there is no such relation? One can go different ways. One possibility is to say that the predicate then has an empty extension. Another possibility is to adopt a more liberal view and say that the predicate can still have a non-empty extension: it can ascribe a relation that is sufficiently like the relation that so to speak would be the most fitting semantic value for the predicate.

[36] Wedgwood (2001), p. 20.

[37] Wedgwood himself says,

> The possibility of such moral disagreement [as is found in cases like Moral Twin Earth cases of the kind directed against Jackson-style analyses] casts serious doubt on all noncircular conceptual analyses. But the possibility of such disagreement casts no doubt on the conceptual role semantics that I have proposed. According to my semantics, you and your friend both mean the same thing by the term "wrong," because you both master the rule according to which certain moral beliefs commit one to a certain sort of *preference* or endorsement of *attitude*. That is, for both of you, sincere acceptance of a sentence involving "wrong" has the same *consequences* for *practical reasoning* even if your moral thought is guided by different fundamental moral intuitions, so that you form opposite moral beliefs on the basis of the same nonmoral beliefs. (2001, p. 29)

Wedgwood talks about "consequences for practical reasoning" where I would talk about normative role.

[38] Wedgwood (2001), p. 29 himself makes essentially this point.

It may be thought that non-naturalist realist views generally are like Wedgwood's view in being Alternative-unfriendly. But that need not be so, as stressed already in Chapter 1. Suppose that we accept the non-naturalist realist's metaphysics of normative properties. There still remains the separate question: by virtue of what does a given predicate refer to a given normative property? If the non-naturalist rejects Wedgwood's view on reference-determination, then, regardless of how special and normative the properties she postulates are, she does not offer anything that immediately gets around the problem posed by Moral Twin Earth arguments. Absent a suitable view on reference-determination, it can still be that predicates with the same normative role are not coextensive.

Wedgwood's own outlook incorporates many more elements than the ones I mentioned; elements I will abstract away from in my discussion.[39] For example, Wedgwood endorses a form of normative judgment internalism, and he holds that "the intentional is normative" (and moreover that this is the key to metaethics).[40]

What I claim is that the only reasonable way for the ardent realist to deal with the dilemma I have been concerned to stress in this chapter is to avoid it by appealing to Alternative-unfriendliness. This is not to defend Alternative-unfriendliness outright. There may be general reasons for skepticism about the prospects of Alternative-unfriendly theories. There may also be worries not unlike those that have been in focus here that do arise for Alternative-unfriendly theories. I will turn to this in Chapter 3.

The way that many contemporary metaethicists see it, an important fault line between different realist views is that between naturalist and non-naturalist views. This is illustrated by, for example, the non-naturalist arguments discussed above. But there are two importantly different distinctions in the vicinity. One has to do exclusively with metaphysics, while the other, although likewise with metaphysical implications, has to do with language, more specifically with reference-determination. The metaphysical distinction is between the *metaphysically moderate* views according to which to allow normative properties and facts is not to introduce anything alien to an ordinary naturalistic worldview, and *metaphysically radical* views according to which it is to introduce something thus alien. Naturalist views are metaphysically moderate views and non-naturalist views are metaphysically radical views. The distinction that has to do with reference-determination is best explained by appeal to the notion of referential normativity. To hold that normative predicates are referentially normative is to hold that they have their reference determined in a way importantly different from that in which ordinary descriptive predicates get their reference determined.[41] It is, to be sure, a generalization of the

---

[39] Relatedly, I will not discuss at any length the criticisms of the specific aspects of Wedgwood's view that have appeared in the literature. For such criticisms, see, for example, Schroeter and Schroeter (2003), Schroeder (2008), and Holton (2010).

[40] Compare Enoch (2011), pp. 179ff, who relies on Wedgwood's view on reference-determination but also abstracts away from these further commitments on Wedgwood's part.

[41] I don't mean to imply that all descriptive predicates get their reference determined in the same way. Surely there can be, and arguably is, diversity in that regard. Especially given the fact of diversity in how

fairly commonplace idea of conceptual-role semantics; but that *normative* role as opposed to descriptive role could determine reference is a much less commonplace idea. To hold that normative predicates have their reference determined causally in the way that Cornell realists like Boyd (1988) and Brink (1989) hold, or to hold that they have their reference determined by descriptive folk theories in the way Jackson (1998) holds, is to hold that they have their reference determined in the same kind of way that descriptive predicates have their reference determined. To be *metasemantically moderate* is to go along with the Cornell realists or with Jackson on this, and not just regarding actual normative predicates but all possible non-defective normative predicates; if one holds that some possible non-defective normative predicates are referentially normative, then one is *metasemantically radical*. While it may seem most natural to either be moderate along both dimensions or radical along both dimensions, mixed views are certainly possible. It is, for example, a substantive hypothesis that any property ascribed by a referentially normative predicate would have to be non-naturalistic. What this turns on is whether any property that is fit to be picked out by such a predicate would have to be so special that it could not simply be another part of the naturalistic world order.[42]

---

descriptive predicates get their reference determined, the talk of metasemantic radicalness cannot be expected to be particularly precise.

[42] Compare in this connection Moore's open question argument. In brief, the argument runs as follows. Consider any purported naturalistic analysis of goodness, for example one according to which something's being good is the same thing as our desiring to desire it. The open question argument says that even having determined that something is such that we desire to desire it, the question of whether this something is good is not settled—this question remains open. But since the question remains open, something's being good cannot be the same thing as our desiring to desire it. This naturalistic analysis of goodness fails, and all other naturalistic analyses of goodness fail for the same reason.

Moore's open question argument does not successfully establish that the property of being good cannot be a naturalistically acceptable property; at most it establishes that the concept of being good cannot be analyzed in terms of non-normative concepts. This point has been made by many theorists criticizing Moore's argument. And I am unsure how much force to accord to the argument, even understood only as an argument regarding the unanalyzability of the concept of being good (despite being sympathetic to its conclusion): concerning the felt distance between the concept of being good and the proposed analyses, one can just say that some correct analyses are not obviously correct. But for what it is worth, many metaethicists have seen something compelling there, and they have taken the argument to indicate something that is not just another instance of the general fact that it is hard to come up with acceptable analysis. In principle, a metasemantically radical view is well placed to accommodate this. A friend of such a view can say that the reason why the felt distance between the concept of being good and any purported naturalistic descriptive analysis of it is greater than the felt distance in other cases of concepts we have failed to analyze is that the concept of being good has its reference determined in a way that is different in kind from how descriptive concepts have their reference determined. If one could further argue that metasemantic radicalness entails metaphysical radicalness—that if a metasemantically radical view is true of normative concepts then the properties they ascribe, if any, would have to be non-natural, then one would have an argument for non-naturalism (or for the claim that any acceptable realist view would have to be non-naturalist) that makes essential use of something much like the open-question argument. The strategy behind this possible argument again illustrates the usefulness of distinguishing being metasemantically radical/moderate from being metaphysically radical/moderate. That distinction is central to the strategy of the argument.

2.7 Concluding Remarks

Either Alternative is possible or not. If it is not possible, a number of theories of the semantics of normative terms, the Alternative-friendly views, are false. If it is possible, difficult questions arise concerning what to say about the issue of whether any actual or possible terms are in any way objectively normatively privileged.

The problems I have been concerned with are problems that arise for Alternative-friendly theories. If one instead embraces Alternative-unfriendliness and says that some possible non-defective thin normative terms, the kind we have been concerned with, have their reference determined by normative role, then one quite obviously avoids these problems in their present guise. The overall picture would be that the properties ascribed by terms whose reference is determined by normative role are normatively privileged: there is something about how these properties are in themselves that make them fit to be picked out by these normative roles. One needn't face the choice of either saying that there is an ineffable Further Question of the kind discussed or embracing a deflationary attitude.

Of course, that Alternative-unfriendly views avoid the specific problems I have been concerned with here does not mean that they are not problematic in other ways, or even that they avoid all nearby problems. In Chapter 3 I will, among other things, discuss some problems for Alternative-unfriendly theories.

3

Qualifications and Objections

The arguments in Chapter 2 drive at the idea that there is an important dividing line in metaethics between Alternative-friendly and Alternative-unfriendly theories. Only given an Alternative-unfriendly theory can ardent realism be defended.

In this chapter I will pick up some loose ends from Chapter 2. I will introduce some needed qualifications, compare some (seemingly) similar considerations from the literature, respond to some mistaken objections—and, lastly, discuss an objection I am not sure there is a good response to. The objection concerns whether a version of the same problem discussed in Chapter 2 arises for the Alternative-unfriendly theories.

3.1 Some Qualifications

I have said that a theory like Wedgwood's is Alternative-unfriendly in the sense characterized. I basically want to stand by that. But I need to be more careful regarding the characterization of Alternative-unfriendliness.

When speaking about Alternative-friendliness and Alternative-unfriendliness, I have so far spoken about the normative roles "associated with" terms. But there are important distinctions to draw when it comes to the "associated with." Compare the ordinary descriptive case. Suppose it is indeed part of the meaning of "bachelor" that "all bachelors are unmarried men" is true. Then the description "unmarried man" is associated with "bachelor." But "bachelor" can also be associated with terms in a different way. For every sentence "All bachelors are F" that is generally regarded as true, "bachelor" is in some way associated with being F. "Unmarried man" is *conventionally* associated with "bachelor" but in some other cases the association is not conventional; we just tend to link the items in our thinking. Similarly, one and the same normative role can be associated with different expressions in different ways. Consider some seemingly purely descriptive predicate "D." If we generally believe that all and only things that are D are right, then the same normative role that is associated with "right" is, in some sense, associated also with "D." Given our convictions, considerations about what is D are action-guiding. But no one could reasonably hold that just because "D" is associated with the normative role in this way, it must have the same semantic value as "right." After all, we can be wrong. So if one speaks of Alternative-friendliness in the careless way I have so far, speaking merely of normative roles "associated with" terms, then all reasonable theories are Alternative-friendly—and Wedgwood's theory certainly is Alternative-friendly.

An obvious fix is to replace the talk of merely being "associated with" with talk of what is *conventionally* or *semantically* associated with a term. Then it is more plausible that Wedgwood's theory is Alternative-unfriendly. The extended argument against "Alternative-friendly" theories that I have given is then to be seen as an argument against theories given which the thinnest terms can have the same normative roles conventionally associated with them, and yet differ in reference.

There is also another complication. It is best explained by consideration of a different case. Suppose I define an ordinary descriptive predicate F by saying that something is F exactly if it is both G and H. Then descriptions G and H are conventionally associated with F, and they intuitively determine its reference. But now consider a different predicate F+ governed by the same stipulation but for which it is also stipulated that some particular object b is F+, where b fails to be both G and H. In some way, F+ is defective. Whatever exactly should be said about F+'s semantic value, it seems plausible that F and F+ are not coextensive. (F+ might have an empty extension, or it might be indeterminate what its extension is, or its extension can be what in some sense comes closest to satisfying the inconsistent stipulations.)

Just to take an example, suppose I introduce the predicate "bachelor*" by the stipulation that something is a bachelor just in case it is both unmarried and a man, but also make the stipulation that Sarah Palin, who is neither, is a bachelor*. There may be difficult theoretical questions about what exactly to say about the extension of "bachelor*." But one thing that is not clear, at least, is that "bachelor*" is true of exactly the unmarried men.

Consider now a predicate B+ which relates to Wedgwood's B in the way that F+ relates to F. It is governed by the same rule as F but by some other rule as well, perhaps to the effect that what satisfies such-and-such descriptive conditions is B+. Whatever exactly should be said about B+'s semantic value, B+ and B are not coextensive. But then there can be predicates conventionally associated with the same normative role but that still are not coextensive—and for general reasons, so it seems genuine Alternative-unfriendliness still cannot be achieved.

If it could be insisted that F+ and B+ are meaningless—that the inconsistent stipulations fail to endow them with meanings—then the problem is averted. One could say that according to an Alternative-unfriendly theory, all *meaningful* terms associated with the same normative role have the same semantic value. But I don't think it can plausibly be said that all expressions like F+ and B+ are meaningless. In general, there can be perfectly meaningful terms governed by inconsistent stipulations.[1] What one can try to say is that F+ and B+ are semantically defective, and that according to an Alternative-unfriendly theory all semantically non-defective

---

[1] See e.g. Eklund (2002a).

terms conventionally associated with the same normative role have the semantic value. Taking this route, one would need to spell out exactly what semantic defectiveness is. A different option still would be to consider only those terms that have conventionally associated with them only a given normative role and nothing else. The relevant question about these terms would be if they could have non-defective semantic values, as opposed to being empty or meaningless or radically semantically indeterminate.

When considering how to understand referential normativity, it is important to remember that we have been concerned with the thinnest normative terms. Consider some other normative terms, e.g. terms of the form "good F" ("good tennis player," "good administrator," "good sniper"), or thick normative terms like "courageous," "brutal," "cruel," etc. Just as in the case of the thinnest terms, one can ask whether the reference of one of these expressions is determined by normative role. But whereas in the case of the thinnest terms it is intuitively relatively clear what the question amounts to—witness the lively discussion of Moral Twin Earth cases, comparing our "good" and "right" with the counterpart terms of the Moral Twin Earthlings—it is unclear even how to approach this question in the case of these other normative terms. Consider:

There is a linguistic community speaking a language much like English, except for the following differences (and whatever differences are directly entailed). While their word "___" is associated with the same normative role as our word "___" is associated with, their word is not coextensive with our "___." So even if they are exactly right about what is ___ in their sense, and they seek to promote and to do what is ___ in their sense, they do not seek to promote what is ___.

If one tries to replace "___" with "good tennis player" or "courageous," one runs into trouble when trying to evaluate whether a scenario of this kind is possible. There are two ways of thinking about the normative roles of these expressions. First, one may be content with a coarse-grained individuation of normative roles, and, for example, think of the normative role associated with "courageous" as simply being, roughly, *favorably assessing the action, agent, or character trait involved.* But in that case, "courageous" and "modest" will have the same normative role, and it is quite obvious that this normative role does not determine reference. Second, one can instead think of normative roles in a more fine-grained way, such that the normative role of "courageous" is different from that of other positive normative terms used to assess actions, agents, and character traits. The problem is that thus conceived, the normative roles of these terms seem inseparable from descriptive aspects of their use. The fine-grained normative role of "good tennis player" is inseparable from what it is to play tennis. It is unintelligible how these thicker or more complex terms could have the same fine-grained normative role yet differ in descriptive respects.

If one speaks of "normative role" in the fine-grained way, then perhaps one should for this reason say that in the case of these expressions normative role determines reference, and rather trivially so. One cannot even make sense of different expressions of "good tennis player" with the same normative role but different reference, so one cannot intelligibly engage in the thought experiment of considering whether the scenario envisaged is possible. However, that the normative roles of these terms determine reference is no immediate comfort for the would-be ardent realist. I might aspire to be a good democrat while someone else aspires to be a good fascist. Maybe both "good democrat" and "good fascist" are referentially normative—the reference of these complex expressions is determined by normative role—but there is another question of whether either of our aims is to be valued simpliciter.

The question of how best to distinguish between, on the one hand, the kind of normativity that pertains to the thinnest possible terms and, on the other, the kind of normativity that pertains to, for example, many terms of the form "good F" is difficult. I will turn to issues in the vicinity in Chapter 9, but will not resolve this issue even then. Regardless of how the distinction is best drawn, it is the referential normativity of possible terms in the former class that is relevant to the aims of ardent realism.

Some theorists might wish to maintain that *all our non-defective normative terms* are like terms in the second class. If those theorists are right, as they may well be for all that I am concerned to argue in this book, then none of our actual terms expresses what is of relevance to the ardent normative realist's aims. Even so, the ardent normative realist's aims could be satisfied so long as some *possible* normative terms belong in the former of the two categories distinguished, and those terms are referentially normative. That is what I am concerned with. Of course, a theorist could in principle maintain that not only all actual normative terms but also all possible ones belong in the second class. But such a claim—as opposed to the importantly different claim that all *non-defective* possible normative terms belong in the second class—beggars belief.

One thing that emerges as the earlier somewhat careless talk of normative roles associated with terms is scrutinized in more detail is that the idea of Alternative-unfriendliness is beholden to controversial claims in general philosophy of language concerning something going beyond reference that is part of the meanings of expressions. Both *Quineans*, who reject the idea that there is any reasonable distinction to be drawn between what is part of meaning and what is not, and the theorists we, following Williamson, can call *referentialists*, who insist that there is nothing more to meaning than reference, will take issue with that.[2] Rather than address these issues in general philosophy of language head on, let me just say this. The most plausible view I can see on what it is for an expression or concept to be normative is that the expression is semantically associated with a normative role, and the most plausible view that I can see on what properties are normative is that a property is normative just in case it is apt to be ascribed by a referentially normative expression. I will present considerations in favor of these views in Chapters 4 and 5. My concern

---

[2] Williamson (2009).

with Quineanism and referentialism has to do with how these theories can make sense of what it is for an expression or concept to be normative, and of what it is for a property to be normative.

3.2 The Extent of the Divergence

I have said that some theories of normative semantics are Alternative-friendly: on these theories it holds for the thinnest possible normative roles that two terms can have the same role of this kind yet differ in extension. But I have left open the *extent* to which they can differ in extension. It may be thought that if the extensions of predicates with the same normative role can only differ slightly, then the problems I have discussed are not very serious. The normative predicates corresponding to each other in normative role may by and large agree with each other in their application, and if some proposed action is in the extension of all the counterparts of "right," then we can say that this action is licensed as right in a way that can be thought to give comfort to the ardent realist. Maybe there are actions such that they are in the extensions of some but not all counterparts of "right," and in *some* sense there may be no objective fact of the matter about how to act, but so long as these actions are *fairly few and far between* that need not be of great concern. One can then avoid both the idea of a Further Question, apparently ineffable, and the threatening deflationary consequences of denying that there is such a question. The whole problematic is, one may think, defused.

Nothing I have said so far blocks this strategy. But if the proponent of a supposedly Alternative-friendly theory attempts this as a way out, she is for all important intents and purposes abandoning her Alternative-friendliness. She is emphasizing that "right" and its counterparts divide actions into three classes—(i) the class of those actions falling under all of them (let us say that these actions are *superright*), (ii) the class of those actions falling under some but not all of them, and (iii) the class of those actions falling under none of them—and what is more, she accords a certain importance to this tripartite distinction. There is something important that distinguishes those actions that are superright; and the question of which actions are superright is privileged over the question of what actions fall under our "right." But if she holds this, nothing of importance separates her from a theorist who rather says that the extension of "right" is completely determined by the predicate's normative role but allows that the normative role does not determine a fully determinate extension. Of course, she says something different about the specific semantics of "right" than does this other theorist. But by her own lights, the normatively central question in the vicinity is not about what happens to fall under our "right" but instead about what is superright; what is guaranteed to fall under all these predicates because of the normative role associated with them all.

Alternative-friendliness cannot be defended by appeal to the notion of what is superright. In fact, the notion of superrightness can be appealed to in an independent argument which in its own way presents problems for Alternative-friendly theories. I do not myself think that the argument in the end works, but it deserves mentioning. The argument is this: So long as the notion of the normative role associated with a predicate is in good standing (and there is no *immediate* reason why the friend of an Alternative-friendly theory would have to deny that), a notion of superrightness can be defined—but it cannot plausibly be denied that what is superright is thereby normatively privileged, since what is superright falls under every predicate associated in the right way with the normative role of "right." And what is more, superrightness is an Alternative-unfriendly notion. Or so the argument runs.

There are several different possible responses available to the theorist who wishes to remain genuinely Alternative-friendly. She might, for example, question the very notion of normative role, or insist that a superrightness predicate would be gerrymandered and of no real normative import. To see the motivation for saying this, compare another thin predicate, "permissible." What is superpermissible would be what falls under all concepts of permissibility. But to go with what is superpermissible when addressing matters of permissibility is to adopt a particular, very restrictive stance—and there is nothing that warrants the claim that the agent who uses superpermissibility as her notion of permissibility uses a particularly privileged notion of permissibility. Indeed, it can be that no notion of permissibility with the same normative role as ours is coextensive with the notion of superpermissibility.[3]

3.3 All Things Considered

Granted a conceptual difference between all-things-considered terms and moral terms, I focus on the all-things-considered terms, as mentioned early on in this chapter. But some philosophers are skeptical of the idea of all-things-considered normative terms such as the all-things-considered ought and the all-things-considered right. And such skepticism is sometimes associated with the naturalist realism that often goes together with Alternative-friendliness. The theorists I have discussed as defending causal and descriptivist theories of reference-determination do tend in fact to speak specifically of morality. One might worry that by focusing on what Alternative-friendly theories say about the all-things-considered terms, I am discussing something with only rather limited interest.

A first response to this charge is that even if Alternative-friendliness does in fact tend to go together with skepticism about an all-things-considered ought, the overall theme of the present discussion has to do with things like what is required for what I called ardent realism. It is then relevant to demonstrate that not even allowing an all-things-considered ought suffices for ardent realism. Given Alternative-friendliness, the ardent realist is still not home free.

---

[3] Compare perhaps the in some ways parallel remarks concerning supervaluationism about vagueness in my (2010).

But let me also address doubts about the all-things-considered ought. Before doing so, however, let me note a certain ambiguity in the question of whether there can be an all-things-considered ought. One question in the vicinity is that of whether there can be an all-things-considered ought; another can be stated as one of whether there can be an all-things-considered "ought," quotes added. What I mean is this. Distinguishing between representations (like expressions and concepts) and the things in the world our representations stand for, one question is whether there can be a representation with certain features, a certain kind of "ought"; another is whether there can be something in the world that this representation stands for, a certain kind of ought. One possible view is that there is such a thing as the concept all things considered-"ought," but since all the ought-facts in the world are specific ought-facts of the kind *ought in order to...*,[4] there is nothing in the world that corresponds to that concept. However, having noted the ambiguity, I will speak throughout of the "all-things considered ought," omitting quotation marks to avoid clutter, and letting context disambiguate when necessary.

There are in principle two importantly different ways of rejecting the all-things-considered ought. A *radical* way of rejecting it involves saying that various oughts that are in different ways relativized are *all there are*—there's what one morally ought to do, what one prudentially ought to do, what one ought to do for one's mother's sake, and also what one ought to do to benefit the 1 percent, or the Nazi cause. And if one tries to ask: but what *ought* I really to do, what I morally ought to do, or what benefits the 1 percent, or what furthers the Nazi cause, etc.?—then the first italicized "ought" is in fact always used with some relativized meaning or other, the relativization being supplied by context, and the thought that some of these oughts are objectively privileged over others is deemed a myth. A more *moderate* way of rejecting the idea of an all-things-considered ought involves still *privileging* some oughts over others. The view would be that there still is something that privileges (say) the moral ought over the, so to speak, unsavory oughts, and makes it objectively correct to be moved by the moral ought but not by the unsavory oughts—and it is not simply that *morality* enjoins us to be more concerned with what we morally ought to do.

These two ways of rejecting the notion of an all-things-considered ought are importantly different. Focus first on the more radical kind of rejection. There is a clear, intuitive sense in which this jettisons what one might want to get out of normative realism. It is clearly unsatisfactory from the point of view of the ardent realist. While there may be facts about what I morally ought to do, they are in no way objectively normatively privileged over facts about what I ought to do to further this-or-that unsavory cause. I might happen to be such as to be more moved by some considerations over others, but that is a different matter. Turn then to the view of someone who rejects the all-things-considered "ought" only in the more moderate

---

[4] Or however best to characterize the relativized or specific ought-facts.

kind of way. One worry about this kind of view concerns whether it is stable. Is not the view in effect that I *ought all-things-considered* to be moved by considerations about what I morally ought to do but not about considerations about what one ought to do to further the Nazi cause? Moreover, suppose, contrary to what I have just suggested, that the kind of view just described is indeed stable, and a reasonable view. Then note that the considerations discussed in this chapter can be presented directly for, e.g., the moral case, if need be. I can ask whether a given theory of how the *moral* "ought" and *moral* "right" get their reference determined is Alternative-friendly (that is, whether it allows for there being alternative terms with the same normative role but different reference), and proceed from there. If it is assumed that there is an all-things-considered ought, then running the argument directly concerning the moral ought would not be very attractive, for the reason that even if there are non-coextensive *moral* "oughts" with the same normative role, one can, for all that the argument pertaining to the moral case says, go on to ask the "further" question about whether one *ought* to be concerned with what one "morally ought" to do or with what one "morally ought*" to do, employing the all-things-considered "ought." But if, as we are now considering, there is no all-things-considered ought, then the argument can usefully be run with the moral "ought" as its target.

3.4 Normative Theory

My discussion is and has been very abstract, and proceeds at a certain remove from actual normative theorizing. One impatient response to my suggestion that comparing "ought" and its would-be counterpart "ought*" presents interesting puzzles is that if indeed there are these two different notions then we simply get our hands dirty and do *normative theory* to decide in favor of one over the other. Taken in the most straightforward way, this suggestion is clearly wrongheaded. What normative theory does is to figure out the truth about (the principles regarding) what we ought to do. Normative theory as carried out by members of the alternative community would aim to figure out the truth about (the principles regarding) what one ought* to do. The puzzles that I have been concerned with have to do with how to decide between focusing on ought-facts and focusing on ought*-facts. Neither our normative theorizing nor theirs helps with that decision. (Our normative theory says which facts one *ought* to be concerned with and their normative theory says which facts one *ought** to be concerned with.)

The response is the same if the complaint is put not in terms of normative theory but in terms of *reflective equilibrium*.[5] It is a point often repeated that in normative theorizing the proper method is one of getting our different beliefs into such an equilibrium. But whatever the virtues may be in general of appealing to this method,

---

[5] The classic references are Rawls (1971) and Goodman (1955). See Daniels (2011) for a recent overview.

QUALIFICATIONS AND OBJECTIONS 53

it is beside the point in the present context. If, as is *stipulated* to be the case in the set-up of the problem, "ought" and "ought*" are not coextensive, then *any* fully reliable method for arriving at answers as to what ought to be done and as to what ought* to be done will yield that what ought to be done is not the same as what ought* to be done.

There is a somewhat better version of the "can't we just do normative theory?"-complaint. The complaint can be answered also when raised in this way, but the issues brought up are interesting. It is a commonplace that various theoretical enterprises are such that they also involve conceptual improvement. Physical theorizing may have begun with the concept of weight, but that concept has been abandoned in favor of different mass concepts. It is a natural thought—and I believe a correct one—that philosophy too should involve conceptual improvement.[6] In branches of philosophy, as in branches of science, we can abandon folk concepts for serious inquiry and instead use technical concepts specially crafted for the theoretical purposes in question. In metaphysics we can come up with new concepts, better suited for the theoretical purposes at hand. Maybe normative theorizing should be seen that way too, in which case even if we start with (say) the folk concept *right*, a process of conceptual improvement can yield that we instead should use a somewhat different concept. Moreover, it can be said that the history of philosophy already to a significant extent is a history of conceptual improvement: philosophical theorizing regularly can and does lead to improved ideology, improvements in the tools we use. The "can't we just do normative theory?"-complaint can be rephrased as: through normative theorizing we arrive at the normatively better concepts.

But there is an interesting disanalogy between the case of thin normative concepts like the concept *right* and the other cases brought up. In each of the other cases where we consider whether to use concept C or concept C*, we can ask in suitably independent terms which concept to use. When comparing two scientific concepts, one can ask which concept is such that its use would produce a more theoretically virtuous theory. Sometimes in the case of normative expressions and concepts, we can ask ourselves a somewhat related question. When we consider whether we ought to use such terms as "slutty," "chaste," "perverted," etc., or whether some other terms, with different meaning, what we ask are which terms we ought to use for the purposes of evaluating sexual behavior. But when we try to turn to the thinnest normative expressions and ask whether to, for example, use "ought" or "ought*," we are asking, well, which one we *ought* to use, or which one we have *most reason* to use, etc. The general point is that we will use one or other of the thin normative expressions we have when trying to raise the issue. If we were instead asking whether a theory using one of these concepts was more explanatory or otherwise theoretically virtuous in the standard sense than a theory using the other concept, we just would

---

[6] See e.g. Burgess and Plunkett (2013a, 2013b). I will return to this issue, and focus more on it, in Chapter 10.

not be asking the normatively relevant question. One of these "oughts" could be more useful for these theoretical purposes even while it is not therefore the one that is, so to speak, privileged for normative purposes. So when we try to ask what would constitute conceptual improvement when it comes to what normative conceptual tools to use when engaging in normative discourse, we either frame the question so as to favor one set of normative conceptual tools over another or we frame the question in such a way that it does not capture what we want to ask—it ends up being about something other than what pertains to the specifically normative. This is the ineffability concern from earlier, in a different guise.

3.5 Embarrassment of Riches

In this section I wish to turn to what I see as a very serious objection to the positive suggestion I have been highlighting and defending, that appeal to Alternative-unfriendliness gets around the problems for ardent realism. I call the problem *embarrassment of riches*. The discussion of this objection will be inconclusive. But toward the end of the discussion of the objection, I will present the type of answer that I favor.

Suppose that all terms that have their reference determined by some specific associated normative role, R, are indeed coextensional. It is still possible for a term to have a *slightly different* normative role R*—it does not have the exact same action-guiding role, or link to motivation—and fail to be coextensional with the terms with normative role R. And it is still possible that a term associated with the slightly different role R* has a significantly different extension from R.

If so, one community could use normative terms with some normative roles, and another could use normative terms with other normative roles. The members of these communities are guided by their deliberations to perform different actions. There is no sense to be made of whether to use a term with role R or a term with role R*. A problem similar to that faced by Alternative-friendly theories arises even if normative role determines reference.

The point can be put in terms of what would satisfy the ardent realist. Suppose that the ardent realist is granted everything, when it comes to issues brought up in Chapter 1. All standard forms of antirealism are ruled out. Humeanism about reasons is ruled out. There is an all-things-considered ought. And—adding the condition motivated by much of the discussion up to this point—normative predicates are referentially normative, in the sense introduced. But suppose that Bad Guy has normative predicates with *slightly* different normative roles from ours, and his positive normative predicates are true of the actions he tends to perform and false of the actions we tend to value. This possibility is not ruled out by anything said so far. And this kind of case does seem, in the abstract, to present the same sort of parity problem that the earlier scenarios involving alternative communities do. We can state normative justifications for our actions using our terms; Bad Guy can state normative justifications for his actions using his terms. But is there any way to make a case that our way of valuing is privileged (or even to provide content to the claim that it is privileged)?

It is important to be clear on exactly what the problem we are currently considering is a problem for. It is a problem for the ardent realist: is there any way at all to get the ardent realist what this realist desires? The working hypothesis was that Alternative-unfriendliness could be sufficient for the ardent realist. But now the worry arises that maybe not even this would be sufficient. It is also a problem as far as a suggested take-home lesson from the earlier discussion is concerned. The earlier discussion has suggested that there is a crucially relevant difference between metasemantically radical Alternative-unfriendly theories on the one hand and metasemantically moderate Alternative-friendly theories on the other. But what the present problem points to is that the same sort of problem that afflicts metasemantically moderate theories also afflicts at least a particular class of metasemantically radical theories. However, even should there be no acceptable reply to the present problem, that does not show that something is amiss with the present type of investigation. The negative points, about what does not suffice for the purposes of ardent realism, still stand. It is only that the outcome of the discussion is somewhat different from what the earlier discussion may have suggested. The upshot is not that ardent realism requires Alternative-unfriendliness. Instead, the upshot is that nothing could satisfy the ardent realist.

Of course, it is in itself not a problem that there may be different normative predicates associated with different normative roles. That is our actual situation. We have different normative predicates, and they are associated with different normative roles. Nor is it itself a problem if we have an expression associated with a given normative role and some other community has normative expressions but none associated with that same normative role. What is problematic is if there is some other possible community with an expression sufficiently much like our "ought" (say) in its associated normative role that intuitively their predicate is in *normative competition* with ours, while still the normative role is not exactly the same: if using that expression instead of "ought" for action-guiding purposes has a different practical upshot and one cannot easily combine using that expression and using "ought." The concern is abstract: I don't have a neat example of a possible expression fitting the bill.

In response to general concerns about what sameness of normative role might be, I brought up Wedgwood's view. Although I do not want to tie the discussion to this view, it may be again be useful to illustrate by considering it. The problem arises if there are predicates with slightly different normative roles from Wedgwood's "B(x, y, z, t)," governed by the rule:

Acceptance of "B(x, y, me, t)" commits one to having a preference for doing x over doing y at time t.

Are there such slightly different predicates? Well, there are such different predicates if there are, for example, notions of *commitment* or of *preference* somewhat different from ours: if, for example, there is a possible notion preference* much like our notion of preference but such that there are cases where someone prefers *a* to *b* but does not prefer* *a* to *b*, or vice versa. (Arguably the expression "preference" is vague, as are nearly all natural language expressions. Some different alternative notions of preference could correspond to possible precisifications of the actual vague notion.)

The embarrassment of riches problem is stated in terms of how terms with slightly different normative roles can have different extensions even if normative role determines reference. How serious the problem is depends on how referentially different the relevant terms can be. If the extensions are only barely different, then, it may be thought, there may be no cause for concern. But even if normative role determines reference, terms with only slightly different normative roles can in principle have even radically different extensions. (But compare earlier remarks on superrightness.)

The problem posed by consideration of terms with slightly different normative roles is not only a problem for certain aspects of what I have suggested on behalf of the ardent realist. It presents a problem also for others. Consider Gibbard's (2003) defense of a certain form of sophisticated expressivism. Much of Gibbard's discussion concerns a particular purported normative concept functioning a particular way. This concept is the concept of what Gibbard elsewhere calls the last "ought" before action. In the very first two paragraphs of his (2003), Gibbard says:

Holmes is stalked by Moriarty. He plans to escape by train, packing as late as possible to conceal his intentions. But by now it may be too late to catch the train, in which case packing is useless. If he has enough time, on the other hand, he might take a hansom cab and stop on the way by the river to investigate. Thinking through the considerations, he decides to starts packing.

What kind of thought is his decision to pack? What kind of utterance would express it—"express", that is, in the way a statement of fact expresses a belief in that fact? What kinds of reasoning can figure in his decision? Will his reasonings be confined to the facts, or are there special kinds of reasoning that enter into deciding?[7]

Gibbard uses this example to illustrate what the concept he wishes to focus on, the last "ought" before action, is supposed to be like. It is supposed to be this concept that figures in the reasoning indicated here. On Gibbard's view, Holmes can tell himself, equivalently, either "I ought to pack now," "So start packing now," or "I must pack now," or "packing is the thing to do." Different forms of words get at the same thing. Gibbard appropriates the phrase "what to do" and sometimes uses that to express the concept he is concerned with.

One thing Gibbard fails to ask—and the question is in a way so peculiar that it may only be natural to fail to ask it—is whether there is, instead of a unique possible

---

[7] Gibbard (2003), p. 3.

concept that is the last "ought" before action, a number of slightly different, non-coextensive concepts each with an equal claim to be the last "ought" before action, and different thinkers can employ different ones among these non-coextensive concepts. This question is essentially that of whether there are these different thinnest concepts with only slightly different normative roles. Gibbard presents parts of his discussion as a *possibility proof*: whether or not any concept we have is the "what to do" concept that Gibbard is talking about, it is possible for there to be such a concept. What the present discussion indicates is that there is also reason to wonder about the availability of something like a *uniqueness* proof. Can it be shown that there is only one concept with a claim to express a last ought before action?

One way to respond to the threat that there are these slightly different normative roles, and that Bad Guy can simply use concepts with slightly different normative roles, would be to seek to deny that there are these slightly different normative roles. I think this is somewhat attractive. Gibbard's talk of *the* last ought before action intuitively sounds persuasive. But one would like more of an argument.

In his (2001), Richard Joyce compares morality and practical rationality. He thinks while the former can be coherently questioned, the latter cannot. It is incoherent, Joyce says, to reason: "Yes, I recognize that there is practical reason for me to φ, but what is that to me?—Why should I adopt that set of rules?".[8] He elaborates,

Practical reasons are, by definition, those which guide our actions when everything has been taken into account: if the rules of chess are telling me to move my rook straight, the rules of etiquette telling me that I ought to let my opponent win, the rules of prudence telling me that I ought to move the rook diagonally (thereby annoying my opponent thereby winning a bet), then practical rationality is not a *further* consideration. Rather, when I have weighed all these claims and come up with an answer to what is to be done, then that is the judgment of practical rationality.[9]

In one sense, Joyce is right, and the point he makes relates to points I have been making. It seems impossible to rationally question one's thinnest normative terms. But there is a kind of complication that Joyce's discussion slides over. He goes on to conclude from the claim that practical rationality cannot be intelligibly questioned that practical reasons "cannot be legitimately ignored."[10] The complication is this. Following Joyce, let us use "should$_P$" for the "should" of practical rationality. Then there is a question of whether there are alternative terms that are in normative competition with "should$_P$"—whether some community could use some notion "should$_{P*}$" such that while this too is an all-things-considered notion, it is not coextensive with "should$_P$." If there is such an alternative possible notion, then while reasonable debate over whether to deliberate about what "should$_{P*}$" be done instead of above what "should$_P$" be done may be impossible (compare what I said in Chapter 2 about possible debates between us and users of alternative normative terms), maybe considerations of what one

---

[8] Joyce (2001), p. 49.   [9] Ibid., p. 50f.   [10] Ibid., p. 51.

"should$_P$" ought to be abandoned in favor of what one "should$_{P*}$" do. (Here, as many times earlier, ineffability rears its head. What about the "ought" in this last sentence? Is that not the ordinary "ought"? The point that I intend to make is that it could be that "should$_{P*}$" is normatively privileged over "should$_P$." As before, the talk of normative privilege does not by itself get around the ineffability worries.) Joyce, like Gibbard, in effect relies on a uniqueness assumption. If there are different "shoulds" of practical rationality, then although raising the question of which one to use is problematic, for reasons I have earlier belabored, there is a decision there to be made, regarding which possible "should" of practical rationality to employ.

How might one respond to the embarrassment of riches argument?

One possible way to go would be to provide a theory of what normative roles are such that expressions associated with different normative roles cannot be in normative competition. I mention this as a possibility. But fleshing out the idea would require going into more detail about normative role than I can manage—and I anyway do not know how plausible this would be.

Let me then turn to a second possible type of response. Grant, at least for the sake of argument, that there can be expressions in normative competition, associated with slightly different normative roles, in the way that the objection supposes. But turn to the question of how things look on the worldly side of things. If normative role does not succeed in non-defectively determining reference to begin with, then the ardent realist has anyway lost. So suppose normative roles sometimes succeed in non-defectively determining reference; there are properties that by their very nature are apt to be ascribed by predicates associated with such normative roles. And consider "ought" and the supposed alternative expressions associated with slightly different normative roles. The embarrassment of riches objection assumes that all, or at least several, of these different normative roles are non-defectively reference-determining. For suppose, to the contrary, that only one of the expressions in normative competition is non-defectively reference-determining. Then the property that this expression is normatively privileged over the others: this property is in and of itself apt to be picked out by the normative role. Even if the other expressions in normative competition ascribe properties and have non-empty extensions, these properties are, under the supposition, not such that an expression's being associated with a normative role (in the right way) suffices for the property to be picked out by the expression.

To assume, with the embarrassment of riches objection, that several of these normative roles are non-defectively reference-determining is to assume that while there are properties that are normatively privileged in the way just described, some of these properties that are so privileged are in normative competition with each other. Perhaps it is so. Perhaps the world is a normatively messy place—and if the world is a normatively messy in the way now at issue, that is bad news for the ardent realist. I don't see a neat way to rule out the possibility that it is. But it is more natural to think that if there is normativity in the world at all, only one of "ought" and its normative competitors is associated with a reference-determining normative role. If the others have non-trivial semantic values, those semantic values are not determined by normative role alone; for the world does not supply such semantic values. Even if there is an embarrassment of riches when it comes to the different normative roles that can be associated with a predicate, it can be that some but not all of these normative roles have normative properties corresponding to them. Call this *the normative sparseness reply*. The normative sparseness reply is both elegant and natural.

Of course, the normative sparseness reply involves some speculative metaphysical assumptions. But in the context, it is perfectly in order. I am only concerned with laying out what sort of account *would* give the ardent realist what she wants.

Embarrassment of riches problems arise for other ideas as much as for my preferred suggestion. I have earlier discussed, and rejected, the suggestions that the ardent realist should say that elite properties are normatively privileged, and that normative privilege simply has to do with ascribing normative properties (that the rightness concepts that are privileged are the ones ascribing normative properties). It may be worth remarking that the theorist who wishes to appeal to eliteness in the context will be in trouble if there are too many similar elite properties: for example, if there are different elite properties ascribed by concepts with the same or only slightly different normative roles. Similarly, the theorist who wishes to appeal to normativity of properties will be in trouble if there are different normative properties ascribed by concepts with the same or only slightly different normative roles.

3.6 Pluralism About Reference

I have been talking about normative roles determining reference and about the properties corresponding to these reference-determining normative roles. A property corresponds to a normative role just in case this property is ascribed by any expression associated with that normative role in the relevant way. But it would be in the spirit of the present investigation, where we are considering not just the ordinary expressions we have and what they stand for but also what in some sense better alternatives to these expressions might be, to ask whether there are *alternative possible notions of reference and ascription*—and, if so, whether there is an in some relevant sense *best* notion of reference. This spells trouble for the idea that appeal to referential normativity might be a way out for the ardent realist faced with the problem posed by the possibility of alternative normative concepts. If there simply are alternative notions of reference and none stands out as the best, then although some but not all properties correspond to normative roles, other properties corres-pond* to normative roles (where a property corresponds* to a normative role just in case every predicate associated with this normative role in the right way ascribes* that property), and there is no reason why standing in one correspondence relation takes precedence over standing in another. So suppose then that there is one in some relevant sense best notion of reference. One will then want to ask: best in what sense?

If the "best" notion simply is the one that is more *elite*, then it may appear that problems I have earlier brought up regarding appeal to such features in this dialectical context—see the discussion of Sider's suggestion in Chapter 2—are again relevant.

One question that can be raised regarding the considerations of the previous paragraph concerns what the talk of alternative notions of reference comes to. Talk of reference is obviously bound up with talk of truth, and since the case of truth has been discussed more prominently, it may be wise to approach the issue via considering truth.

Truth pluralism as it tends to be discussed is the idea that different truth predicates are suitable for different discourses (perhaps this kind of pluralism could aptly be called *discourse pluralism*). Truth pluralists of this kind tend to hold that different truth predicates are suitable for, say, moral or mathematical discourse than for the most paradigmatic kinds of descriptive discourse. Perhaps truth for ordinary descriptive discourse is correspondence, but truth for moral discourse is something else.[11] But there are different possible kinds of truth pluralism. One—which we might call *multipurpose pluralism*—is that different kinds of truth predicates are best suited to different tasks. (E.g.: it is sometimes said that we need a disquotational truth predicate for some tasks and a substantive truth predicate for other tasks.) Another—call this *egalitarian pluralism*—is that even bracketing the pluralism just pointed to, there is no unique best truth predicate. Corresponding to these different forms of truth pluralism are different forms of pluralism about reference and ascription.

It is the themes that come up in connection with egalitarian pluralism that now emerges as highly germane to the issues centrally dealt with in this book.

There are certain problems regarding the idea of talk of alternative notions of truth and reference, in the sense of egalitarian pluralism. I don't think the problems are sufficiently serious that one can simply dismiss such talk of alternative notions as unintelligible—so I wouldn't respond to the embarrassment of riches objection simply by appeal to these problems—but they are worth bringing up. They illustrate what one would need to get into when trying properly to evaluate the egalitarian truth pluralism. If we try to imagine a community whose members aim to judge that p not when p is true but when p is true* (where truth* is not coextensive with truth), are we not really imagining a community that judges something with a different content, that p*, instead of that p? After all, somehow or other—with details to be filled in depending on which theory of content one prefers—the content of a judgment somehow depends on use and the judgment's relations to the world, and this community's judgments of the relevant kind are correlated with it being the case that p* and not with it being the case that p. (Let me illustrate this using an especially stark example. Suppose we want to say that they aim to judge that p when p is *false*. Then they will make the relevant judgments when we in the corresponding situation

---

[11] See e.g. Wright (1992), Lynch (2009), and the essays collected in Nikolaj Pedersen and Cory Wright (2013).

would judge that not-p. Do they not then judge *that not-p* instead of judging *that p*?) But if so, such a community seems not to be possible. And if a community operating with a truth-like norm different from a norm of ordinary truth is not possible, then it is not possible to have an aim of inquiry other than truth.[12]

If we think of something's being a possible alternative concept of truth as its being an alternative aim of judgment, then the idea that there are possible alternative notions of truth is jeopardized by the kind of argument I have just sketched. But while being the aim of judgment may be one thing that can be thought to be constitutive of the notion of truth, it still is not obvious that the antecedent could be discharged. That depends on contested issues relating to the philosophy of truth: what makes something a concept of truth to begin with? Is it the relation to the aim of judgment or something else entirely? The points about truth are of relevance to reference given the way the truth of sentences is determined by the reference of the parts. It does not follow that there cannot be different concepts of reference. A lesson of Quinean permutation arguments regarding reference is that different assignments of reference can issue in the same truth conditions; correspondingly, one can, for all that the argument sketched promises to show, envisage different concepts of reference so long as truth conditions are not affected. But there cannot be any greater divergence than that between different concepts of reference, if the argument works.

The appeal to Alternative-unfriendliness was an attempt to salvage ardent realism by appealing to something in some relevant sense non-arbitrary that could serve to single out particular concepts of rightness and goodness as normatively privileged. What attention to truth and reference does is to highlight that even if reference works in such a way that all thin normative concepts with the same normative role are coextensive, there can be arbitrariness. There can be alternative notions of reference. Suppose that there in fact are. What might in the relevant sense privilege one possible notion of reference over others?

If one asked that question in a general setting, it would be natural for many philosophers to appeal to some notion of eliteness. Some possible notion of reference might be more elite than competitors; and we can be in a position to reasonably judge it to be so by, say, noting its usefulness in semantic theorizing. But even granting that some possible notion of reference is more elite than others, and that this is of relevance to some theoretical questions we might ask ourselves about reference, there remains a question over the relevance of such considerations in the present context. Earlier I argued that one concept of rightness being more elite than another does not speak to the question of whether it is normatively privileged. One may think that if this argument is persuasive, then by parity of reason the fact that some rightness property is ascribed or referred to, where the relevant relation of ascription or reference is the most elite, does not speak to the question of whether this property

---

[12] See further Eklund (2012b). Stich (1990, pp. 115–27) tries to compare different concepts of truth in precisely the way that seems problematic given the brief argument sketched.

of rightness is normatively privileged. On the other hand, it can be retorted to this that the cases are different. It surely would be wrong to hold that the eliteness of some reference relation means that this reference relation is itself normatively privileged (whatever this would mean). But all we do is rely on the in fact elite reference relation when theorizing about how language relates to the world, including when theorizing about how normative language relates to the world. (Compare perhaps the doctrine of double effect. The suggestion mentioned amounts to saying that although a normative upshot may be a foreseeable side effect of giving preference to a particular reference relation, it matters that this is not the chief reason for giving preference to the reference relation in question.)

3.7 Concluding Remarks

In this chapter I have further elaborated on the themes from Chapter 2, and discussed a number of objections to what I proposed could be sufficient for ardent realism. Of the greatest importance are the last two objections, what I called the embarrass-ment of riches objection, and objection from pluralism about reference. As I made clear, I am not convinced that are satisfactory answers to these objections. If the objections stand, then the ardent realist is not out of the woods even if it is the case that normative role can determine reference. My suggestion that the question of whether normative role can determine reference is pivotal for metaethics is on the wrong track. So long as one of the objections stand, a more radical conclusion is suggested: no matter what, there is no way to make good on ardent realism.

4

Normative Concepts

In Chapters 1 through 3, I have been concerned with the possibility of alternative normative concepts and the theoretical problems that this carries with it, specifically when it comes to what would be sufficient for what I have called ardent realism. I presented what I see as the best way out for the ardent realist: appeal to referential normativity. But I have also presented some objections to this suggestion. I have not argued either for or against ardent realism. But some possible positions should stand out starkly given the preceding discussion. One is that ardent realism is true, and there is referential normativity. Another is that ardent realism is false, and moreover, that it is fundamentally unclear how the world could be such as to vindicate ardent realism.

In this chapter and the following ones, I will elaborate on themes related to what has come up earlier. In the present chapter and Chapter 5 I will discuss the question of in virtue of what properties are concepts normative. I will argue that the notion of normative role is central here: so central that if by the end of the day we would want to reject the notion of normative role as objectionably unclear, we should likewise reject questions about the normativity of properties and concepts as objectionably unclear. In Chapter 6 I will highlight what I call presentationalism, the view that there is no normativity in the world but ordinary normative sentences are nevertheless true, and true in as robust a sense one can ask for. In Chapter 7 I will relate a number of the views that are rendered salient by the present theoretical framework to what is sometimes called immoralism, suggested by passages from Marx and Nietzsche. Chapter 8 will relate to a number of different specific issues in the metaethical literature. In Chapter 9 I will turn to thick concepts as well as to what is sometimes called formal normativity. When discussing what ardent realism requires I have, for reasons mentioned, focused on what characterizes the so-called thin normative terms. But any comprehensive account of what distinguishes the normative must take into account all different broad kinds of normativity. Chapter 10 will be devoted to broader metaphilosophical issues. Chapter 11 contains brief concluding remarks.

I have been concerned with what it takes for ardent realism to be true. I have stressed that even if all ongoing debates were settled in a way favorable to the ardent realist, something else is needed. What I have pointed to is what I have called referential normativity. However, as mentioned, there is another reply that may be tempting: what the ardent realist needs is that in addition to there being normative predicates objectively true of things, etc., there are genuinely normative properties. I have already given one response to this: appeal to normativity of properties does not help by itself, simply inviting the further question of what it is for a property to be normative.

In this chapter I explicitly turn to the question of what it is for something to be normative. There are in fact two questions here. One is what it is for a *property* or a *fact* to be normative (as opposed to, e.g., simply being something we value or disvalue). Another is what it is for a *linguistic expression* or a *concept* to be normative (again as opposed to, e.g., simply being something that stands for something we value or disvalue, or being something we use to recommend or warn). Let us call the former *the property question* and the latter *the concept question*. The property question is the most germane to other concerns, for example because it can be suggested that what ardent realism requires is that there be some properties that are in and of themselves normative. However, I will discuss both questions. In this chapter I discuss the concept question and in Chapter 5 I turn to the property question.

My answer to the concept question will be that an expression or concept is normative by virtue of being conventionally associated with a normative role. It is being conventionally associated with normative use—whatever renders use normative—that marks an expression or concept as normative. The upshot of my discussion of the property question will be that a property is normative exactly if it can be ascribed by some possible referentially normative predicate. This does not amount to a proper answer to the question: the question asks what it is for a property to be normative, and all that is offered is an extensionally correct characterization. It would be implausible to claim that what it is for a property to be normative is for it to be ascribed by some possible predicate of a given kind. But although the suggestion does not answer the property question as formulated, it is still an informative claim.

As just mentioned, I earlier (Chapter 1) discussed the view that what ardent realism requires, in addition to there being some true atomic normative sentences, etc., is that some properties are in and of themselves normative. This was there discussed as an alternative to the suggestion that one appeal to referential normativity. If normativity of properties is best elucidated by appeal to referential normativity, then appeal to normativity of properties does not in fact represent an *alternative* route for the ardent realist.

There will be many distinctions to keep track of as the property and concept questions are discussed, and those distinctions will be introduced in due course. But some distinctions I will slide over. Among them, again to emphasize, is a distinction which for some purposes may be crucial. It is the distinction sometimes drawn between the normative and the evaluative. As I have done throughout my discussion, I will use "normative" as a general term encompassing all this. While a distinction between the evaluative and the normative may be important for some purposes, the considerations I will present apply equally in both cases.

It is possible to adopt a *dismissive* view on both the property question and the concept question, and hold that properties and concepts are not in themselves normative. All there is to it is that there are some properties or facts that we tend to value, and some expressions that we tend to use for normative purposes. Speaking of the properties or of the expressions or concepts themselves as normative is to mistake for a feature of them what is merely something that has to do with us. The possibility of a dismissive answer to the property question will loom large in the discussion, and occasionally I will also bring up the possibility of a dismissive answer to the concept question. But I may sometimes talk as if I simply presuppose that there really are normative properties and normative concepts.

Another kind of dismissive attitude toward these two questions is that of the sort of primitivist who holds that even if there is something that distinguishes normative properties and facts, and something that distinguishes normative concepts and expressions, normativity is such a basic feature that it is simply not possible to say what is distinctive about the normative. However, given the high level of abstraction at which the present discussion will be conducted, it is hard to see what such primitivism could have going for it. The sorts of questions I will be asking are abstract ones such as (in the case of the concept question): is the normativity of a predicate explained by the normativity of what it stands for in the world, or is it rather a matter of its characteristic use? Even if it is hard to say anything very informative about what about a property makes it normative or what about the use of a predicate makes that predicate normative—so primitivism of some flavor is defensible—one can still take a stand on these questions.

It may also be worth stressing that the question of whether normativity is a primitive feature of properties or concepts is one thing, and the question of whether particular normative properties and concepts are in some sense primitive is quite another.[1] Even if our basic normative concepts are primitive, one can in principle say something informative about what distinguishes them all as normative. That an informative analysis of the concepts is impossible does not mean that nothing informative can be said about the features they share. (Conversely, it could be that the basic normative concepts are not primitive in this way, but their normativity is a feature of them that cannot be further elucidated.)

I will often simply talk about predicates and the concepts that predicates express, assuming that the lessons of the discussion of predicates carry over to linguistic expressions of other kinds. Moreover, I will often speak of linguistic expressions rather than concepts. The reason is that I will occasionally bring up the question of

---

[1] Sometimes this distinction is not heeded. Witness, e.g., Parfit (2006): "Rather than merely saying where normativity can be found, some writers try to explain what normativity is. But...that cannot be helpfully done. We can ask what normative concepts, such as *ought* and *reason* mean. But there are no answers to these questions that are both interesting and true" (p. 331). Here Parfit proceeds without comment from considering the primitiveness of normativity to considering the primitiveness of *ought* and *reason*.

whether the normativity of a predicate is a matter of sense or reference or instead is a matter of something like conventional implicature; and given one entrenched way of talking about concepts, the concept expressed by the predicate is in the latter case not itself normative. For ease of expression, I will sometimes go back and forth between talking about predicates and talking about concepts, trusting that it will be clear that this is justified in the context. I will for the most part simply assume that the predicates concerned ascribe properties. In so doing I set aside prominent versions of expressivism, precisely those versions according to which normative predicates do not ascribe properties, as well as semantic views on normative expressions to the effect that the semantics of these expressions is more complicated in important ways. When it comes to expressivism it should be noted that the property question anyway does not arise for these versions of expressivism; and what it comes to the concept question I myself favor the answer that would anyway be favored by the expressivist, that the normativity of an expression or concept has to do with certain kinds of features of its use—its normative role.

There are different kinds of normative expressions, and one can reasonably suspect that they are importantly different, so that we shouldn't simply assume that the same view on what makes an expression normative applies to all. There are many different distinctions within the class of normative expressions that can be proposed, but let me here use a fairly coarse-grained classification of purportedly normative expressions as *thin* ("good," "bad," "right," "wrong," "ought"...), *thick* ("brutal," "generous," "lewd," "courageous"...), and *slurs* ("chink," "nigger," "kike," "faggot"...). In provisionally drawing these distinctions, I do not mean to commit myself to the view that by the end of the day the distinctions between these classes of expressions and concepts will prove especially important, or that these distinctions between normative expressions can be usefully and unproblematically drawn. More importantly, perhaps, I do not mean to commit to the claim that all these expressions should in the end count as normative. One might, for example, be skeptical as to whether slurs really should be grouped with the normative expressions, and one might also be skeptical as to whether the so-called thick expressions really are normative.[2] (Though do keep in mind that I use "normative" as a catch-all term, to apply also to what may more naturally be called evaluative expressions.) For most of the discussion I will speak as if they are, but at appropriate points skepticism will be brought up. I will also tend to speak as if the same account of normativity will be true for all normative expressions, even if, as noted, one can reasonably be skeptical of this. At appropriate points, doubts will be brought up.

Among expressions and concepts we would regard as normative are "good," "right," "ought," "just," and the concepts they express—goodness, rightness, justice, and the concept expressed by "ought," which does not have a convenient name.

---

[2] About the latter issue, see e.g. Blackburn (1992). This issue is discussed further in Chapter 9.

Speaking in this way, I am sliding over difficulties. The expressions are arguably context-sensitive, and express different things in different contexts. But even if the expressions are context-sensitive, we may for present purposes think of what the expressions semantically express as used in a relevant type of context. Among *properties* regarded as normative are the properties these expressions ascribe—the property of being good, the property of being right, and the property of being just.[3] Whatever type of thing "ought" stands for would also standardly be regarded as normative.

But are various sorts of *mismatch* cases possible?

First, is it possible for there to be normative predicates or concepts that ascribe non-normative properties? There are different sorts of putative cases of this kind that must be distinguished. One may think that normativity generally is something that characterizes only our devices for representing the world and not what these devices stand for. Or one may think that even while there also is normativity in what expressions and concepts stand for, *some* normative expressions and concepts may fail to stand for something normative. Further distinctions can be drawn among cases of this latter kind. One view can be that slurs and thick concepts can fail to ascribe anything normative, but the thinnest normative concepts are constrained to ascribe something normative. Another, more radical view may be that even some possible expressions and concepts that intuitively are of the same type as our "good," "right," etc. stand for non-normative properties. For example, it may be—perhaps— that some community uses a predicate to ascribe some non-normative property, but the way they *use* this predicate is characteristically normative so that the expression qualifies as normative anyway, and as normative in just the way, whichever it is, that our "right" is normative. Compare again the Alternative scenario. Maybe there are these different, non-coextensive predicates with the same normative role—and only one predicate ascribes a normative property? If so, then the others can count as normative because of their role, although they do not ascribe normative properties.

Or is the suggestion just presented incoherent? Perhaps the characteristically normative use of a normative expression precludes that it ascribes a non-normative property? Or perhaps what it is for an expression to be normative is for it to stand for something normative, so that even a conventionally normatively used expression standing for a non-normative property will not properly count as normative.

If it is possible for normative predicates to ascribe non-normative properties, might that possibly be the case for some of *our* normative expressions? Consider first slurs. On one popular view, to use a slur for a given group of people is equivalent to using a non-normative word, "—" ("black," "Jewish" ...), but with a negative or

---

[3] Of course it can be denied that these expressions ascribe properties. Most famously, it has been argued that "good" does not ascribe a property. See e.g. Geach (1956), Thomson (e.g. 2008), Szabó (2001), and Finlay (2014). My concerns here are orthogonal to what comes up in these debates, and hence in the main text I speak in the simple way I do here and elsewhere.

contemptuous tone of voice; it is only that the negativity is conventionally associated with the word. Less metaphorically put, the evaluation can be held to reside not in what is *said*, in Grice's favored sense, but in some other feature of how what is said is communicated. Perhaps there is a conventional implicature: the speaker's use of the slur conventionally implicates that the speaker has a negative attitude toward —s. Conventional implicature is an aspect of meaning that does not directly affect reference: a standard purported example concerns how "but" relates to "and." The thought is that both expressions make the same contribution to truth-conditions, but the use of "but" conveys something more in addition. According to the suggestion at hand, slurs stand for the same properties as their non-loaded counterparts. But then their normativity is not simply a matter of what property they stand for. Call the kind of view on slurs just sketched *the tone view*.[4] The tone view is by no means an uncontroversial view on slurs. But it is a common view (and although I will not argue the case here I am inclined to believe it to be correct). Of slightly greater interest is the possibility that some thick terms—terms that express so-called thick concepts— might fail to ascribe normative properties. Maybe, for example, "chaste" in fact just stands for a particular way of conducting one's sex life which does not have any immediate normative significance at all, even though the word "chaste" in some way presents what it stands for in a positive light. One reason that this is potentially of interest is that thick concepts are regularly focused on and employed in normative theorizing: but if this sort of case can obtain, one should be alive to the possibility that what goes for "chaste" in this case might go for other thick terms.

Might *our* thin terms ascribe non-normative properties? That suggestion offhand sounds more strange. Of course, one may think, the property of rightness (if there is one) is a normative property! But consider again the Alternative scenario, and the possibility that there are non-coextensive predicates having the same normative role, but only one ascribes a normative property. If it can be so, can we really be confident that it is our normative predicates and not their rivals that ascribe normative properties?

A different kind of question concerns whether it is possible for non-normative predicates and concepts to ascribe normative properties. For example, might it be possible for some community to use a predicate that in fact ascribes the property of being right, but their use of the predicate is such that the expression is not normative? Relevant to this question is, again, the issue of whether the normativity of an expression

---

[4] "Tone" is the common English rendering of Frege's "Färbung" (literally: coloring). Frege held that "horse" and "nag" have the same sense but still differ in tone. The tone view is embraced by, e.g., Boisvert (2008), Copp (2009), McCready (2010), Schroeder (2009), Whiting (2007), and Williamson (2003).

Conventional implicature is a linguistic phenomenon, and anyone who defends a conventional implicature view on the normativity of slurs or any other linguistic expressions faces questions about the employment of the corresponding concept in thought—surely it seems one can use slurs in thought and still one would thereby think whatever negative thing is associated with the slur. For relevant discussion see Williamson (2009), p. 154f.

is best seen as going together with how the expression is conventionally used. Also relevant is whether there might be something about the normativity of a normative property that makes it impossible for a non-normatively used expression to ascribe such a property. Some authors have thought so, but I will argue that for every normative property, it is possible for a non-normatively used expression to ascribe that property.

As should be clear from my formulations of the concept question and the property question and from my discussion of the possibility of mismatch cases, the distinction between concepts and properties is crucial for the discussion. Properties are had by entities, concepts are not (although they are true of entities and entities fall under concepts); concepts are tools for representing the world, properties are not (although we use concepts of properties when representing the world). Different concepts can ascribe the same property. There is no doubt that the concept of being water and the concept of being H_2O are different concepts; but for all that, the property of being water and the property of being H_2O can be the same property. The distinction between concepts and properties has been prominently highlighted in metaethics, for example in that one popular answer to Moore's open question argument is that Moore's considerations at best show that the concept goodness cannot be identical to any naturalistic concept, but that is compatible with the property goodness being identical to some naturalistic property. Even so, I think the distinction is not always properly heeded, and a theme in the discussion will be how normative concepts and normative properties relate.

Some theorists deny that there are such things as properties, and others hold that even if there are properties, properties are just "shadows" of concepts, so that an independent investigation into how concepts relate to properties is misbegotten.[5] These are respectable metaphysical views which should not be dismissed out of hand. And each of these views might seem to be in some tension with the distinction between properties and concepts that I will rely on. But more precisely, what I will rely on is that it is one thing for two predicates to be synonymous and another for them to behave extensionally in the same way. Hence, I will assume that referentialism is false. A convenient way to express this is in terms of concepts and properties.[6] I will presuppose that any friend of a view on concepts or properties that rules out drawing the distinction this way will want to find another way to draw the distinction in question; and that hence, in a work not primarily devoted to straight metaphysics, I can legitimately speak of the distinction in terms of concepts and properties.

---

[5] See e.g. Schiffer (2003) and Hofweber (2006).

[6] If one posits both concepts and properties, one can at least in principle draw a tripartite distinction, between (a) two predicates expressing the same concept, (b) two predicates standing for the same property, and (c) two predicates having the same intension (being true of the same things, across possible worlds). If one abandons property talk, one will have to try to find some other way to distinguish between (b) and (c), if one allows that there is a distinction there to keep track of.

Incidentally, complications in this vicinity are relevant to other themes in the metaethics literature. Debates over naturalism and non-naturalism are standardly conducted in terms of what the metaphysics of normative properties is. But suppose you are a nominalist metaethicist and you deny the existence of properties. You can still think it a significant question whether naturalist or non-naturalist realism is preferred, but you cannot state the question the way it is standardly stated. If you still believe in facts, you can state the question as concerning what normative facts are like and if your nominalism only yields that predicates don't ascribe anything, you can still state the question as concerning what "rightness," "goodness," etc. stand for. But even if you don't believe in facts and even if, because of your nominalism, you believe the terms mentioned don't refer to anything, you can still be a normative realist and you can still find it a significant question whether the normative realism is best construed as naturalist or non-naturalist. But how exactly can you state the question? One special reason this is an interesting problem is that in the discussion of arguments to the effect that if the normative supervenes on the natural, then a version of naturalism is correct, arguments tend to turn on finer issues regarding the metaphysics of properties, such as whether necessarily coextensive properties can still be distinct.[7] If there are no properties, how can this debate instead be conducted? I do not mean this to be a merely rhetorical question. Someone rejecting the existence of properties can, for example, make use of a binary sentential operator, *just is* (or, more idiomatically, *for it to be the case that ... just is for it to be the case that* ___), and conduct the discussion in terms of whether it is sufficient for the truth of something of the form ... *F* ... *just is* ... *G* ... and that the predicates "F" and "G" are necessarily coextensive.[8]

The concept question and the property question will be central to the discussion in this chapter and Chapter 5. But it is natural to feel somewhat uneasy about how they are framed. For example, one may think that even if we do speak of expressions and properties as normative, such talk is not sufficiently regimented and disciplined for one to reasonably argue for and against various definite answers about the sorts of cases I have described. It will simply be a matter of terminological legislation how to decide how to speak about these cases. Such worries are not unreasonable. But rather than attempt to address them in the abstract, I will let the specific discussion of purported answers speak for itself. It will be clear from the discussion that there are reasonable questions there, and questions that admit of reasoned answers. It is possible that the label "normative" is actually used in such a way that some regimentation is needed. I do not think that means that the discussion of what is normative is so unconstrained that it cannot be conducted in a reasonable fashion. But the proof of this contention will lie in the discussion itself.

[7] See e.g. Jackson (1998).
[8] See Rayo (2013) for employment of a "just is" operator in metaphysics.

4.1 The Metaphysical View on the Concept Question

Let us start with the concept question, the question of what it is for an expression or a concept to be normative. And consider first what I will call the *metaphysical* view on the concept question: the view that a predicate is positively (negatively) normative by virtue of ascribing a property that is itself positively (negatively) normative. A consequence of the metaphysical view is that any predicate that ascribes the same property that a given positively (negatively) normative predicate ascribes must itself be positively (negatively) normative. Sometimes the metaphysical view is accepted as an obvious concomitant of realism. In a recent survey article, Stephen Finlay (2010) writes,

> On a realist view of normativity, a concept or word is normative in virtue of being about a normative part or feature of the world—a normative fact, entity, property, function, or relation.... For realists, normativity is in the first place something metaphysical, and only derivatively a feature of normative thought and discourse.[9]

Finlay notes that antirealists may hold a different view on normativity. But the metaphysical view faces problems which should make even a realist want to reject it. In this section I will present some arguments against the metaphysical view.[10]

Before turning to specific arguments against the metaphysical view, it may be worth stressing how it is natural to talk about concepts outside the realm of the normative. Suppose (to use the standard, discredited example in philosophical discussions of the matter) that the pain is C-fiber firing, so that the property of being in pain is identical to the property of having ones C-fibers firing. Then a given mental property is identical to a given physiological property. One and the same property is itself both mental and physiological. But one would not say that the concept of being in pain and the concept of having one's C-fibers firing are identical, and one would not say that the concept of being in pain had turned out to be a physiological concept, or that the concept of having one's C-fibers firing had turned out to be a mental concept. A concept's ascribing a mental property does not suffice for the concept being mental; a concept's ascribing a physiological property does not suffice for the concept being physiological.

Compare too another analogous case. Consider $\aleph_0$, the smallest infinite cardinal. The standard concept of this number is mathematical. Now suppose theologians discuss what God's favorite entity is, and use "Favorite" as a name for this entity, whichever it is. Suppose further (you guessed it) that in fact Favorite=$\aleph_0$. Then the

---

[9] Finlay (2010), p. 334.

[10] If Finlay simply stipulatively uses "realism" for the position on normativity that he describes, of course my criticism is beside the point. But it is clear from Finlay's discussion that he wishes to use "realism" in accordance with its standard use in the metaethical literature.

   Similarly, some might be inclined to think that Finlay may be trivially right, for he could simply be using "normative concept" to mean *concept that ascribes a normative property*. But as is clear from Finlay's restriction to realist views, this is not Finlay's usage (else Finlay should hold open that on antirealist views there just are no normative concepts).

mathematicians' "$\aleph_0$" stands for something of theological significance and the theologians' "Favorite" stands for a mathematical entity. It would still ring odd to speak of the mathematicians' concept $\aleph_0$ as being theological, or to speak of the theologians' concept Favorite as a mathematical concept.

Return now to the concept question, and normative concepts. Saying what I have just said about mental, physiological, mathematical, and theological concepts sounds natural, and while "normative" could work differently, it seems one would need special reason for thinking that it does. Moreover, saying what I have just said about mental, physiological, mathematical, and theological concepts does not seem by itself to be to compromise with realism about any of these domains.

Let me now turn to specific arguments against the metaphysical view.

The metaphysical view is not true of slurs given the popular tone view introduced earlier in this chapter. However, the tone view on slurs can be resisted.[11] One might instead hold, for example, that a slur stands for a property different from the one its neutral counterpart stands for—perhaps something like ___-and-therefore-worthy-of-contempt. This property would in all the ordinary cases be uninstantiated: no one is worthy of contempt on account of being a ___. Or one can hold that slurs are defective in such a way that they fail to ascribe any properties at all. Another possible view is that slurs simply are taboo words. Their use causes offense but not because of anything conventionally associated with the term's meaning but simply because their use violates a taboo. On this *prohibitionist* view, slurs are hardly even properly classed as normative expressions: their supposedly normative aspect consists in their use violating taboos, and that is a sociological and not a semantic fact regarding these terms.[12] And even should the tone view be correct, one can reasonably maintain that this counterexample to the metaphysical view relies on facts specific to the case of slurs, and does not generalize to other types of normative expressions. Maybe different views on what it is for an expression to be normative are true of different classes of normative expressions. A restricted version of the metaphysical view might be that predicates that are, so to speak, *normative by virtue of sense* are so by virtue of ascribing normative properties. The idea would be that some predicates are

[11] For criticisms of the view, see e.g. Richard (2008), Anderson and Lepore (2013), and Hom (2008). For responses to those criticisms see e.g. Whiting (2013).

[12] The prohibitionist view is defended in Anderson and Lepore (2013). One main argument Anderson and Lepore provide has to do with the fact that we are so hesitant to use slurs even in indirect and quotational contexts. For criticism, see Whiting (2013). I myself think that one reason why appeal to taboos cannot be the whole story comes from comparison of dirty words. Take the dirtiest, most inappropriate words for the genitals. It seems very plausible that the use of these words is taboo in much the way Anderson and Lepore describe, if any words are. What's wrong isn't in what is said or conventionally implicated. (What would be said or implicated by these dirty words that isn't said or implicated by their more clinical counterparts?) So something else must explain their status as prohibited words. But the case of dirty words is strikingly disanalogous to the case of racist slurs. While a precise statement of what the use of racist slurs conveys is hard to come by, one can at least provide rough glosses of what kind of normative judgment is conveyed. By contrast, it would be hard even to begin addressing the question of what normative judgment the use of a dirty word serves to convey.

normative as a matter of their Fregean senses or truth-conditional meanings, while other normative predicates are normative as a matter of something semantically associated with them some other way—for example, they are normative by virtue of what conventional implicatures are associated with them. The tone view is true of slurs and is not in conflict with the claim that a metaphysical view is true of predicates that are normative by virtue of sense.

However, thick terms also present potential problems for the metaphysical view, and while one can adopt something like a tone view on thick terms, that has not tended to be as popular. Let a normative term or concept be *objectionable* iff, roughly, its use in some sense presupposes a false normative claim. This characterization of objectionableness is intentionally left rather tough. I wish to remain neutral between different views on meaning. Many or all slurs are objectionable: they are such that anyone who uses them thereby commits herself to a false normative claim (that the targets of the slur are worthy of the negative view or attitude that use of the slur expresses).[13] The point is also sometimes made that there appear to be objectionable thick concepts. Allan Gibbard (1992) has prominently argued that "lewd" expresses an objectionable thick concept, for its use presupposes a false negative view on overt displays of sexuality.[14] Whether or not Gibbard is right about this specific example, surely the phenomenon of objectionableness cannot reasonably be denied.[15] (Here are other candidates for objectionableness: "chaste" may be thought to falsely presuppose that abstaining from sex is in and of itself good; and "(sexually) perverted" may be thought to falsely presuppose that sex has some particular purpose such that sex that doesn't serve that purpose is thereby bad. It is perhaps not surprising that the examples are all terms pertaining to sexual morality.)

Blackburn (1998, 2013) discusses the example of "cute," as used to describe young women.[16] In conversation I have heard it suggested that this might be another example of an objectionable thick concept. But as Blackburn himself notes, there is nothing correspondingly objectionable about calling puppies and kittens "cute." (It may be somewhat *cloying* but that is another matter.) What may be objectionable about calling young women "cute" is that someone who talks about them this way is talking about them in the same way one finds it natural to talk about puppies and kittens—and this is different from the concept itself being objectionable. (Compare: if someone calls a dead serious philosophy paper of mine "hilarious," I find that

---

[13] "Some or all": if "facho," applied to fascists, counts as a slur, that is arguably a counterexample to the universal claim. For the normative claim that its use communicates, this is arguably simply true. However, "slur" tends to be used in such a way that if a word's use is not objectionable then it is not a slur—and so if "facho" is not objectionable then that suffices for the word's not being a slur.

[14] Of course, and as Gibbard is well aware, this is a much simplified account of what use of "lewd" signals.

[15] See Chapter 9 and Väyrynen (2009, 2013) for more on objectionable thick concepts. Gibbard (1992) also argues that the phenomenon obtains by considering a fictional example, "gopa," meaning roughly *glorious killing*.

[16] Blackburn (1998), p. 201 and (2013), p. 123f.

objectionable and perhaps offensive. But this is not because there is something objectionable about "hilarious." Instead it is because my serious philosophy papers ought not to be evaluated in terms more properly used to evaluate slapstick.)

What should be said about the *extension* of an objectionable thick concept? One possibility is that if a thick concept is objectionable, then it is *empty*; another possibility is that even if a thick concept is objectionable, it is actually true of pretty much what it would be true of if it weren't—its objectionableness effectively doesn't matter to its extension. Let us say that on the second hypothesis, objectionable thick concepts *misevaluate*, the idea behind this label being that such a concept is true of things that do not "fit" the evaluation associated with the concept, it misevaluates. It can be that I should agree that such-and-such behavior is lewd, even while I should not agree that the behavior is in any way *bad*.

My own preferred view, which I will return to in Chapter 9, is that objectionable thick concepts misevaluate. Here is the straightforward way in which I would motivate the view. Whatever else may be true of the concepts *perverted*, *lewd*, and *chaste*—in particular, even if these are objectionable concepts—behaviors which would paradigmatically be regarded as perverted or lewd or chaste do occur, and when one considers the question of how one would answer if forced to answer the question of whether the behaviors are or are not perverted (lewd, chaste,...) one will intuitively have to answer in the positive.

Some theorists would oppose the misevaluation view. I suspect that much of this opposition comes from two sources.

First, it may derive from the sense that one would wish to *avoid using the words* to describe anything in light of what use of these words would convey. But it is important to distinguish the question of the reasonableness of such a policy from the question of whether the words actually are true of some things. Moreover, our reluctance to use these words extends beyond the contexts where they are positively applied to things: we are likewise reluctant to use them in various embedded contexts.[17] This reluctance is not explained by supposing the words are not true of anything; and one may suppose that our reluctance to use the words has some form of unified explanation.

Second, one may presuppose a view on meaning on which if some principle, P, is in some sense part of the meaning of a predicate, then if P isn't true then the predicate cannot be true of anything—and rely on this to conclude that whatever exactly to say about objectionable thick concepts, these concepts do not misevaluate. I think there are good reasons to dispute the general view on meaning and reference-determination, and will return to this in section 4.3, when talking about what I will call semantic analyticity. Absent this general view on meaning and reference-determination, I see no reason why there could not possibly be misevaluating thick concepts; and if there

---

[17] See e.g. Väyrynen (2013).

are some possible misevaluating thick concepts then I do not see any good reasons why our actual ones should not be among them.

Misevaluating thick concepts presents another problem for the metaphysical view: a misevaluating thick concept can be positively (negatively) normative even while the *property* it ascribes is not in fact so. The concept chaste is a positive normative concept but if in fact nothing is praiseworthy precisely on account of being chaste, then the property that the concept ascribes is not necessarily a normative property. The concept presents the property it ascribes in a positive light, but that does not reflect any feature intrinsic to the property. (I say that the property is "not necessarily" a normative property. The reason for the caution is that the property ascribed, for example, even could be a negative normative property: the property we have a positive normative concept for is actually a negative feature of whatever possesses it.)

Turn lastly to a different argument against the metaphysical view. I think this is the strongest of the arguments, and also the one that best illustrates *why* the metaphysical view is mistaken. The two previous arguments have been conditional upon assumptions about slurs and about objectionable thick concepts that have not been properly defended. This last argument will be more unconditional. Besides, it will target sufficiency while the previous considerations targeted necessity. The preceding arguments were to the effect that some normative predicates can fail to ascribe normative properties; this argument is to the effect that a non-normative predicate can ascribe a normative property.

Suppose that an alien linguistic community introduces into their language a word—"thgir"—with the stipulation that "thgir" is to ascribe *the property that our "right" ascribes*, but this community does not in any way use their word "thgir" normatively.[18] Suppose, for example, that one of them, when learning English, has overheard English speakers speaking of what is "right," having only an unspecific or mistaken idea of what the word might stand for—and introduced into her community's own language a new expression, "thgir," with the stipulation that "thgir" is to ascribe the property, whichever it is, that "right" ascribes, and then uses "thgir" in accordance with the stipulation. "Thgir" is then meaningful, but the meaning with which it is endowed does not guarantee that it plays the role in deliberation characteristic of normative concepts. "Thgir" ascribes the same property as "right," but it is hardly a normative predicate. "Thgir" ascribes the same property as our "right" does, a *property* that in fact is normative, but there is no reason to hold that the *predicate* is (positively) normative.[19]

---

[18] The point made by "thgir" could not equally well have been made by, e.g., "has the property ascribed by the actual English 'right'." For even if this complex predicate is necessarily coextensive with "right," it arguably ascribes a different property from rightness—the property of having the property ascribed by the actual English "right." Of course, some theorists hold that necessarily coextensive properties are identical, but that idea is controversial—and appealing to "thgir" sidesteps that issue.

[19] For examples somewhat similar to that of "thgir" (but used for different purposes), see Hay (2013), p. 455f, Millgram (1995), and Väyrynen (2013), p. 102.

The alien community, as described, can certainly have the description "the property ascribed by 'right'," and this description can denote the property that "right" ascribes. Why should they not also be able to introduce a predicate ascribing this property? ("Let 'thgir' ascribe the property ascribed by 'right'.")[20]

If it can happen in this way that a non-normative term ascribes the same property as a thin term like "right" does, then one can present similar examples with respect to arbitrary thin and thick terms. (It is sometimes alleged, among those who think that normative and non-normative aspects of a thick term's meaning cannot be pried apart, that a thick term cannot have the same reference as a non-normative term. I think those who go on to make the latter claim have not properly taken into account the possibility of the sort of case I am here considering. Even if thick terms can, by the argument given, have the same reference as descriptive terms, that does not mean that thick terms can be informatively analyzed partly in descriptive terms. Just as an analysis of what is right as what is thgir is not informative, an analysis of what is lewd in terms of what is *dwel* would not be.)

It is important to this argument that what is stipulated is exactly that "thgir" *is to ascribe the same property as* "right." The counterexample to the metaphysical view that I am presenting would not work if the stipulation was that "thgir" *is to have the same meaning as* "right," for it would be more questionable in that case that the stipulation worked.

The friend of the metaphysical view might point out that how an expression is introduced and how it later is used are two different things, and that it is compatible with the "thgir" example as, so far presented, the alien community's use of "thgir" is such that it in fact ascribes a different property from that which our term "right" ascribes, the explicit stipulation to the contrary. After all, a term's actual use need not match what it is originally stipulated to mean. But this is hardly a very deep response: we can just explicitly add that it is a feature of the aliens' use of "thgir" that it is in accordance with the stipulation.

Another response to the argument is to insist that if "right" and "thgir" ascribe the same property, then they are not merely coreferential but they must be synonymous,

---

[20] Roberts (2013) suggests that "thgir" "does not *ascribe* the property of rightness, but ascribes the property of being whatever our RIGHT ascribes" (p. 87; Roberts uses capitals when naming concepts). My immediate reaction to a suggestion like this is I don't see what such a suggestion can have going for it—and besides, wouldn't it generalize so as to yield the bizarre conclusion that whenever one introduces a predicate "F" with the stipulation that it ascribe a property P, it really instead ascribes the property of being whatever "F" ascribes?

The main aim of Roberts' article is to argue that there are normative predicates such that they have no set valence: they are neither inherently positive nor inherently negative, but instead they have variant valence. Specifically, she argues that some thick normative predicates are like this. She indicates that she thinks this matters for arguments such as the "thgir" argument. But first, "right" is anyway a different case, since "right" is not thick. Second, I don't see why one couldn't run an argument analogous to the "thgir" argument for a thick predicate supposed to have variant valence. Also for such a predicate, F, one could imagine an alien linguistic community introducing a predicate—non-normative for the same reasons "thgir" is—with the stipulation that their predicate ascribe whatever property F ascribes.

so that if one is normative then so is the other. But even if the synonymy claim could be defended—and clearly this is far from obvious—this is not sufficient for the metaphysical view. One might also take the lesson to be that we should adopt a *dismissive* view: a predicate with the meaning shared by "right" and "thgir" can perhaps often be *used* normatively, but the predicate is not *itself* normative. (One could in principle hold that "right" and "thgir" have the same sense, in Fregean terminology, but at the same time insist that they differ in, for example, what their use conventionally implicates, and that it is in virtue of this difference that "right" is normative but "thgir" is not. If so, then again "right" and "thgir" ascribe the same property but differ in that where the former is normative, the latter isn't.)

William FitzPatrick (2011) holds that when a property is irreducibly normative, there cannot be a non-normative concept for the property.[21] (He only explicitly says that "we" cannot have such a concept, but I take it he means that there *cannot be* a non-normative concept for that property.) If my point about "thgir" is correct, then FitzPatrick is wrong. To resist arguments like the "thgir" argument, FitzPatrick would have to either deny that "thgir" ascribes the property that "right" ascribes despite how it is introduced and used, or else insist that "thgir" is normative after all. I take it that the former strategy must be regarded as entirely lacking in plausibility on anybody's view. The introduction of "thgir" follows a general recipe for how to introduce new expressions having the same reference as old ones. One thing to stress regarding the latter strategy is that some features of FitzPatrick's own view make it *especially* uncomfortable for him to adopt that strategy. He thinks that normative predicates are characterized by their playing a special kind of role in deliberation.[22] FitzPatrick thinks this underlies the intuitive force of the open question argument. But "thgir" does not have this special role in deliberation. To rescue the idea that

---

[21] FitzPatrick (2011), p. 8f. One interesting question regarding FitzPatrick's view is what he would say about the properties ascribed by normative concepts other than the thinnest ones. Can they too only be ascribed by normative concepts? Or are those properties simply not irreducibly normative?

Dancy (2006) also seems to commit himself to the thesis I argue against here. He says that "[t]he question is whether we can or cannot argue directly from the normativity of such facts as that one ought to do A to their nonidentity with *any* fact capturable in ways that employ no normative concept" (p. 141), suggesting that he thinks that the non-naturalism he embraces commits him to answering this question in the affirmative.

Heathwood (2015) even thinks that the claim that a property is unnatural can be explicated in terms of it not being possible to ascribe it using descriptive terms. Because of complications like those brought up here, he qualifies the thesis somewhat, but I am skeptical also of the revised thesis.

Compare also Mackie's (1977) presentation of the argument from queerness. Mackie describes the realist view he opposes as one according to which moral facts are somehow intrinsically motivating, and *acquaintance* with a moral fact is sufficient to motivate. There are of course questions about whether Mackie's realist is a mere straw man, but still it can be thought relevant that Mackie's realist would be committed to what FitzPatrick commits himself to. However, it seems what FitzPatrick commits himself to is something more extreme than what Mackie's realist is committed to. For Mackie's realist can say that in the example given above, the speakers of the "thgir" community are not related to the rightness facts in the right way to be motivated; they manage to *talk about* them but they are not genuinely *acquainted* with them.

[22] See FitzPatrick (2008), p. 176, and FitzPatrick (2014), p. 566.

"thgir" is normative, one would have to downplay what it takes for an expression or concept to be normative, for example through by fiat equating the normativity of a concept with the normativity of the property it stands for. But no one who takes that line can subscribe to what FitzPatrick says when presenting his version of an open question argument. For FitzPatrick's point with respect to that argument is that a distinguishing feature of normative concepts is that they play a special role in deliberation.

One might also try to get around the argument by appealing to how, *once the speaker finds out the true nature of the property that "thgir" stands for,* "thgir" will for her play the role in deliberation characteristic of normative properties. But first, FitzPatrick and other theorists who hold that no non-normative predicate can stand for a normative property are non-naturalists, and take their view to be bound up with their non-naturalism. But if the thesis is defended in this way, there is nothing that immediately prevents it from being equally defensible from a naturalist standpoint. Second, even if one can make good on this suggestion, it is unclear how it supports the metaphysical view on the concept question. The metaphysical view says that a normative predicate or concept is one that ascribes a normative property; it says nothing about finding out the true nature of the property in question.

A potentially striking fact concerning "thgir" is that given the way it is introduced, its reference is derivative upon that of "right." Let us say that while "right" *directly* ascribes the property of rightness, "thgir" only *derivatively* ascribes it. (Whatever exactly direct ascription and derivative ascription comes to. I am sure that can be problematized. But the remarks to follow are independent of the details.) One of Debbie Roberts' (2013) replies to my "thgir" argument, as this argument was presented in my (2013), involves relying on a distinction like the one described.[23] But this is not immediately a defense of the metaphysical view. So long as derivative ascription is a form of ascription, "thgir" is still a counterexample to that view. But one can suggest a modified metaphysical view, according to which a predicate is normative iff it directly ascribes a normative property. The modified view still faces potential problems with slurs and objectionable thick concepts. One might also worry about whether the direct/derivative distinction is a semantic or a metasemantic distinction: whether it is a distinction between semantic features of expressions or instead between ways in which semantic features can be determined. There is some reason to think it is the latter: that it has to do with how an expression has come to have the semantic features it has rather than with what semantic features an expression has. If so, then the modified view would have it that the difference between an intuitively normative predicate such as "right" and an intuitively non-normative one such as "thgir" is in fact metasemantic rather than semantic.

---

[23] For more on how Roberts (2013) replies to the "thgir" argument, see footnote 20.

I think the best defense of the letter of the metaphysical view against examples like "thgir" would involve denying that it is a characterizing feature of normative predicates that they play a special role in our thinking and deliberation, and maintaining instead that the *only* unifying feature of normative predicates is in what they stand for. But first, to stress, this view too is put under pressure by consideration of slurs and objectionable thick terms. Second, given this underlying view, it seems that it will just be a matter of theoretical bookkeeping whether one describes the resulting view as a metaphysical view or one that involves dismissing the concept question. One can use "normative predicate" in such a way that all and only predicates that ascribe normative properties count as normative, or one can choose to use "normative" only to apply to worldly items, given that this is where the similarities are supposed to lie.

To relate back to Finlay's remarks, quoted early in this section, none of the problems with the metaphysical view need in themselves be a problem with normative realism broadly construed—the view that some (atomic) normative sentences are mind-independently true. And even if we take normative realism also to involve the claim that some properties are in and of themselves normative, rejection of the metaphysical view is compatible with normative realism. One possible view is that what the problems discussed in this section point to is that there can be a kind of mismatch between a language's predicates and what properties in the world really are normative. That view is a normative realist view and it is perfectly compatible with the view that some properties are in and of themselves normative.

4.2 The Normative Role View on the Concept Question

If one accepts the above arguments against the metaphysical view, then one will think that something other than what they stand for makes slurs and objectionable thick concepts normative, and one will naturally think despite standing for something normative, something else about "thgir" makes it non-normative. It is natural to think that this other something is *use*. Something about how slurs and thick concepts are used makes them normative despite not standing for anything normative, and certain facts about how "thgir" is, or is not, used make it non-normative despite standing for something normative. This brings us to the next view on the concept question, the *normative role view*, according to which what makes a predicate normative is the *normative use* semantically associated with it, whether this use is understood in terms of *expression of an attitude* or to, say, *recommending* or *prohibiting*. In my discussion I have used *normative role* as an umbrella label for this normative use, abstracting away from questions about how to describe it more precisely. I will continue speaking in terms of this notion of normative role.

There are a number of different ways to think about meaning. I earlier mentioned *referentialism*, according to which meaning is exhausted by reference. *Fregeans*, by contrast, hold that meaning goes beyond reference. An immediate complication regarding how to draw the theoretical map arises if there are such aspects of meaning as conventional implicature, or what Frege called tone. Frege famously distinguished between reference, sense (which is the truth-conditionally relevant aspect of meaning, and together with the world determines reference), tone (roughly: conventional implicature), and also force (what semantically distinguishes, e.g., indicative sentences from imperative ones). A truly radical referentialist would eschew all aspects of meaning beyond reference. A less radical referentialist would only object to sense as distinct from reference, and allow that expressions can be associated with tone and force as well as reference. A natural question to ask about these possibilities is what it takes for something to affect sense rather than tone. At least for Frege and those following him, sense is distinguished from tone by being reference-determining. One can say that on a normative role view according to which normative role is reference-determining, normative role is part of sense. Someone who disagrees with Frege over the need to postulate something like Frege's notion of sense can still appeal to tone and force. Coreferential terms can be said to differ in meaning because they differ with respect to tone or force. The relevance of these considerations to the normative role view is that the friend of the normative role view has some different theoretical options. She can say that differences between normative expressions and non-normative ones, or between different normative expressions, are differences having to do with sense, or she can say they have to do with tone. Or she can say that it is sometimes the one and sometimes the other. As discussed earlier in this chapter, the tone view is a popular view on slurs. One can accept a tone view across the board or one can think normative role sometimes is a matter of sense. On some possible views on how so-called normative terms work, the normativity enters in through *conversational* rather than conventional implicature. It is a pragmatic feature, not immediately tied to any conventional aspect of meaning. The way I prefer to talk of these things, such a view would not be a version of the normative role view. Instead it is a view on which there aren't any normative terms. A radical referentialist who refuses to appeal to either sense or tone or force would have to say that the only way a term can be in and of itself normative is in virtue of having a normative referent. In other words, the metaphysical view, earlier rejected, would be the only option.

It should be obvious that the normative role view avoids the problems faced by the metaphysical view. "Thgir" fails to be positively normative despite ascribing the property of rightness, since it is not associated with a normative role. Objectionable thick terms and slurs are associated with normative roles and can hence be normative despite not ascribing normative properties. I find the normative role view attractive, in part because of how it deals with the examples discussed. In what follows I will discuss some important choice points for friends of this view.

There are many questions that can be raised about the notion of normative role to which the normative role view appeals. I will for now pause only on those clarificatory questions that are relevant for present purposes. One question regards how fine-grainedly to think of normative roles. A *coarse-grained* view would be that there are only two kinds of normative roles for an expression to be associated with, *positive* and *negative*. A more *fine-grained* view would make more fine-grained distinctions between the roles associated with different terms. The normative role with which "beautiful" is associated is different from that with which "tasty" is associated; and these two are in turn quite different from that with which "good" is associated. I favor the latter view, and have indeed presupposed it throughout when speaking of normative role.

A friend of the normative role view can in principle maintain that it is just not possible for two predicates to relate to each other in the way just sketched, for the normative differences between the predicates necessitate differences in extension. That is, a friend of the normative role view can insist that (all or some) normative predicates are referentially normative, in the way earlier outlined: their normative roles determine reference. But the phenomenon of referential normativity is in tension with a coarse-grained view, for the idea that normative role is reference-determining goes more naturally with drawing the finer distinctions drawn on a fine-grained view. (The coarse-grained view cannot plausibly be combined with the view that the normative role of some predicates can suffice to solely determine reference.) Of course one might in principle hold that the normative roles of some expressions are reference-determining while the normative roles of other expressions are not.

One may think that normative terms are not always used normatively in the way they would have to be for the normative role view to be correct. Thick terms certainly can be used in ways apparently contrary to their intuitive valence. Blackburn's example, "last year's carnival wasn't lewd enough," makes this point.[24] More generally, it has been argued, for example by appeal to the "amoralist," that one can felicitously use even thin terms without expressing attitudes.[25] But to the extent that this actually does problematize the normative role view—and that demands that a term's having a normative role and its use expressing an attitude go together, and this is not obvious—it problematizes quite generally the idea that some terms can be in and of themselves normative. The point does not do anything to address the problems for other views that have been brought up. Moreover, I think that appeal to social externalism helps blunt the force of the amoralist example. Generally, social externalism is the thesis that what a word, as employed by a speaker, expresses can depend on facts about the speaker's social environment—her community. The classic example is Putnam's "elm"/"beech" case.[26] Putnam says that he possesses no information associated with "elm" or "beech" that serves to distinguish elms from beeches. All he knows is that they are trees with leaves. Yet "elm" as used by Putnam is true of

---

[24] Blackburn (1992), p. 296. One may think one can get around the problem by emphasizing the work done by "enough" in Blackburn's sentence. But the same point can be made by appeal to a speech like "Last year's carnival was a success in all sorts of ways. But there was something missing. It just wasn't lewd."
[25] The classic reference is Brink (1989).   [26] See Putnam (1975).

some trees, the elms, and "beech" as used by Putnam is true of some other trees, the beeches. Why? The reason, Putnam says, is that he is part of a linguistic community where some speakers, the experts, do possess the relevant information distinguishing these trees from each other, and in virtue of this, "elm" and "beech" also as used by Putnam have different semantic properties. (Arguably what matters is not only that Putnam in some sense belongs to this community, but that Putnam is prepared to defer to the relevant experts in this matter.) Once social externalism is accepted as a live possibility, one needs to distinguish between different kinds of scenarios involving amoralists. Even if one can imagine individual users of the terms normally regarded as thin normative terms who do not use them with the accompanying attitudes or normative roles, and who still use these terms with the same meanings the rest of us use them with, maybe those speakers are like Putnam in the "elm"/ "beech" case. But consider then a whole supposed community of amoralists, and for simplicity suppose that this community is not in contact with us. I am inclined to say such a community would not be using normative terms. And if that is what to say about an amoralist community, then an amoralist in our community using a normative term with its conventional meaning only does so by virtue of facts having to do with her community.[27]

Roughly, for a feature to be semantically associated with a term is for it to be the case that were that feature missing, the term would not have the meaning it actually has. To consider whether some moral term would have the same meaning as used by an amoralist community is to consider whether those aspects of use that would be different in such a community are essential to it. To say that the normative use of a term is semantically associated with it is not, or is not immediately, to say that every individual competent use of it would have to be accompanied by the right attitudes.

On some possible versions of a normative role view, normative role is at least sometimes reference-determining (and at least some normative predicates are referentially normative); on other versions it is not so. On the latter kind of normative role view we have what I have called Alternative-friendliness, and the puzzles that attend to all Alternative-friendly views arise: are we to say that there somehow is a Further Question as to which normative concepts are privileged? The supposed Further Question threatens to be ineffable; but if we say that there is no Further Question, we give up on something that would seem dear to the ardent realist.

Just as the normative role view is compatible with either view on Alternative-friendliness, so is the metaphysical view earlier discussed. It may perhaps be tempting to think that the metaphysical view is incompatible with Alternative-friendliness: if certain features of a property are what accounts for the normativity of a predicate that ascribes the property, then it is natural to think these same features also explain the predicate's specific normative role; and then for any two predicates

[27] For related discussions in the literature, see e.g. Bedke (2009), pp. 191–5, Blackburn (1998), pp. 59–68, Dreier (1990), pp. 9–14, and Tresan (2009), pp. 185–93.

with the same normative role, we will have that in each case the normative role is explained by the property the predicate stands for, and the property will be the same in both cases. But while this train of thought may be tempting, it is not an inevitable concomitant of the metaphysical view, and the metaphysical view is compatible with Alternative-friendliness.

As already mentioned, I am inclined to favor the normative role view. What makes a predicate normative is that it as a matter of semantics is associated with a normative role. One main motivation is negative: I see serious problems with all other alternative views. As for problems for the normative role view, the main concern would be that there is no workable notion of normative role such that normative expressions all can be said to be associated with normative roles. If for this reason the normative role view were to be found untenable, I would favor a dismissive view, and say that the idea that some concepts and expressions are in and of themselves normative, as opposed to simply generally being used normatively, is misguided.

The normative role view yields that expressions are normative only if their associated normative roles are associated with the meaning of the expressions. Both referentialists and Quineans may have problems with such a view—referentialists because they identify meaning with reference and Quineans because they don't think there is any reasonable distinction to be drawn between what is part of meaning and what is not.[28]

A referentialist can, to be sure, insist that a normative role is *metasemantically* associated with a given term and plays a role in determining its reference. She can mimic much of what is said by someone who takes normative roles to be semantically associated with terms. She can then say that a term's normativity is not strictly part of the meaning and that the pretheoretic conviction that some terms are normative as a matter of meaning blurs matters of semantics and matters of metasemantics. This may not be unreasonable, but it is a revisionary stance. Anyone inclined to take that stance can read "metasemantics" for semantics at appropriate places.

Moreover, as earlier touched upon, a referentialist or Quinean can, while eschewing anything like a Fregean notion of sense, accept a notion of conventional implicature and say that what renders an expression normative is a matter of what it conventionally implicates. Timothy Williamson (2009) adopts a kind of conventional implicature view on slurs.

In his (forthcoming), Williamson remarks, surely rightly,

One of the main sources of resistance to a robustly realist and cognitivist conception of normativity, and indeed of morality, has been the difficulty of explaining on its term the supposed conceptual ties from moral thought to action. If there are no such conceptual ties to

---

[28] This is emphatically not to say that there is no way that they can accommodate such a view. For example, Williamson (2009) appeals to conventional implicature in the specific case of slurs, and this strategy can be applied more broadly.

explain, then one of the main sources of resistance to a robustly realist and cognitivist conception of normativity, and indeed of morality, is an illusion.

This is in the context of a discussion casting doubt on "conceptual ties" in general. But if there are no conceptual ties linking moral thought—or, generally, normative thought—to action, what distinguishes moral or normative thought as such? One natural thing for a referentialist to say may be that what characterizes normative thought is its subject matter: it is thought that is about normative properties. But this just is the metaphysical view, earlier rejected.

The same issues that normativity presents here arise also in other cases. Compare vagueness.[29] Vagueness is the feature of expressions dramatically illustrated by different versions of the sorites paradox. Here is one version of the paradox:

> Someone who has lived 1 second is not old.
> For any n, if someone who has lived n seconds is not old, then someone who has lived n+1
> seconds is not old.
> So, for any finite n, someone who has lived n seconds is not old.

This is a paradox, for the conclusion appears to follow from the premises—and yet the premises are eminently plausible but the conclusion manifestly implausible. Vagueness enters in because it is the vagueness of "old" that is responsible for the attractiveness of the second premise. Witness how if one replaced "old" with a predicate that is not vague in the relevant respect, say "has lived for a million seconds or less," then the second premise loses its plausibility.[30] It is standard to respond to the sorites paradox that it is the second premise that should be rejected as untrue. The question is how this can be reasonably done, given the vagueness of the key predicate, in this case "old." Much of the discussion of the sorites paradox in effect revolves around questions about the nature of vagueness. What is it for an expression to be vague?

Although I won't fully argue the point here, I think vagueness cannot be characterized solely by appeal to referential properties of vague expressions: a non-vague expression can have the same referential properties as a vague expression.[31] Suppose, for example, that a simple fuzzy theory is the correct theory of vagueness, and suppose that someone is tall* to degree 1 iff that person is at least 1900 mm, tall* to degree 0 iff that person is 1800 mm or less, and tall* to degree d if in between, where d= (the person's height in mm—1800)/100. "Tall*" is hardly vague despite having a fuzzy semantics. It is a distinguishing characteristic of vague expressions that they give rise to sorites paradoxes. But there is no reason why "tall*" would invite a sorites paradox; the principle that a tiny difference in height makes no difference to tall*ness lacks plausibility. While this example only targets a simple degree theory of

---

[29] See Sorensen (2012) for a helpful overview.
[30] Note the "in the relevant respect." Arguably, "has lived for a million seconds or less" is also vague, due to vagueness in when "living" applies.
[31] See Eklund (2005).

vagueness, I believe the lessons generalize. So, if vagueness is a feature of the meaning of an expression, it must pertain to another aspect of meaning. My own preferred view is to appeal here to the conceptual roles of vague expressions. A referentialist or Quinean will have to look elsewhere. One possibility is to say that vagueness is a metasemantic rather than a semantic feature of expressions, just as one possibility in the case of normativity is to say that normativity is a metasemantic rather than a semantic feature of expressions.

4.3 The Minimalist View on the Concept Question

It is also worth comparing a different kind of view on the concept question, one suggested by some discussions relating to the matter. Consider first the following claim:

(M)   A predicate F is positively (negatively) normative iff "x is F" conceptually entails "x is [to that extent] good" ("bad")

(The "M" is for minimalism. I will get to the minimalism aspect of this shortly.)

What I have in mind by conceptual entailment is what some theorists might instead refer to as analytic entailment. Good questions can be asked about just what this entailment relation is, and skepticism about this entailment relation may be reasonable. But let me for argument's sake take the general idea of such an entailment relation on board. Briefly, not all necessary entailments are conceptual entailments. A paradigmatic example of a conceptual entailment would be from ___ is a bachelor to ___ is unmarried. A paradigmatic example of a necessary entailment that is not a conceptual entailment would be that from ___ is water to ___ is H_2O. What distinguishes conceptual entailments from merely necessary entailments is supposed to be, roughly, that the former entailments can be known on the basis of conceptual competence alone. (Of course, more would need to be said in a proper defense of the idea of conceptual entailment. All I am trying to do is to say enough to provide a sense of what conceptual entailment is supposed to be.)

Maybe a distinction should be drawn between conceptually entailing something about goodness/badness and conceptually entailing something about rightness/wrongness. Such distinctions are orthogonal to my present concerns, and I will happily slide over such complications, just as I generally slide over distinctions between the evaluative and the normative. But I do bother with the "to that extent." One might reasonably be concerned that positive (negative) thick concepts may be true of some behavior which is all things considered pretty bad (good). The "to that extent" is there to ward off this kind of concern.

"Thgir" does not present a problem for (M). Even if "thgir" and "right" ascribe the same property, so that necessarily something is thgir iff it is right, one can maintain that "x is thgir" does not *conceptually* entail "x is right" or "x is good."

Given (M), one can suggest a certain kind of minimalist view on the concept question, according to which for a concept to be normative just is for it to stand in the right entailment relations to the concept *goodness* or the concept *badness*. Merely to accept (M) is not immediately to subscribe to this minimalist view: it is only to state necessary and sufficient conditions for a predicate to be normative. But unless the friend of (M) subscribes to this view, she does not offer an account of what it is to be normative, even if she offers a non-trivial purportedly extensionally adequate characterization. What is special about the minimalist view is its insistence that (M), or something like it, provides a *full* explanation of what it is to be normative. This is what makes the view a genuinely *minimalist* view. For any predicate F, we can define a notion, "F-ish," such that a predicate G is F-ish iff "x is G" conceptually entails "x is F." While such notions can be defined, they do not generally carve out classes of predicates in any interesting way.

It may be worth comparing a rather different case. Consider one gloss on the notion of analyticity, sometimes called *Frege-analyticity*.[32] For a sentence to be Frege-analytic is for it to be either a logical truth or something that can be transformed into a logical truth by substitution of synonyms for synonyms. (Quine prominently discusses this conception of analyticity in his (1951).) One consequence of conceiving of analyticity as Frege-analyticity is that it is then trivial that logical truths are analytic. This is striking, for one might have thought that to characterize logical truths as analytic is to say something distinctive and controversial about their metaphysical status and/or their epistemological status.[33] The similarities to the present case ought to be obvious. Even if the concept of being good or the concept of being a reason for desiring that such-and-such is held to be, rather clearly, a normative concept, one might have thought that in so characterizing the concept, one is not saying anything completely trivial.[34]

Michael Smith (2013) suggests that "a concept is an ethical concept if and only if, if someone believes that that concept is instantiated, then that person believes that there is a reason for him to desire that the world be a certain way,"[35] and it is clear from the context that Smith takes this characterization to not only be extensionally adequate but also to speak to the question of by virtue of what a concept is an ethical concept. (For example, the characterization is presented in a section of Smith's article titled "What makes a concept an ethical concept?"[36]) One concern about Smith's character-ization derives from considerations familiar from the debate over social externalism. If a thinker can have beliefs involving a particular concept even while under some important misapprehension regarding the conditions for something to fall under that

---

[32] See e.g. Boghossian (1996).   [33] See Boghossian (1996), p. 367.
[34] As Dancy (2006) says about a view like the minimalist view considered, "We still haven't learned what normativity is. To say that 'ought' is a normative notion was supposed to be informative, not merely to say that 'ought' lies at the center of a group of notions that cluster around it. Effectively, we were trying to say what normativity is, and all we have achieved is to point to one central notion that has got it, or from whose presence in a fact the normativity of that fact is derived" (p. 136). To my mind it is unfortunate that Dancy says that "notions" are present in "facts," but the main point he is making survives cleaning up such things.
[35] Smith (2013), p. 105.   [36] Ibid., p. 99.

concept, then in relevant cases it appears a thinker can have beliefs to the effect that some ethical concept is instantiated without believing that there is reason for her to desire that the world be a certain way. Suppose, however, that Smith successfully can evade this problem. Then there is a different concern, and it is that concern I wish to emphasize. Smith's characterization, which is in the tradition of explaining the normative or the ethical in terms of reasons, is minimalistic in the sense character-ized here. When it comes to why the concept of a reason for desiring something is an ethical concept, Smith's account only says: the concept of a reason for desiring something is an ethical concept because if someone believes that this concept is instantiated, then this person believes that there is a reason for her to have some non-belief judgment-sensitive attitude. To say that this concept is ethical is then to say something rather trivial, only in a very limited way going beyond the bare claim that the concept of a reason for desiring something is linked to the concept of a reason for desiring something.

It is important when evaluating these remarks to distinguish between a view that purports to give a characterization like Smith's of what it is for a concept to be ethical, and a genuinely primitivist view. If a theorist said that she just cannot give an informative account of why the concept of a reason is normative, but only argues that other concepts are normative by virtue of their connections to the concept of a reason, then her view is not minimalistic in the sense my discussion has sought to illustrate. When she says that the concept of a reason is a normative concept, she is not only saying that it is linked to the concept of a reason. To take a characterization in the style of (M) to state *what makes something a normative concept* is to adopt a minimalist view.

An even clearer instance of the phenomenon I wish to illustrate comes from Mark Schroeder (2007). Schroeder says, "What it is to be normative, is to be analyzed in terms of reasons." This suggests something stronger than merely that everything that is normative is in fact such that it can be analyzed in terms of reasons. For what Schroeder says is that this is *what it is* to be normative. Applying this to reasons themselves, the claim becomes something like: for reasons to be normative is for them to be analyzed in terms of reasons.[37] It is this stronger claim I see as problematic, for the kinds of reasons given in the previous few paragraphs. The claim that reasons are normative becomes the claim that reasons are analyzed in terms of reasons.

Let me now turn to assess (M). (M) faces some of the same problems that the metaphysical view faces. If the tone view on slurs is correct, (M) is false as it stands.

---

[37] In the context of Schroeder's discussion, the stronger claim stands out, for everything else in the passage is consistent with his only making the weaker claim, and as far as I can see the weaker claim is sufficient for his argumentative purposes.

The stronger remark of Schroeder's echoes Joseph Raz (1999), p. 354 (a passage Schroeder also refers to): "The normativity of all that is normative consists in the way that it is, or provides, or is otherwise related to reasons." One consequence of this claim is that the normativity of reasons *consists in* the way that they are or provide or are related to reasons.

If * is a slur, * is negatively normative but something of the form "__ is *" can be true without "__ is bad" being so, But again, slurs are special, so one might anyway prefer the more restricted:

(M′)   A predicate F is positively (negatively) normative *as a matter of sense* iff "x is F" conceptually entails "x is [to that extent] good" ("bad").

But adding this qualification may not be sufficient to get around all problems in the vicinity. If objectionable thick concepts can misevaluate, there can be behaviors which are, say, lewd or perverted, but which are not *bad*. If thick terms moreover are normative as a matter of sense, terms expressing objectionable thick concepts then present counterexamples to (M′). A friend of (M′) can attempt to respond that if objectionable thick concepts misevaluate, that just shows that a tone view is true of them—and of thick concepts generally (since it would be odd to single out the objectionable thick concepts for special treatment). I believe that someone inclined to take this route will face an uphill battle: paradigmatic thick concepts are sufficiently similar in behavior to thin concepts that it is hard to maintain that a tone view is true of the thick concepts but not the thin; and a tone view does not seem very attractive for the thin concepts. But I may be wrong. Some theorists do appear happy to discuss slurs and thick concepts together, not drawing much of a distinction between the two cases.[38] Moreover, some theorists do defend what are in fact tone views of the thin concepts.[39] One question for the latter theorists concerns how they propose to distinguish slurs and the thick and the thin. (Or might they say that there simply are no differences in kind?) Another possible response for the friend of (M′) is to say that the so-called thick normative terms are not really normative after all.[40] A potential problem for both this suggestion and that previously brought up is that, as is often remarked, it may be that the idea of a thin/thick dichotomy should be abandoned in favor of the idea that this is just a matter of degree.[41] (I discuss these issues regarding the thick in more depth in Chapter 9.)

One interesting response that the friend of (M) or (M′) can make to the problems posed by slurs and thick concepts is to appeal to a non-orthodox view on conceptual entailment—one on which P can conceptually entail Q consistently with P being true and Q untrue. This may initially sound like a complete non-starter, but let me explain.

As theorists like Paul Boghossian (see especially his 1996 and 2003) and Jamie Tappenden (1993a and 1993b) have noted, there are several distinct ideas underlying the traditional notion of analyticity. Two in particular deserve stressing. There is the *metaphysical* idea of truth in virtue of meaning. And then there is the *epistemological* idea of—roughly—something's being a sentence such that it is part of competence

---

[38] See e.g. Blackburn (1984), Elstein and Hurka (2009), and Scanlon (2003).
[39] See e.g. Barker (2000), Boisvert (2008), and Copp (2001, 2009).
[40] See Blackburn (1992).   [41] See Scheffler (1987).

with the expressions involved to be disposed to accept it, and being pro tanto epistemically justified in accepting it. We can then distinguish two notions of analyticity, one metaphysical and one epistemic. Focus on the epistemic idea. Note that it is possible, at least in principle, that a sentence should be analytic in the epistemic sense without being true at all. There is nothing in the characterization of epistemic analyticity that requires that all epistemically analytic sentences are true. (This last thing is something I have stressed and made use of in earlier work.[42] Boghossian seems to assume that epistemic analyticity entails truth. Tappenden, like me, denies that epistemic analyticity entails truth, but he still thinks epistemic analyticity precludes outright falsity.)

While I wholeheartedly endorse the distinction between metaphysical and epistemic analyticity, I do think that the standard understanding of epistemic analyticity in turn runs together two different ideas, one regarding what competence involves, and one regarding justification. One can in principle hold that semantic competence with some particular expression involves a disposition to accept some given sentence S containing this expression, while refraining from going on to say that the competent speaker's acceptance of S is epistemically justified, even pro tanto. What will matter to my discussion is only the idea regarding competence. I will speak of *semantic* analyticity when talking only about this idea, setting aside the related epistemic claim.

If it is indeed possible that sentences can be semantically analytic without being true, this can provide an important part of the solution to many philosophical puzzles. Consider, for example, the liar and sorites paradoxes.[43] First, the liar paradox. In one of its basic forms, the liar paradox concerns what to say about a sentence that says of itself that it is not true. Let L be such a sentence. Is L true or not true? Well, suppose first that L is true. Then things are as L says they are. But L says that L is not true. So given the supposition, L is not true. From the supposition that L is true, we have derived that L is not true. Hence L is not true. But if L is not true, then things are as L says they are. But if things are the way a sentence says they are, then the sentence is true. So L is true. But then we have concluded both that L is not true and that L is true. Contradiction!

It is widely agreed that one thing the liar paradox is shows that not all instances of the schema "s is true if and only if p" (the *T-schema*), where for "p" a sentence is substituted and for "s" a name of this sentence is substituted, are true. This can be shown easily. If the T-schema is valid, one instance is: L is true iff L. But also, since L says that L is not true, L iff L is not true. By the transitivity of the biconditional, L is true iff L is not true. But this is, classically, a contradiction.[44]

---

[42] Among relevant discussions are my (2002a, 2002b, and 2005).

[43] For helpful overviews of these paradoxes, see Sorensen (2012) and Beall and Glanzberg (2011), respectively. I have discussed these paradoxes at length in, for example, my (2002a, 2002b, and 2005).

[44] Naturally one can also respond to the liar paradox by revising classical logic. I do not here wish to get into details regarding the liar, but only to briefly present the problem.

But it seems somehow meaning-constitutive for "true" that this schema should be valid. We can resolve the conflict by saying that the T-schema, or the instances thereof, are semantically analytic. It is part of competence with "true" to be disposed to accept the T-schema, while yet the T-schema is not actually valid.

Next, the sorites paradox. Consider the following version of the sorites paradox. We have a long (but finite) series of buckets of paint. The leftmost one (bucket #1) contains paradigmatically red paint. In the bucket to the right of that (bucket #2), one drop of yellow paint has been mixed in. In the next bucket (bucket #3) two drops of yellow paint have been mixed in. And so on. Toward the end of the series, the paint looks paradigmatically yellow. Now consider the following reasoning:

> The paint in bucket #1 looks red.
> For any two buckets of paint in the series, if the paint in bucket #n looks red, then the paint in bucket #n+1 looks red.
> So the paint in each of the buckets in the series looks red.

The premises seem very plausible and the conclusion appears to follow from the premises, yet the conclusion is clearly unacceptable. It is standard to resist the sorites reasoning by finding a way to resist accepting the second premise. But how can the second premise be rejected compatibly with the vagueness in "looks red"? More specifically, "looks red" is not only vague but observational, and the second premise can be motivated by the principle "if x and y are indistinguishable with respect to color to casual observation then if one looks red then so does the other." So if the second premise is rejected, so must this principle be. But how is rejection of the principle stated compatible with using "looks red" with the actual meaning it has?

We can resolve the conflict by saying that the relevant principle, and analogous principles—so-called *tolerance principles*—for other vague expressions are semantically analytic.[45] More generally, a tolerance principle for a predicate is a principle stating that for some possible parameter of application (say, height for "tall" and age for "old"), some small enough difference in the parameter of application never matters to the predicate's applicability, while some large enough difference sometimes matters. The sorites paradox shows that tolerance principles fail where the small differences that never matter can add up to a difference large enough to matter.

An immediate objection to these suggestions is that it seems clearly possible for speakers to deny instances of the T-schema, or tolerance principles, without displaying incompetence. For example, experts on the liar and sorites paradoxes routinely deny these things! This observation might be generalized. One might think that for any purported untrue semantic analyticity, if someone can recognize that it is untrue, she can thereby come to reject it without manifesting incompetence.

The most important response to this objection is the following. What underlies the idea that there is a non-trivial notion of semantic analyticity is that there are

---

[45] See e.g. Eklund (2002a, 2005).

sentences such that competence with the expressions involved entails standing in some distinguished cognitive relation R to these sentences. It is common to identify R as *believing* or *accepting*, or *being disposed to* believe or accept. When introducing semantic analyticity, I have followed suit. But already independent considerations show that such an identification is too simple-minded. If anything has the status of semantic analyticity, the sentences expressing basic logical laws surely do. But for pretty much any basic logical law, one can find logicians and philosophers denying it.[46] (Call this the phenomenon of *radicalism*.) Hence, the identification of R is somewhat trickier than might have been expected. And given that the simple-minded suggestions regarding R do not work, the path to untrue semantic analyticities lies open, where a sentence is semantically analytic just in case full competence with the constituent expressions entails standing in relation R to this sentence. If, simple-mindedly, we identified R with belief, the account would not be plausible. But crude suggestions like that are anyway ruled out.

I mentioned earlier in this section that there is nothing in the characterization of semantic analyticity that immediately guarantees that what is semantically analytic is true. But how might reference-determination work such that what is semantically analytic may fail to be true? There are different ways, but one example is provided by a view on reference-determination inspired by what Lewis says about terms getting their reference determined by false theories.[47] According to Lewis, the terms refer to what comes closest and close enough to what satisfies the relevant theories. The referents are imperfect satisfiers of the theories. This can be straightforwardly extended to where the theory in question is or contains semantic analyticities, and where the theory is inconsistent and not simply false. An alternative, more strict view on reference would be that the referent of a term, if any, would have to be such as to make true associated semantic analyticities.

After this long detour into semantic analyticity, let me now relate back to the immediate topic, the viability of (M) and (M′). If, as I hold, there in fact can be semantic analyticities that are untrue, and known to be untrue, then the would-be friend of (M) or (M′) can understand "conceptually entails" to mean *semantically analytically entails* and respond to the problems posed by slurs and thick concepts by appeal to how semantic analyticities may be untrue. That something is C, where C is a slur or thick concept, and can semantically analytically entail that this something is F without it being the case that necessarily if something is C then it is F.

Let me now turn to a different potential problem for (M) and (M′). Some writers have insisted that many thick concepts do not have invariant normative valence, but instead have *variant valence*: for example, that while it may perhaps *typically* be the case that something's being a courageous thing to do counts in its favor, sometimes this can count against it.[48] One may try to account for this by saying that even if x's

---

[46] See Williamson (2003, 2006, and 2007), who uses this fact in arguments for referentialism.
[47] See e.g. Lewis (1997).   [48] See Dancy (1996) and Roberts (2013).

being courageous is in and of itself something that is good-making, this feature can in combination with x's other features make x less good than it would otherwise be. But *suppose* the phenomenon of variant valence obtains and cannot be accounted for in this way: that for some instances of, say, courage, not only make the possessor less good than the possessor would otherwise be, in combination with some of the possessor's other features, but they are not even in and of themselves something good. This presents a possible problem for (M′). But we must be careful here. Bearing in mind the concept/property distinction, there are two different variant valence-theses:

> (PV)   For some property that a thick concept ascribes, sometimes this property is a good-making (bad-making) feature of what has it and sometimes not.
>
> (PC)   Some thick concept C is such that sometimes to say "___ is C" is to say something positive (negative) about ___ and sometimes not.

("PV" for property variance and "PC" for concept variance.) As stated, (PC) may suggest the view that "___ is C" simply is context-sensitive: in some contexts, the predicate expresses a positive concept and in others it expresses a negative one. But if what is going on is simply that the predicate is context-sensitive, then it is unclear how we are dealing with a concept with variable valence, rather than with a term that expresses different concepts in different contexts. But the intended understanding, however we are best to make sense of it, is that what (PC) says is to be the case even while this cannot simply be traced to such context-sensitivity. The idea is that the concept includes evaluation, in some way, but this evaluation is not inherently either of positive or of negative valence, but acquires different valence in different contexts.

(PV) and (PC) do not necessarily stand and fall together. It is possible, for example, that (PV) is true but (PC) is not: that while something's having the property in question is not always a good-making feature, to say of it that it is "C," where C is a thick concept which ascribes the property, is always to evaluate it positively.

The thesis that is of relevance to (M′) is (PC). It would be natural for someone subscribing to (PC), and who holds that thick concepts satisfying (PC) are normative, to reject (M′): these thick concepts do not stand in simple conceptual relationships to the concepts *goodness* and *badness*. The examples used to motivate variant valence in the first instance justify (PV). And as noted, (PV) can be true without (PC) being so.

Even if (PC) holds and (M′) should be rejected, the friend of (PC) can in principle accept a different kind of minimalist view. For example, it can be maintained that for a predicate to be normative just is for it to be one of the predicates on a *big list*: there is nothing deeper that unites these predicates; not even their conceptual entailment relations to the concepts *goodness* and *badness*.[49]

---

[49] For this kind of list view, see Jackson (1998), p. 120. However, Jackson's motivation for accepting such a view is different.

My own view, moreover, would be that if some, or all, thick concepts really verify (PC) then we should simply question whether these concepts really are normative. Whatever the fate of a view that is generally dismissive of there being normative expressions or normative properties, one should be open to the possibility that some expressions or properties that intuitively are to be regarded as normative ought not in the end to be so classified.

None of the problems discussed shows that (M) and (M') *must* be rejected. Even if the tone view of slurs is accepted, that only casts doubt on the fully general (M); (M') is a natural revision. The phenomenon of misevaluating thick concepts, if genuine, casts doubt on (M') only on the assumption that thick concepts are normative as a matter of sense. As for variant valence, I have just outlined my preferred response. Even if the doubts about the extensional adequacy of (M) and (M') can all be removed, I would myself be concerned about the minimalistic character of any theory which says that (M) or (M') provides the full story about the normativity of concepts.

The minimalist view has some striking consequences with respect to the possible normative concepts of other communities. Suppose first that an Alternative-friendly view is true, and consider the alternative normative concepts of some other community. Given the minimalist view, these (supposed) alternative normative concepts would not be classified as normative at all. Suppose next that an Alternative-*unfriendly* view is true, and that the reference of our normative predicates is determined by the normative roles of our predicates. And consider the alternative normative concepts of some other community, and suppose that the reference of these concepts is determined by their normative roles, so that they are coreferential with our concepts. It is actually not obvious that these alternative normative concepts would be classified as normative given the minimalist view. For example, having the same normative role as our concept of being good might not amount to being conceptually linked to that concept in the way required by (M'). That depends on how the conceptual entailment talk is cashed out. But if conceptual entailment relations require that someone competent with the concepts in question must thereby be in a position to know the entailment in question, the counterpart of our concept of being good might well not stand in a conceptual entailment relation to our actual concept of being good.

A possible reaction to the potential problems faced by the different constructive answers to the concept question is to embrace a dismissive attitude toward this question. While we can sometimes use some expressions and concepts to evaluate, speaking of some expressions and concepts as in and of themselves normative is misguided. Importantly, however, taking such a stance does not mean that one must adopt a dismissive attitude toward the property question. One can say that the only things properly called normative are properties; there is no reasonable notion of normativity that properly applies to concepts.

4.4 Concluding Remarks

I have gone through a number of views on the concept question: the metaphysical view, the normative role view, the minimalist view, and, to some extent, the dismissive view. I spent some time arguing against the metaphysical view. The view I favor is the normative role view. I have gone through some potentially serious problems for the minimalist view, but have not presented anything that even purports to be a decisive argument against it.

5

Normative Properties

5.1 The Property Question

Let us now turn to the property question: what is it for a property to be normative?
One simple suggestion appeals to the following equivalence:

(P1)   A property is normative iff it can be ascribed by a normative predicate.[1]

Someone who holds that there is this equivalence can also hold that something
stronger than the equivalence would be true: that this states what it is for a property
to be normative. But (P1) faces a host of potential problems. First, when we take into
account slurs and objectionable thick concepts, we should be open to the possibility
of normative predicates ascribing non-normative properties. For example, it may
be true that some behaviors are lewd, but the property ascribed by "lewd," lewdness,
is not a normative property. (Although at least in the case of slurs, an "as a matter of
sense"-clause would address the problem.) Second, on any Alternative-friendly
version of the normative role view, (P1) will yield that there are *very many* normative
properties—all the properties ascribed by all the different alternative normative
predicates are normative. While opinions may vary, one may be concerned about
this consequence. Third, recall presentationalism, briefly introduced in Chapter 1.
The presentationalist holds that normativity resides only in representations and not
in what is represented, and holds that normative predicates ascribe properties that
are not normative. Only in Chapter 6 will presentationalism be our main topic. I will
not outright defend presentationalism, but I will argue that the view has rather
obvious attractive features. (P1) pretty immediately rules out the presentationalist
view, since (P1) rules out that there are non-empty normative predicates but no
normative properties. Fourth, (P1) threatens to be incompatible with any view on the
concept question which picks out normative predicates in terms of the normativity of
the properties they ascribe, such as the metaphysical view. One cannot both say that
what it is for a property to be normative is for it to be ascribed by some normative
predicate and what it is for a predicate to be normative is for it to ascribe some
normative property. In sum, (P1) is in conflict with a large variety of views. Needless

---

[1] The idea is common. One recent discussion where it receives expression is Streumer (2011); see
p. 326.

to say, this by no means immediately dooms (P1). It goes without saying that a thesis can be true even though it conflicts with many views. But the variety of views, and views on other issues than those immediately addressed by (P1), with which (P1) is incompatible makes it hard to see what comprehensive theoretical framework (P1) might comfortably fit into.

There is also a general theoretical reason for discomfort with (P1), having to do with metasemantics. In general, a predicate can present the property it ascribes as being a particular way while the property it ascribes can fail to be exactly that way. I am putting this impressionistically as I don't want to tie the point to any particular way of theorizing about meaning.[2] The general point is that on any view on meaning that can allow for a discrepancy between how the predicate presents the property and the actual nature of the property, there is some reason to be suspicious of (P1). For might it not be that a predicate then presents the property it ascribes as normative, while the property is not in fact normative? Even if so, that does not immediately mean that (P1) is false, for a predicate's presenting the property it ascribes as normative need not amount to the predicate itself being normative. I just wish to point to one possible theoretical reason for dissatisfaction with (P1).

A suggestion like (P1) can be put forward in two different spirits. One can think that there is something metaphysically distinctive about normative properties and that (P1) is a promising way to get at what this is. Or alternatively one can think that there is no notion of a normative property that picks out an interesting class of properties, and one puts forward (P1) as a suggestion for how anyway to pick out some sort of notion of a normative property.[3] I think (P1) at least would be more palatable if taken in the second spirit.

A different view on the property question centers on:

(P2)   Property F is positively (negatively) normative iff for all x, if x is F then necessarily x is [to that extent] good (bad).

(As earlier, one might worry about, for example, the relation between what is good/bad and what is right/wrong. As earlier, I will slide over such concerns.[4]) To illustrate how (P2) works, let me note how it deals with some things that have come up earlier. Suggestion (P2) deals nicely with examples like "thgir." To be thgir is to be right, even if "right" is normative and "thgir" is not. The property of being thgir is a normative property (even if the "thgir"-users may be unaware of the fact that it is). That consequence sounds correct to me. (P2) also deals well with objectionable thick

---

[2] But recall what I said in Chapter 4 about there being possibly untrue semantic analyticities. This provides one way to undergird what is suggested in the text. If "All Fs are Gs" is semantically analytic but untrue, then the predicate "F" presents the Fs in one way—as being G—although as a matter of fact not all Fs are Gs.

[3] Analogously, one can put forward the metaphysical view on the concept question in two different spirits.

[4] Copp (2013), p. 32f, discusses a criterion like (P2) but focuses on reasons instead.

concepts. An objectionable thick positively (negatively) normative concept (or a slur) may ascribe a property that fails to be positively (negatively) normative. (P2) does pretty immediately rule out possible views such as presentationalism—it does so together with the assumption that some things are good (/bad). Note also that combining (P2) with an Alternative-friendly normative role view has the consequence that the normative terms of alternative communities cannot be expected generally to ascribe "normative" properties. One may differ regarding how agreeable this consequence is. (The friend of a view of the kind in question might point out that in the alternative community's corresponding sense of "normative," *our* normative terms cannot be expected generally to ascribe "normative" properties.)

(P2) is arguably much too permissive as it stands. One might want to leave room for there to be a purely descriptive property F such that something's being F necessitates this thing's having a normative property. Indeed, if the normative *supervenes* on the non-normative, as is widely believed, then there will, under suitably liberal assumptions about property existence (that the set of descriptive properties is closed under Boolean operations), certainly be such necessitation relations. But by (P2), F is then a normative property after all. Someone who finds (P2) too permissive might try to appeal to the distinction between *essential* features on the one hand and merely *metaphysically necessary* ones on the other. The essential features of something are those of its necessary features that make this something what it is. A well-known example, due to Kit Fine, is that while it is a metaphysically necessary feature of Socrates that he is a member of his singleton set, this is intuitively not an essential feature of Socrates.[5] Fine's distinction has become very influential. Given this distinction, one can say that some properties F are such that it is an *essential* feature of F that if something is F then it is good (bad), while others fail to be such even though *necessarily*, if something is F then it is good (bad). The normative properties can be identified as the ones in the former category. Suppose, to illustrate, that goodness supervenes on some descriptive feature G. Then, necessarily, if something is G then it is good. One can still avoid the conclusion that G is really a normative property by saying that it is not essential to G that if something is G then it is good.

Even if some modified version of (P2) is extensionally adequate, the view that (P2) or some suitably revised version succeeds in spelling out what it is to be normative may be regarded as being too beholden to an overly minimalistic view on what it is for properties to be normative. For any property F, we can define a notion of being F-ish such that a property G is F-ish if and only if (it is an essential feature of ψ that) something's being G necessitates its being F. That does not mean that the notion of being an F-ish property carves out any interesting class of properties. Moreover, it will be trivial that F is F-ish. Compare the above remarks on the minimalist view on the concept question.

---

[5] Fine (1994).

Recall also the possibility that there are alternative normative concepts, in the sense of concepts with the same normative roles as ours but with different extensions. Let "good*" express such a concept. By (P2), the property that "good*" ascribes need not be a normative property. (Even though, of course, the community using "good*" can use a concept of normativity*, where a property is normative* if it stands in the right relation to goodness*.)

What might a suitable non-minimalistic view on the property question be like? A primitivist view according to which the normative properties form a significant metaphysical kind but which eschews any sort of informative characterization of what makes a property normative would be one such view. This view may well be correct. But when we are only talking about characterizations given in such broad strokes as here, one may be skeptical of a primitivist view, even if one may share the primitivist's doubts about the possibility of giving any detailed informative characterization of what distinguishes normative properties from other properties. Note too that while it is possible to be a primitivist both when it comes to the property question and when it comes to the concept question, someone who is a primitivist when it comes to both these questions will be hard pressed to say what the relation is between normative properties and normative concepts.

Another type of non-minimalistic view focuses on *motivation*. There are two different kinds of view of this general type. On one kind of view, normative properties are such that recognition that they are instantiated is somehow in and of itself motivating. On another kind of view, normative properties are such that recognition of their being instantiated *ought* to be motivating. The latter kind of view is in effect a kind of primitivist or minimalist view in light of its focus on what *ought* to motivate. Turn then to the former kind of view. A first problem is that it is rather obviously somewhat Panglossian as it stands. Worries on this score can be softened by the addition of a "ceteris paribus" clause, even though probing questions could be asked about how such a clause is best understood. Even supposing such questions could be adequately dealt with, a second, more serious problem remains. Suppose there were intrinsically motivating facts: facts the mere acquaintance with which served to motivate. There still is the question of whether one ought to act in the way in which one is thereby motivated to act. Maybe one is motivated to do something one really ought not to do. Motivation and normativity are different things.

In his (2006), Derek Parfit defends his brand of irreductive normative realism by going through and rebutting various objections to it. A common theme to many of the objections he considers is that the irreducibly normative facts that a realist like Parfit postulates cannot motivate. Parfit's response to such objections is that they are beside the point. Normativity is one thing and motivation another. So long as the realist can establish that it is a truth that we have reason to do so-and-so, she has won. If that reason does not necessarily motivate, then so be it. Thus far I am with Parfit: he is making the correct point that motivation and normativity are different issues.

Even if one is convinced by Parfit's point, however, worries may linger. Even while avoiding the motivation talk, one may still think: so maybe there are in some sense irreducible facts about what one has reason to do—*but so what*?

However, the difficulty for anyone with this sort of concern is how to spell out the "so what." A friend of Parfit's view can respond by presenting a dilemma: What is the "so what" question all about? One possibility is that it amounts to a concern about the motivational force of normative facts all over again. But that concern, we assume, has already been dealt with. Or the "so what" question asks whether we really have reason to do what we have reason to do. But spelled out that way, the question seems toothless. Of course, if I have reason to φ, I have reason to φ.

The considerations that have been brought up earlier in this book, regarding communities with alternative normative concepts, are relevant here. They serve to put some pressure on, for example, a normative realist of Parfit's kind. If there is another possible linguistic community, using notions of "reason" and "ought" with the same normative roles as our notions but with different extensions, then we can note that whereas we can comfort ourselves by saying "of course if I have reason to φ, then I have reason to φ," they can comfort themselves the same way by saying "of course if I have reason* to φ, then I have reason* to φ," where reason* is their notion of reason. If there is something in the world itself that favors our way of going about things over theirs, that is not shown by little speeches like this. To show this, one would need to show that there is something privileged about our notion of reason.

5.2 Normative Properties and Referential Normativity

Another type of non-minimalistic view on the property question, one toward which I am more attracted, appeals to the notion of referential normativity. Recall, a predicate is referentially normative if its reference is non-defectively determined by its normative role. The general idea is that there is something in the role of a predicate which makes it normative, and a referentially normative predicate is such that those aspects of a predicate's role suffice to determine reference. Then consider the following suggestion:

(P3)   Property F is positively (negatively) normative iff it can be ascribed using a non-defective referentially normative predicate.

(P3) is like (P1) except that the predicates (P3) speaks of are referentially normative predicates rather than normative predicates generally. Given that the notion of a referentially normative predicate is more restrictive than that of a normative predicate, many of the problems regarding (P1) are avoided. If, for example, Wedgwood's general semantic theory is attractive, then (P3) may likewise be attractive.

The property question concerned *what it is* for a property to be normative. Unfortunately, (P3) is not plausibly an answer to that question, even if extensionally adequate. The intuitive idea behind (P3) is that a property's normativity is what makes it fit to be ascribed by a referentially normative predicate. One might wish for a more direct characterization of what makes a property normative than (P3). However, condition (P3) is still informative, and it is possible that the sort of indirect characterization of property normativity that (P3) provides is the best that can reasonably be hoped for.

Once one sees (P3) as an option, one can further appreciate what is wrong with (P1): (P1) does not care, so to speak, about just *how* a property comes to be ascribed by a given normative predicate. That is why the properties ascribed by slurs and objectionable thick concepts would count as normative by (P1). By contrast, what (P3) says is, in general terms, that a property is normative if it is ascribed by a normative predicate, and is so by virtue of a feature of the property which makes it well suited to be ascribed by a predicate which is such that what it ascribes is determined by its normative role.

Once one has distinguished between the concept question and the property question, it may be natural to suspect that either properties will be what are fundamentally normative and a concept is derivatively normative by virtue of ascribing a normative property, or concepts will be what are fundamentally normative and a property is derivatively normative by virtue of being ascribed by a normative concept. If one accepts the normative role view on the concept question, accepts (P3) as satisfactory, as far as it goes, as an answer to the property question, and moreover takes some non-deficient predicates to be referentially normative, then one embraces neither of these views. There are normative properties and normative concepts, and neither type of normativity is merely derivative.

Adherence to (P3) is compatible with a number of different metanormative views. This may be obvious, but let me anyway go through it. Non-naturalist realists can adhere to (P3). They can insist that only non-natural properties can be ascribed by referentially normative predicates: only those properties are such that a predicate's normative role determines that this property is what the predicate ascribes. Naturalist realists can adhere to (P3) too. They would have to resist the non-naturalist reasoning just sketched. One can also adhere to (P3) while denying that any property satisfies the condition stated there. Recall presentationalism: the view that it is only representations and not what is represented that is normative. (P3) is consistent with the possibility that there are no normative properties as characterized. A presentationalist could appeal to (P3) to defend her view. The presentationalist can say that (P3) states the condition for a property to be normative but nothing meets it.

A reader might reasonably worry, for all I have said, that the proposal I favor—that normativity in the world is bound up with there being possible non-defective referentially normative predicates—makes normativity in the world problematically bound up with issues in the theory of reference. Shouldn't one's views on normativity in the world be independent of what one thinks about reference? But first, again to stress, the claim at issue is not that it is *in virtue of* being ascribed by a referentially normative predicate that a property is normative. As already conceded, I am not strictly offering an answer to the property question as originally stated (what is it for a property to be normative?), but only offering an informative, necessarily true biconditional.

5.3 More on Referential Normativity

There are some ways in which we might be more careful about what referential normativity is. Let a term be *fully referentially normative* if its normative role is sufficient to determine reference: any two terms with the same normative role associated with them must have the same reference. Let a term be *partially referentially normative* if its reference given its associated normative role is different from what it would have been if it didn't have this associated normative role but all else was equal. Given the distinction between full and partial referential normativity, there are really two versions of (P3), depending on how we understand the referential normativity at issue:

> (P3-FULL)   A property is positively (negatively) normative iff it can be ascribed using a non-defective fully referentially normative predicate.
>
> (P3-PARTIAL)   A property is positively (negatively) normative iff it can be ascribed using a non-defective partially referentially normative predicate.

(P3-PARTIAL) provides an in principle considerably weaker condition on the normativity of properties than does (P3-FULL). I see no particular reason to decide between them. One need only keep in mind that there are these two versions of the condition, one weaker and one stronger. If only (P3-PARTIAL) holds, then one should properly speak of normativity as *constraining* rather than as *determining* reference.

Referential normativity also comes up in connection with the distinction between Alternative-friendly and Alternative-unfriendly theories. There it is full referential normativity that is at issue. To accept an Alternative-unfriendly view is to accept that the predicates in question are fully referentially normative; to accept an Alternative-friendly view is to deny this. But given the distinction between partial and full referential normativity, one can wonder whether one ought instead to draw a distinction in terms of partial referential normativity. It is reasonable to think that if there is partial referential normativity, then there is a correlated metaphysical feature: some properties are more apt to be ascribed by predicates associated with a given normative role than others, even if not all predicates associated with this normative role are guaranteed to ascribe the same property. Introducing some terminology, let us say that the properties in question are partially normative and that partial normativity comes in degrees. And anyone who thinks there is, or would be, something objectively normatively privileged about properties ascribed by fully referentially normative predicates should find it natural to think a property that is partially normative to a degree greater than another property is objectively normatively privileged over this other property.

One might also ask what exactly it is for normative role to *determine reference*. As earlier discussed, some theorists hold, following Lewis, that we can classify possible meanings in terms of how elite they are. This thought is often accompanied by the idea that what is more elite is more reference-magnetic: the more elite meanings are more intrinsically eligible to be meant than others. This complicates a number of the things I want to say. For example, take an intuitively Alternative-friendly theory, for example a naturalist theory which appeals to a causal theory of reference-determination or a descriptivist theory of reference-determination. On the face of it, there will, given such a theory, be different alternative notions of "right." But if the friend of such a theory also appeals to reference magnetism, she can insist that because a particular supposed referent of "right" is reference-magnetic, that is in fact the referent of the predicates "right" used by all the supposed communities. Does this mean that on her view the normative role associated with "right" determines the predicate's reference? What it does do is force us to be clearer on what it is for the normative role associated with a predicate to determine the predicate's reference. On a relatively non-demanding conception of determination, it is sufficient for a predicate's normative role to determine its reference that as a matter of fact all (non-defective) terms conventionally associated with this normative role have the same reference. Given this conception of determination, what we are considering is that reference magnetism helps make it the case that the predicate's normative role does determine its reference after all. But on a more demanding conception of what it takes for a predicate's normative role to determine its reference, what has just been sketched is not sufficient: it must also be that it is the normative role that does the determination in question—and not something different. And given the more demanding conception, one can think that a predicate's normative role determines its reference only if it isn't extraneous factors that do the job—and reference magnetism may be thought to be just such an extraneous factor.

I think the appropriate conception of determination for present purposes is the more demanding conception. Think about it this way. If it weren't for reference magnetism, there would be (at least) two properties that are candidates for being what we should take to play the rightness role, rightness and rightness*. They are both, at least reference magnetism aside, apt to be picked out by a predicate associated with the normative role associated with "right." Then suppose rightness is in fact more elite and more reference-magnetic than rightness* and is what is ascribed by all normative predicates with this normative role. Why should this be taken to matter to the normative question of what to do? Why would the supposed fact that rightness is more elite and more reference-magnetic than rightness* make it make more sense for me to structure my actions around what is right than around what is right*? When discussing this matter in Chapter 2, I distinguished between different conceptions of eliteness, and concluded in each case that appeal to eliteness is problematic.

A different complication regarding appeal to (P3) is that a term's referent may be only an imperfect satisfier of the conditions semantically associated with the term. The referent may, for example, be such that it does not completely satisfy or fit the associated description of conceptual role but only comes nearest or near enough. In principle, one could favor something like (P3) but think a property that is the referent of a referentially normatively predicate but which is only an imperfect satisfier is not normative: only a property which is a perfect fit would be. I won't try to resolve this issue here; I am only concerned to flag it.

A related complication is that a predicate whose reference is determined by normative role may be semantically indeterminate: there are a number of different properties that are candidate referents of the predicate. There is no property that the predicate determinately refers to, but there are several such that it is indeterminate whether the predicate refers to them. This indeterminacy may, for example, arise because there is no property that perfectly fits the normative role, and different properties come close enough and maximally close to fitting the role. Suppose for simplicity that none of the properties has an independent claim to be normative. Should the friend of (P3) say that these properties are all normative on account of being candidate referents? Or should she say that none of them is? Or should she perhaps say that for each of them, it is indeterminate whether it is normative? Perhaps the best option is the last one. Again this is an issue I am more concerned to flag than to attempt to resolve.

5.4 Concluding Remarks

In this chapter I have addressed the property question regarding what normativity is. In Chapter 4 I addressed the concept question. The proposed answers to the property and concept questions nicely dovetail with other themes and arguments. My proposed answer to the concept question crucially relies on the notion of normative role—the supposed characteristically normative use, however this is to be precisely specified, of normative expressions. This notion of normative role was also crucial to a central suggestion brought up in response to the problems presented by alternative concepts: that what the ardent realist needs is that some possible normative expressions are referentially normative, in the sense that their reference is determined by normative role. Referential normativity, moreover, is what the proposed answer to the property question revolves around, as that answer was that a property is normative exactly if it can be ascribed by some possible referentially normative predicate. (Though recall that this is not strictly an answer to the property question, since it does not plausibly speak to what *makes* a property normative.)

All this makes use of the notion of normative role. Readers may naturally be uneasy about this, especially since I have not been very specific about the notion of normative role. I believe that this notion is in good standing. But the skeptic can take my claims as conditional. If some concepts are normative, they are so by being associated with normative roles. If some properties are normative, then they can be ascribed using referentially normative predicates; and no other properties can be ascribed using such predicates. If ardent realism is true, then some predicates are referentially normative. The skeptic could draw the conclusion that no concepts or properties can be said to be normative; and that ardent realism cannot be vindicated.

It would be consistent with all of the main points from the chapters preceding Chapters 4 and the present chapter to simply treat questions about what properties and concepts are properly labeled as "normative" to be theoretical *don't cares*; and the main arguments Chapter 4 and the present chapter could be resisted without detriment to the rest of the book. However, what I do see as important is that there is a potentially theoretically important distinction between the properties I have called normative and other properties, whether or not this is labeled a normative/non-normative distinction, similarly for what I have said regarding concepts.

6

Presentationalism

At some points earlier in the book I have had occasion to relate to the *presentationalist* view, according to which there is no normativity in the world itself; all the norma-tivity there is resides in our representations of the world. In this chapter I will further explain presentationalism, discuss some of its virtues, and illustrate how the possibility of a view of this kind is neglected in the literature.

If there is normativity in the world only if some possible non-defective predicates are referentially normative, then even if there are non-empty normative predicates, there can fail to be normativity that does not simply reside in our representations of the world. This complicates the theoretical map.

6.1 What is Presentationalism?

I would like to consider the view that there are no normative facts or properties—as I shall sometimes put it, that there is no *normativity in the world*—but the only normativity there is resides in our representations of the world.[1] This view, as stated, could be true for reasons independent of metanormative theorizing: for example, it can be held that there are no such entities as properties or facts. But suppose that the view holds for reasons specifically related to the normative.[2]

Just *why* would there be no normativity in the world? There are different possible reasons. One well-known consideration here is Mackie's "argument from queerness"—normative facts would have a mysterious kind of to-be-doneness about them.[3] I don't think myself that Mackie's own reasoning is very persuasive, or very

---

[1] "But our representations too are part of the world so if our representations are normative then there is normativity in the world!"—True but irrelevant. First, if necessary one could replace talk of normativity in the world with talk of normativity of properties and facts. Second, compare the case of vagueness. One prominent view on vagueness, arguably the orthodox view, is that vagueness is semantic (or generally, representational): it resides in our representations, not the world represented. If the objection we're considering is sound, it equally swiftly disposes of the view that vagueness is semantic. I take it that whatever the fate of that view on vagueness, it cannot be this easily disposed of.

[2] In Chapter 4, I paused on the issue that the way issues related to normative realism are often stated—in terms of the existence of normative properties and facts—is problematized by the possibility that there may be independent qualms about normative and facts. (It would also be problematized by the general ontological view that there *really* only exist *fundamental* properties, and a great many would-be properties, not just would-be normative ones, are not fundamental.)

[3] Mackie (1977), ch. 1.

clear, but it still helps indicate roughly what sort of reason there can be.[4] One might also be led to skepticism about normativity in the world by consideration of the property question, from Chapter 5: either because one despairs about the possibility of a satisfactory answer to the property question or because one favors a given answer but thinks nothing in the world meets the condition in question. For example, I favored an answer to the property question that appeals to referential normativity— a property is normative exactly if it can be ascribed using a non-defective referentially normative predicate.[5] One can agree that this is the correct answer to this question but go on to add that no possible predicates could be referentially normative given the way the world is.

Given the assumption that there is no normativity in the world, what should we conclude about *normative language*? One possibility is of course to adopt some sort of traditional antirealist view, for example an error-theoretic view that denies that atomic normative sentences are true or a traditional expressivist view, denying that normative sentences even are truth-apt. However, I will explore the possibility that (atomic) normative sentences still can be true. There are a few different views that allow for this, in some way or other. Let me start by briefly listing some such views, indicating what sorts of views of that general kind I will here explore further.

One option is to combine traditional expressivism with a deflationary view on truth and truth-aptness; a view given which meaningful declarative sentences are rather trivially apt for truth. If so, the thought is, one can justifiably describe normative sentences as true or false, even if they don't express genuine propositions, or generally don't stand in the same sort of relation to the world that ordinary descriptive sentences do. This kind of view could perhaps be a viable option. But I mention this view only to set it aside. Whatever the fate of the expressivist-deflationist view, my concern will be with the possibility of normative sentences being non-deflationarily true even if there is no normativity in the world. A second option is to maintain that some atomic sentences under discussion are true even if there is no normativity in the world, and maintain that these sentences are not really normative as a matter of meaning, contrary to how they are commonly seen. Call this the *hyperdescriptivist* view.[6] Compare speaking of something as philosophy.

---

[4] Although here's an adaptation of Mackie's queerness argument using the tools of the present discussion. As presented in Olson (2014), Mackie is best understood as saying that irreducible normativity in the world is queer. However, the targets of Mackie's argument can reply by simply insisting that irreducible normativity is not queer and it is unclear what can be said to sway them if they adopt this stance. I take it that "queerness" here is shorthand for: has a feature such that we ought not accept that the world contains anything like that. As for irreducible normativity, the question in the debate is what that should be taken to be. Here my preferred characterization of what it is for a property to be normative can be wheeled in. The queerness charge is then: how could a property be such that it is fit to be picked out by all predicates having the same normative role?

[5] It was not quite an answer, as it was at best a necessarily true biconditional, not quite addressing the question of *what it is* for something to be normative.

[6] I include the "hyper" since the bare label "descriptivism" has so many different uses.

"Philosophy" is not reasonably thought to be a normative predicate. One can speak normatively using the predicate: a philosopher speaking of a colleague's work as "not philosophy" is naturally seen as disparaging her colleague's work; a physicist who speaks of a colleague's work as "philosophy" can likewise be seen as disparaging her colleague's work.[7] But the evaluation is communicated as a mere *pragmatic* matter. It has no effect on the truth-value of what is said, and more generally, it is not conventionally attached to the word. Compare, too, a perhaps more interesting example. I have heard it claimed that "girl" is a slur, because of its use in contexts like "he throws like a girl." But in the first instance, such uses are just examples of slurring *uses* of "girl." And someone who in some cases says "he throws like a girl," using the expression slurringly, can, for example, lovingly say of his newborn, "It's a girl!". Even if "girl" has slurring uses, the word is arguably not itself a slur and is not normative. The hyperdescriptivist says that all normative uses of language are like this. The expressions themselves are not normative; only individual uses of them are. To relate to the suggested answer to the concept question in Chapter 4: the hyperdescriptivist may deny that any expressions are associated with normative roles as a matter of meaning. The hyperdescriptivist holds that some atomic sentences that typically are classed as normative still are true even if there is no normativity in the world. But she does not strictly hold that genuinely normative atomic sentences still can be true despite there being no normativity in the world. Rather, she denies that the sentences genuinely are normative. This view too I will simply set aside for now. My concern will be with the possibility of genuinely normative sentences being true, even if there is no normativity in the world.

What I will be concerned with are, as already indicated, *presentationalist* views. On any presentationalist view, some predicates genuinely are normative but the normativity of a predicate is a feature of how the property that the predicate ascribes is represented, rather than a feature of the property that the predicate stands for.[8] Contemporary expressivists, who do not deny that normative sentences are truth-apt (in a deflationary sense) and that normative predicate ascribe properties, sometimes say things that suggest presentationalism. But presentationalism as we will discuss it will not be tied to expressivism, or to a deflationary notion of truth.

Here is one presentationalist view, the *imperfect satisfier view*. As mentioned in Chapter 4, David Lewis has prominently defended a kind of liberalized descriptivist theory such that the semantic value of an expression needn't satisfy every element in the theory associated with it; it is sufficient that it satisfy a weighted most.[9]

---

[7] Recall, I am using "normative" widely, to cover also what is sometimes called evaluative rather than normative.

[8] Tiffany (2007) defends a version of what I am calling presentationalism, and Baker (forthcoming) and Copp (2004, 2013) also explicitly bring up this type of view. Moreover, it is in general natural to see some "hybrid expressivists" as defending a view of this kind—I will discuss that issue later.

[9] See e.g. Lewis (1997). It might also be worth comparing what to say about a friend of a causal theory of reference who denies normativity in the world. If she still thinks some atomic purported normative

As descriptivists about reference, they hold that terms get their reference determined by associated theories; as *neo*-descriptivists (as I will use the label) they allow that the associated theory can be false and yet determine the term's reference. Suppose we work with this idea. Then we can say that in the case of normative predicates, normativity is one central part of the theory associated with the predicates; but if there are no normative properties, the predicates can stand for non-normative properties and be true of what has these non-normative properties. Another presentationalist view, the *additional element view*, maintains that even if there is no normativity in the world, atomic normative sentences can still be true, and not because the notion of truth is deflationary or because the so-called normative sentences are not really normative, and not because there are still sufficiently good satisfiers of the theories associated with the predicates, even if there is no normativity in the world, but because their normativity is a feature of the meanings of normative predicates, which is not connected with their reference and the contributions they make to truth conditions. For example, the normativity of an expression might instead be a matter of conventional implicature.

Compare here Mackie's queerness argument as it is often rendered. Here is Miller's (2014) presentation of it:

Conceptual Claim: our concept of a moral fact is a concept of an objectively prescriptive fact, so that the truth of an atomic, declarative moral sentence would require the existence of objectively and categorically prescriptive facts.

Ontological Claim: there are no objectively and categorically prescriptive facts. So,

Conclusion: there are no moral facts; atomic, declarative moral sentences are systematically and uniformly false.

While the argument as presented concerns moral facts, one could easily present the argument as being concerned with normativity generally rather than with morality specifically.

In a book-length treatment of error theory, Olson (2014) distinguishes between different kinds of error theories in metaethics. According to what he calls standard error theory, "moral thinking involves systematically false beliefs...and...as a consequence, all moral judgments, or some significant subset thereof, are false."[10] According to one competing version, moderate error theory, moral judgments are

---

sentences are true, she is either a hyperdescriptivist or a presentationalist. She could certainly be a presentationalist of the additional element variety. Perhaps she could also in principle hold that it is in some way part of the sense of normative predicates that they be normative and qualify as something like an imperfect satisfier presentationalist.

[10]   Olson (2014), p. 8. The reason for the caution—"or some significant subset thereof"—is that one may reasonably think that some moral judgments are negations of others. Olson discusses such complications, pp. 11–15. I shall here set them aside. One way to try to avoid this problem of formulation is to say that the error theorist's claim is that all *atomic* moral judgments are false.

not systematically untrue, even though moral thinking involves systematically false beliefs. Note that a "moderate error theorist" may, for example, be an imperfect satisfier presentationalist. Olson attributes the moderate view to Hume and to (early) Hägerström, but interprets Mackie—I think clearly correctly—as embracing standard error theory.[11] But when Olson later turns to how Mackie argues for his view, he omits to discuss whether Mackie's arguments might only establish moderate error theory. Mackie's various queerness arguments as Olson reconstructs them (Olson rejects all of them but the one that appeals to irreducible normativity) proceed by identifying various properties that moral facts would have to have, and conclude that any facts with such features would have to be queer. Standard error theory is supposed to follow given the additional assumption that we ought not to accept the idea of such queer facts. But first, moral judgments don't necessarily need moral facts to make them true. Presentationalism is an option. Second, independently of what to say about the presentationalist option, the assumptions made in the arguments about what moral facts would have to be like are based on claims about what our conceptions of moral facts are. But it is, or should be, a commonplace that our conception of a type of fact can involve that facts of that type are thus-and-such, but facts of that type aren't actually thus-and-such. The Mackiean arguments need not only that our *conception* of moral facts involve a particular claim. They need moreover that our *concepts* involve this claim. It is common, and reasonable, to draw a distinction between conceptions and concepts. The distinction can be drawn in different ways, but roughly and fairly theory-neutrally, a conception associated with a term is simply the cluster of beliefs involving the term that some person or group has, whereas the concept associated with the term is something attached to the term's meaning. The conception associated with a term can change (beliefs can be revised) without the term changing its meaning, but the concept associated with a term cannot change without the term changing its meaning. Drawing the distinction this way is consistent with identifying the concept associated with a term as a set of beliefs. They can be the beliefs such that it is part of semantic competence with the term to be disposed to have them. Miller's formulation of Mackie's argument correctly speaks of concepts. But the point about the concept/conception distinction is still relevant, for it is incumbent on the friend of Mackie's reasoning to show that the supposedly problematic assumption, in this case objective prescriptivity, is part of the concept and not just of the conception. If it were only part of the conception then it could well be that the assumption is false but moral predicates still are non-empty. Moreover, even if the problematic assumption is indeed part of the concept and not just the conception, it does not immediately follow that what the concept ascribes would need to satisfy the assumption. Recall the discussion of semantic analyticity in Chapter 4. The idea favorably discussed there was that some principles can be such

---

[11] Olson (2014), pp. 39ff.

that it is part of semantic competence with an expression to be disposed to accept them, while still the expression can be non-empty even if the principle is not true. Applied to Mackie's argument: even if it is part of the concept of a moral fact that moral facts are objectively prescriptive, there can be moral facts even if they are not objectively prescriptive.

In what follows I will use the imperfect satisfier view and the additional element view as my examples of presentationalist views. I am intentionally using rather general terms when characterizing these possible forms of presentationalism: I don't want to have to take a stand on theoretical issues I don't see an immediate need to take a stand on. There are important differences between the imperfect satisfier view and the additional element view, but for most present purposes those differences can be disregarded and I will speak of both views under the heading of presentationalism.

Presentationalism is a broadly realist view: normative predicates are objectively true of things in the world. But at the same time, the view undeniably has a rather antirealist flavor to it. It denies that there is normativity in the world. It might be natural at this point to consider whether the view *really* is realist or *really* is antirealist. The case for calling it a realist view is straightforward. It is, as just stated, a view on which some atomic normative sentences are objectively true. Many characterizations of realism that are offered in the literature would because of this have the consequence that presentationalism is a realist view. But there is also precedent for calling it an antirealist view. If one requires for realism not only that there are true atomic normative sentences but moreover that there are normative facts (instantiated) and normative properties, then presentationalism is not a form of realism. Moreover, compare Michael Dummett (1991) on vagueness. Dummett characterizes realism about vagueness as the view that "there is vagueness in reality, not just in our words."[12] Someone who believes that words can be vague but their being vague is just a matter of it being vague what they stand for (contrast: they stand for something vague)—this is a standard view on vagueness as a semantic phenomenon—is then not a realist about vagueness. This despite the fact that this theorist holds that vague representations can be true, and be so by virtue of how things stand in mind-independent reality. If one uses "realism" the way Dummett does when talking about realism about vagueness, then one will say that the presentationalist is not a realist about normativity. She believes some normative representations are true and are so by virtue of how things stand in mind-independent reality—but she thinks the normativity is found only in our words and not in reality.

I don't know how fruitful it would be to launch into an investigation of how best to use the label "realism."[13] The presentationalist view obviously has many of the

[12] Dummett (1991), p. 326.
[13] Though one rather appealing suggestion is that presentationalism vindicates *realism about rightness* but not *realism about normativity*. Thanks here to Jens Johansson.

apparently nice features realist views generally have. It does not run into the kinds of problems that beset traditional expressivist views, such as the Frege-Geach problem. Unlike error-theoretic views, it is compatible with supposed "Moorean" facts about what is right and wrong. The view is, moreover, compatible with the supposed datum that various causal and other explanations make ineliminable reference to facts about what is right and wrong, good and bad, just and unjust, etc. At the same time, the presentationalist view promises to share a nice feature with prominent antirealist views. According to standard realist views, whether non-naturalist or naturalist, there is normativity in reality. Naturalist views face the concern that they do not really respect the fact that there is normativity in reality, even if they insist that there is.[14] Non-naturalist views saying there is non natural normativity in the world invite concerns that they postulate something we should find mysterious. Presentationalism avoids both concerns. The presentationalist doesn't postulate non-natural normativity; she doesn't even purport to make room for normativity in a natural world.

It is quite possible that given the explicit characterization of presentationalism, some naturalist realists might react by thinking that the presentationalist view is what they had in mind all along. When seeking to emphasize presentationalism as a theoretical option, I don't claim that the view is entirely new. But what I focus on is still a theoretical choice seldom stressed: that between presentationalism and naturalist realist views given which there is normativity in the world. (And from now on when I speak of naturalist realism, I will have in mind the latter view.)

Since presentationalism rather obviously meets important desiderata centrally stressed by realists as well as important desiderata centrally stressed by antirealists, I will not spend much more time spelling out the positive case for it. Whatever in the end the proper fate of the presentationalist view, the motivation behind the view ought to be clear. Instead, my main concerns in this chapter will be to clarify the presentationalist view, and to show how awareness of presentationalism as a theoretical option complicates certain arguments in the literature.

Toward the end of this chapter I bring up an objection that it is natural to raise against presentationalism. I will not aim to answer this objection. Instead I will discuss the broader theoretical issues raised, and what the options are if one rejects presentationalism on the basis of that type of objection. I will argue that a host of other theories face the same kind of objection presentationalism faces.

6.2 Some Immediate Concerns

Presentationalism says that there are genuinely normative predicates and that they stand for properties, but denies that the properties they stand for are normative. This might initially sound incoherent, and in conversations about these matters I have

---

[14] See, for example, Dancy (2006), pp. 131–42, Parfit (2011), pp. 324–7, and McPherson (2011).

encountered the suspicion that it is. But whatever in the end the fate of presentationalism, any such quick dismissal of it would be misguided. As was illustrated by
the discussion in Chapter 5, it is by no means clear how to make adequate sense of
talk of the normativity of properties. Moreover, slurs ("nigger," "faggot," "slut"...)
are arguably in some sense normative, but don't plausibly stand for normative
properties, and objectionable thick concepts ("lewd," "perverted," "chaste"...—
thick concepts whose use presupposes objectionable normative views[15]) may be
another case in point. There are of course many different reasonable views on
slurs and on thick concepts, but already the availability of views according to which
these expressions are normative and yet fail to stand for normative properties
shows that no simple incoherence charge will stick. One can hold that normative
concepts always work the way slurs and (objectionable) thick concepts are sometimes
held to do.

In fact, as mentioned in Chapter 1, pejorative expressions—of which slurs are a
subclass[16]—generally provide a model that is helpful to keep in mind when one
considers the possibility of presentationalism. Some expressions are pejorative and
they stand for properties. But to call the properties that such expressions stand for
pejorative sounds misguided. Indeed, it sounds like something of a category mistake.
One can propose that the same is going on with calling properties normative. That
would be (a version of) presentationalism.

A different but related immediate worry about presentationalism is this. Even if
analogies like the ones presented show that there is nothing immediately wrong with
allowing for the possibility that normative predicates may stand for properties that
are not normative, still one can think that "normative," as applied to properties, is
actually used in such a way that it is true as a matter of definition that if a normative
predicate stands for a property then this property is normative. But if so, then there
is no substantive issue of whether there really is normativity in the world if there are
instantiated normative predicates. A theorist is of course free to use the label in
whichever way she prefers; and moreover, perhaps (though I doubt it) the sociological claim about how "normative" is used is correct. But what one cannot
reasonably do is to use the label that way and then go on to reason that since the
property that a normative predicate stands for is normative, it must present some
special metaphysical and epistemic problems; or even, generally speaking, that the
normative properties form a metaphysically unified category in any way. If a "normative property" simply is a property that a normative predicate stands for, a
separate argument would be needed for the claim that there is something objectively
special about "normative properties," something that presents special metaphysical
puzzles. And the presentationalist view can be recast as: there is nothing objectively

---

[15] In Chapter 9 I will elaborate on the idea of there being thick concepts presupposing objectionable
normative views.

[16] See Hom (2010) for the general taxonomy employed here.

special about the properties that fall under the label "normative properties." Importantly, this does not mean that all naturalists automatically are presentationalists. One naturalist can hold that there is something special about those natural properties that are classed as normative even though other naturalists might insist, with the presentationalist, that there is nothing special about those properties. Naturalism does not immediately imply that philosophically significant metaphysical distinctions pertaining to normativity cannot be drawn among the properties there are (although it can of course be *argued* that in the end it does imply that).

6.3 Comparison with Hybrid Expressivism

The presentationalist agrees that predicates standardly held to be normative are indeed normative, and they stand for properties, but insists that the properties they stand for are not normative. One type of presentationalism is the additional element view. Although I have intentionally characterizing the view only in rather general terms, it is natural to understand the additional element view as amounting to something that *hybrid expressivists* have recently defended. There are many importantly different versions of hybrid expressivism, but roughly and generally, hybrid expressivists hold that there are two separate aspects to the meaning of a normative expression, one of which corresponds to what cognitivists tend to postulate and the other of which corresponds to what the expressivist tends to postulate.[17]

It seems to me that anyone who holds such a view should find it natural to hold that such a predicate would be just like an ordinary descriptive predicate were it not for the second, expressivist aspect; and hence that the normativity of the predicate is not a matter of what kind of property it stands for but is instead a matter of, say, what sort of desire or attitude is expressed when it is used. In other words, it seems to me that it would be natural for her to subscribe to an additional element view. One could of course defend a hybrid view of the kind gestured at and hold that there is something distinctly normative in each of the aspects of a normative expression's meaning when taken in isolation. One worry is that this amounts to postulating a kind of *overdetermination* of a predicate's normativity. If already aspects of a normative predicate's meaning relating to its reference suffice to render it normative, why also postulate that there is a separate, unrelated aspect of the predicate's meaning which also pertains to its normativity? Whatever in the end the fate of these doubts—I will later in this chapter discuss similar worries in a different context—the important point for present purposes is simply that it makes sense for

---

[17] See e.g. Boisvert (2008), Barker (2000), Bar-On and Chrisman (2009), Ridge (2006, 2007, 2014a), Copp (2001), Alm (2000), Strandberg (2012), and Schroeder (2009). Other labels besides "hybrid expressivism" have been used for a number of different but related views, and the label "hybrid expressivism" has itself been used in different ways. Here I just use "hybrid expressivism" as an umbrella label, as characterized in the main text.

a hybrid theorist of the kind described to hold an additional element view and thus to be a presentationalist. But curiously, these questions about the metaphysics of normativity do not tend to be highlighted or even noticed in discussions of hybrid theories. Ridge (2014a) does briefly mention the idea that normativity like indexicality is a feature of thoughts, or generally representations, rather than of what they stand for.[18] A thought of mine, *I am scared*, is indexical and arguably thereby different in content from another possible thought of mine, *Matti is scared*, even though I am Matti. When thinking the former I am in some way thinking about the world differently from how I think about it when thinking the latter. But even these thoughts are distinct; there are hardly indexical facts in the world in addition to other kinds of facts—there is no separate fact *I am scared* in addition to the fact *Matti is scared*. However, Ridge does not much elaborate on what he suggests regarding normativity being like indexicality in the relevant respect.

Here is one illustration of how the issue is overlooked. In his important (2009) article surveying various hybrid theories, Mark Schroeder argues that Daniel Boisvert's (2008) hybrid theory, which assimilates normative predicates to slurs, is the best extant theory of this general kind, but raises the following concern regarding Boisvert's view:

> it is important to take stock and see what sorts of proposed advantages might remain for hybrid views in Boisvert's family. If we accept a view like Boisvert's, then we are agreeing that there is a single, invariant, descriptive content of a term like "wrong"—a property that actions can have or lack. But once we concede this much, we must still answer questions like, What property is it? Is it reducible or *sui generis*? How do our words and thoughts manage to be about such a thing? How do we manage to find out what is right or wrong? Why does wrongness supervene on nonnormative properties and relations? These are most of the main challenges facing standard versions of cognitivist realism—in fact, they are some of the problems that ordinary, pure expressivism is motivated precisely in order to avoid having to answer—and [hybrid theories like Boisvert's] do not help us to answer them.[19]

However, on any presentationalist view, the properties that normative predicates stand for are not in and of themselves normative. But then certain puzzles that seemed especially hard when we thought of the properties as normative should dissipate. The properties that the predicates stand for are ordinary, non-normative properties, and there is, for example, no special problem concerning how our words and thoughts manage to be about these properties (no problem, that is, over and above the general problem of how our words and thoughts ever manage to be about any properties). The question of whether the properties that normative predicates stand for are "reducible or *sui generis*" seems serious when we think of these properties as normative. For then if they are held to be reducible, the question arises of how this respects the normativity of the properties; and if they are held to be

---

[18] Ridge (2014a), p. 101.   [19] Schroeder (2009), p. 299.

sui generis, then worries about metaphysical mysteriousness arise. If, on the other hand, the properties are held not to be normative, then the "reducible or *sui generis*" question is no more serious than it would be for any old property. Similarly, questions about how wrongness supervenes on non-normative properties and relations obviously look very different if the property we ascribe using "wrong" is itself a non-normative property. If the property of wrongness is normative, the question arises of how a normative property can supervene on non-normative properties. But if it is non-normative, then trivially it supervenes on non-normative properties. There will of course remain questions about how the property of wrongness supervenes on properties distinct from it, but when the question of the relation between the normative and the non-normative is off the table, this question does not immediately seem more troublesome than other questions about how higher-level properties supervene on lower-level ones. Again, compare how we speak of pejoratives, even if that may be an importantly different case. Given the standard view on pejoratives, it would—obviously—be completely wrongheaded to worry about the normativity of the properties the pejoratives stand for. The property that a pejorative word for, say, the French stands for is the same as the property that "French" stands for—there is nothing normative about it.

None of this is to say that presentationalism avoids all worries often raised regarding concerning popular versions of normative realism. I will turn to one very live worry shortly. The point is just that worries like those Schroeder brings up seem considerably less serious for the presentationalist than for the theorists who believe that the properties in question are normative.

Moreover, while what I have described seems to me the reasonable way for a friend of Boisvert's view as described to reply to Schroeder, it is not clear that this is how Boisvert himself would respond. Boisvert himself happily speaks of the properties that moral predicates stand for on his view as "moral properties," and while he does not pause on their nature, he indicates that an investigation into their nature is a future research project.[20] If he were concerned to say what the presentationalist says, he would indicate that being moral is a feature of predicates and concepts rather than of properties, and that the idea that there are special problems regarding the status of the properties that moral predicates stand for is misguided. Schroeder's concern may then be justified given Boisvert's own understanding of his view. The general point still stands: if one holds a hybrid view and explains the normativity of normative expressions by appeal to a separate, non-referential aspect of their meanings, then there is no reason to think normative expressions also stand for properties that present the metaphysical puzzles normative properties are often thought to present.

---

[20] Boisvert (2008), e.g. p. 171. Compare, too, his (2014), p. 25fn8, where he says "hybrid expressivism requires an ontology of moral properties, a difficulty that may be sufficient for one to ultimately reject hybrid expressivism."

6.4 The Theoretical Map

As should be clear from the above discussion of hybrid expressivist views, there are views defended in the literature that have a good claim to be called presentationalist. So it would clearly be wrong to say that the presentationalist view is completely neglected. But still, presentationalism tends to get overlooked.

It is common in the metaethics literature to present diagrams to display the differences between the different types of realist/antirealist position on offer. But the characterizations of the territory that are provided tend not to make room for presentationalism as a theoretical option. Here is one instructive illustration of this: the diagram used to structure Graham Oddie's (2005) book-length defense of a non-naturalist realism about value. Oddie centers on five questions:

1. *Propositional content*: Do the statements of the discourse really express genuine propositional content?
2. *Presuppositional fulfillment*: Are the existential presuppositions of typical de re statements in the domain actually fulfilled?
3. *Mind-independence*: Are the entities which satisfy these existential presuppositions (call these the *characteristic entities*) mind-independent?
4. *Irreducibility*: Are the characteristic entities irreducible to any more basic category of entities?
5. *Causal networking*: Are the characteristic entities appropriately causally networked?[21]

Oddie uses these questions to distinguish between the main positions in the metaethics literature. The non-cognitivist says no already to question 1. The Mackiean error theorist gives the answer yes to question 1 but the answer no to question 2. The idealist gives the answer yes to the first two questions but the answer no to question 3. The naturalist gives the answer yes to the three first questions but the answer no to question 4. A position Oddie dubs "transcendentist" gives the answer yes to the first four questions but the answer no to question 5. Oddie's own "robust realism" gives the answer yes to all five questions.[22] Where does presentationalism fit in?

As presentationalism is most straightforwardly conceived, the first question the presentationalist gives the answer no to is question 4. In Oddie's taxonomy there is then no difference between, on the one hand, the naturalist realist who believes there are normative properties but holds they are natural properties and, on the other, a presentationalist. That seems wrong.

---

[21] Oddie (2005), p. 22.

[22] Oddie (2005), p. 23. In conversation, several people have suggested that Oddie's question 2 can be read in such a way as to take presentationalism into account. It has been suggested that an "existential presupposition of typical de re statement in the domain" is that there be normativity in the world. However, I understand Oddie to here mean presuppositions necessary for the statements to be true—and then the presentationalist does say yes to question 2. What is more, Oddie does focus on Mackiean error theory in connection with the answer no to this question.

What is more, one can at least envisage a presentationalist who gives the answer yes to all five questions, even if the position of such a theorist might be thought somewhat strange. This presentationalist would hold that the characteristic entities of normative discourse are irreducible to any more basic category but that what distinguishes these entities from more basic entities is not normativity. Oddie's taxonomy provides no resources to distinguish this presentationalist's view from his own preferred robust realism. The same remarks actually apply also to the hyperdescriptivist view. This view too would simply be classed with naturalism in Oddie's scheme, and certain exotic versions of the view would even be classed as robustly realist. What all this points to is that a question is missing from Oddie's scheme: are the entities that satisfy the relevant "existential presuppositions" (to use Oddie's terminology) *normative*?

Parfit (2011) presents a similar map. He classifies views according to their answers to four questions:

1. Are normative claims intended or believed to state truths?
2. Are there any normative truths?
3. Are these truths irreducibly normative?
4. Are the concepts and claims with which we state such truths irreducibly normative?[23]

Anyone whose answer to question 1 is no is a non-cognitivist. Anyone who answers yes to question 1 but no to question 2 is a nihilist. Anyone who answers yes to questions 1–3 is a non-naturalist. Anyone who answers yes to questions 1 and 2 but no to question 3 is a naturalist: and if her answer to question 4 is yes, she is a non-analytic naturalist whereas if her answer to question 4 is no, she is an analytic naturalist.

Where does presentationalism fit in? This is not clear. On one way to understand Parfit, the way he formulates questions 1 and 2 simply overlooks the possibility of presentationalism. On this reading, he presupposes that if some normative claims are true, then there are normative truths in just the way denied by the presentationalist: the normativity in the claim—the representation—has to be accompanied by normativity in the truth—in what is claimed to be. However, more plausibly one can take Parfit to be using "normative truth" in such a way that it is *trivially* true that if there are true normative claims then there are normative truths: normative truths just are true normative claims. Suppose this is how Parfit uses "normative truth." Then my concern about Parfit's taxonomy is different. What does he then do with the difference between the presentationalist and the naturalist who holds that some of the natural properties she believes in also are normative? They both say yes to (1) and (2), given how we now understand "normative truths." The presentationalist certainly

---

[23] Parfit (2011), p. 263.

says no to (3). Parfit seems now just to fail to include a question that serves to distinguish between presentationalism and ordinary naturalist normative realism.[24]

Miller (2003) presents a picture of the theoretical map that is very similar to Oddie's. The only difference is that he does not include a counterpart of Oddie's question 5, and instead of the one question concerning irreducibility he includes one question about whether moral facts are natural facts and a separate question about whether they are reducible to other natural facts. Again, presentationalism is an overlooked option. Railton (1986) presents a considerably more complicated picture, listing no fewer than thirteen questions that can serve to distinguish metaethicists along different realism-relevant dimensions. It would take too long to make the case here, but I think it is clear that Railton too overlooks the possibility of pre-sentationalism. None of the questions Railton discusses serves to distinguish those who hold that some properties and facts are themselves normative from those that instead adopt a presentationalist view. Finlay (2007) separately discusses the question of whether "moral claims aim to describe moral facts involving moral entities/properties," and he recognizes that one can hold that moral claims have attitude-independent truth-values while answering this question in the negative.[25] However, the only position of this kind that he mentions is Hilary Putnam's "pragmatist" position, according to which "moral claims are true not in virtue of there being moral facts involving moral entities like reasons or properties like value, but because there are correct processes for solving practical problems."[26] Finlay notes that also Christine Korsgaard perhaps may be classed as a pragmatist in the sense just described. But presentationalism is not on the map. A different question Finlay brings up is whether "moral entities/properties have attitude-independent authority," and he calls those moral realists who answer this question in the affirmative *normative moral realists*. It is somewhat natural, perhaps, to say that those who answer this question in the affirmative hold that moral entities/properties are normative. However, for all that Finlay says, his question can be paraphrased: *does the fact that X morally ought to φ by itself—and independently of X's attitudes—have consequences for whether X ought to φ, full stop?* But this is just a question about the relation between "morally ought" and "ought full stop," and even a presentationalist may well answer Finlay's question affirmatively. A presentationalist might certainly hold that the relation between the (non-normative) items in the world picked out by "morally ought" and "ought full stop" is such that whenever someone morally ought to φ then she ought full stop to φ.

---

[24] Moreover, Parfit's appeal to commitment to "irreducibly normative" truths as characteristic of non-naturalism, although standard, seems to me problematic. Can I not hold that all truths are natural, but hold that some of the natural truths that exist are also irreducibly normative?

[25] Finlay (2007), p. 821.   [26] Ibid., p. 822f.

6.5 On Some Recent Arguments for Non-Naturalist Realism

Consideration of presentationalism as an option also affects some recent arguments for non-naturalist realism. Presentationalism—and the conceptual framework relevant to seeing presentationalism as an option—problematizes these arguments.

In his (2011), David Enoch argues for non-naturalist realism by employing a kind of indispensability argument for the existence of irreducibly normative truths. He argues that deliberation is a "rationally non-optional project" and that "irreducibly normative truths" are "indispensable for deliberation."[27] On the basis of this we are justified in believing that there are irreducibly normative truths. The way in which these truths are indispensable is not actually held to be that deliberation would be impossible if there were no irreducibly normative truths. Rather, what is held to be going on is that "by deliberating, *you commit yourself to* there being relevant reasons, and so to there being relevant normative truths."[28] One natural objection is that this kind of indispensability is not the relevant one. Only if the existence of normative truths was indispensable would we have a persuasive indispensability argument; but all we have is the indispensability of commitment to normative truths, and that is different. But whatever may be the ultimate fate of this objection—Enoch does bring it up and respond to it—let me set it aside for present purposes. Instead, let us suppose that this is a good indispensability argument for *something*. What exactly is it an argument for?

Enoch happily runs together talk of irreducibly normative *truths* and talk of irreducibly normative *facts*.[29] In many contexts, that may be innocuous. But the distinction matters if, for example, presentationalism is thought of as a live option. Presentationalism is incompatible with there being irreducibly normative *facts*. But one can reasonably understand "irreducibly normative truths" in such a way that presentationalism is fully compatible with there being irreducibly normative truths. The presentationalist can hold that the *ways of presenting* aspects of reality that are associated with normative predicates are irreducibly normative, even if what is presented is not normative.[30] She can say that thinking of some things *under such ways of presenting them* is indispensable for deliberation, and that Enoch provides good reasons for believing that some of what is presented as true is true. She can accordingly hold that there are irreducibly normative thoughts that are true, and she can hold that there are normative truths because there are normative thoughts that are true. So she can agree with much of what Enoch says.

---

[27] Enoch (2011), p. 70.   [28] Ibid., p. 75; my emphasis.

[29] For the most part Enoch uses the locution "normative truths," but in the passage quoted in the next paragraph he also uses "normative facts."

[30] I am using "irreducibly" in the main text to stick as closely as possible to Enoch's formulation. It is actually hard to see what it would be for a way of *presenting* an aspect of reality to be normative but "reducibly" so. This may make the formulation seem a bit awkward.

Enoch does not say much that is directly relevant to excluding the possibility of presentationalism. Presumably, the position is not on his radar. But one potentially relevant remark he makes is:

because the kind of normative facts that are indispensable for deliberation are just so different from naturalist, not-obviously-normative facts and truths, the chances of a naturalistic reduction seem rather grim. . . . The gap between the normative and the natural, considered from the point of view of a deliberating agent, seems unbridgeable.[31]

However, the supposed fact that from the point of view of a deliberating agent the gap between the normative and the natural seems unbridgeable is easily accommodated for a presentationalist: there is an unbridgeable gap between normative and non-normative *thoughts*. It is just that she will resist the further claim that there is a corresponding gap between normative and non-normative aspects of the reality that these thoughts are about. Enoch speaks of the indispensability of normative facts to deliberation, but the question is whether he can help himself to this even if he can make a case for the indispensability of normative thoughts to deliberation, and even if he can help himself to the truth of these normative thoughts.

Already a standard kind of naturalist realist might want to hold that even if the use of normative concepts is indispensable in the way Enoch argues, these normative concepts can stand for properties that while normative, are natural—that Enoch's indispensability argument is compatible with the truth of the (non-analytic) property identifications that the naturalist wants to make. The naturalist would respond to what I quoted Enoch saying about naturalism by insisting that the gap between normative and non-normative *thought* may well be unbridgeable, but this does not mean that there is an unbridgeable gap between normative and non-normative *properties*.

This does not mean that appeal specifically to presentationalism does not serve any worthwhile purpose in the context. The presentationalist can try to insist that Enoch's argument for the indispensability of normative concepts does not even establish that any property is normative. The normativity of a concept does not guarantee that whatever property the concept stands for is normative. Moreover, the presentationalist is especially well placed to respond to a point Enoch raises against naturalism. In the passage quoted above, Enoch says—although he does not much elaborate on the point—that what the indispensable normative concepts stand for would have to be so special that mere natural properties would not fit the bill. But his case for this appears to presuppose just what a presentationalist questions: that there being something quite special about normative concepts means that there will be something correspondingly special about the properties that these concepts ascribe.[32]

---

[31] Enoch (2011), p. 80.

[32] In the main text I am criticizing a certain slide in Enoch's reasoning. When talking interchangeably about normative facts and normative truths, he blurs an important distinction. The carelessness is illustrative, as far as present purposes are concerned, and hence I bring it up. But I should add that for all I say, it could be that Enoch's discussion contains the materials for arguing that the facts themselves

Presentationalism also puts pressure on the naturalist realist; specifically the kind of naturalist realist who appeals to property identifications in the way indicated. The naturalist realist will say that the normative and non-normative concepts differ but they stand for the same property. The naturalist realist must then provide an account of wherein these concepts differ. But it seems that, whatever the details, this would have to involve saying something about how the normative concept is normative in a way that adverts to something other than the property it stands for. And if the naturalist realist provides that kind of explanation, then with what right does she also insist that the property that the concept stands for is normative? Does she not in effect locate the normativity in the way the property is presented? This would appear to be overdetermination of normativity of the kind mentioned in connection with hybrid expressivism: the normativity of the predicate is explained both by appeal to what property the predicate stands for and by appeal to some feature of how the concept presents the property it stands for. Having brought up this potential problem, I should note that there is a reply on offer for the naturalist who wishes to say that there is normativity in the world. It is to appeal to the conception of normativity in the world I favored in Chapter 5, according to which a property is normative if it is ascribed by some possible referentially normative predicate. If she appeals to this conception of normativity, then she can call both the concepts and the properties normative without this being a matter of some theoretically dubious overdetermination, as the representational normativity and the normativity in the world are *linked*. The normativity of the representation is reference-determining; what is represented is constrained to normatively fit the representation. The normativity of the representation and the normativity of what is represented are not independent features.

Remarks analogous to those brought up against Enoch's argument are relevant against arguments for non-naturalist normative realism recently defended by William FitzPatrick and Jonathan Dancy. FitzPatrick attempts to use a version of Moore's open question argument to argue for non-naturalist ethical realism. He says, e.g.,

not even being told what I would desire myself to desire if I deliberated with ethical information and without irrationality will *settle* things, because that misrepresents what we are after when we deliberate: we are not aiming at discovering and conforming to any such hypothetical deliberative results, even in connection with ourselves, but at discovering and conforming to the truth about what is good (or right, or what there is reason to do, and so on), as such.[33]

The response to this is that even if FitzPatrick establishes that genuinely normative thoughts are necessary for deliberation, that does not show that normative concepts

---

must be normative. For example, he argues that the facts in question—the facts making true the normative thoughts we think—must be such that knowledge of their true nature wouldn't make us reevaluate our reasoning. (Compare in this connection Tristram McPherson (2011), who argues that Enoch's claim that the normative and the natural are too different for naturalism to be true overlooks the possibility that it is the concepts that are different, and not the properties they ascribe.)

[33] FitzPatrick (2008), p. 176.

cannot stand for natural properties, or even that the properties these concepts stand for are normative at all. Even if it could be established that the use of genuinely normative concepts is necessary for deliberation, it is a different question whether the properties those concepts stand for would themselves have to be normative. Dancy (2006) identifies certain second-order facts as central normative facts and discusses positively the prospects of arguing against a naturalist that the relevant second-order facts cannot be natural. One central point he makes is that "[i]f we do not use normative concepts, we cannot address the question of what is practically relevant and what is not."[34] A naturalist and a presentationalist can accept this point about *normative concepts*, only disagreeing with Dancy about what this shows about *normative properties*. Compare the claim: "if one does not use the concept water, one cannot address the question of what is water and what is not." Is that claim true or false? Given that the property of being water = the property of being H_2O, does one address the question of what is water and what is not when categorizing things as falling under the concept H_2O or not? This question can be taken in different ways. On one reasonable way of taking the question, one does not address the question of whether something is water by classifying it as H_2O: one only addresses the (different) question of whether it is H_2O. But then, by analogy, one can reply to Dancy by saying that normative and non-normative concepts can corefer even if Dancy is right in what he says about how to address normative questions. If, by contrast, it is maintained that one does address the question of whether something is water by classifying it as H_2O, then it seems the proper reply to Dancy is that just as one can fail to realize that one addresses the question of whether something is water by classifying it as H_2O, one can fail to realize that one addresses a question of whether something is right by doing some thinking that involves only non-normative concepts.[35]

As before, any naturalist, including one who believes in normative properties, can make many or all of the points that a presentationalist can make. But there still is a point to appealing specifically to presentationalism. The presentationalist can completely avoid some objections that—whatever in the end their proper fate—can reasonably be addressed to the naturalist realist.

While we are comparing what various theorists have said, it might also be worth considering the following well-known passage from Gibbard (2006):

There is a property, I say, that constitutes being what one ought to do. This property is, in a broad sense, a natural property. Concepts are another matter: normative concepts are distinct from naturalistic concepts; on this score Moore was quite right. But normative and naturalistic concepts signify properties of the same kinds; indeed a normative and a naturalistic concept might signify the very same property. *What's distinctly normative, then, is not properties but*

---

[34] Dancy (2006), p. 142. In this article, Dancy prominently relates to the arguments against naturalism found in Parfit (2011) (which was circulated in draft form already by the time Dancy wrote his article). I turn to Parfit's arguments in section 6.6.

[35] Copp (2013), p. 49, makes much the same point as I am making in this paragraph.

concepts. It is this set of claims about normative properties—that they exist and are, in a broad sense, natural—that I scrutinize here.[36]

While Gibbard makes his remarks in the context of a discussion of his own favored brand of expressivism, what he gives voice to in the italicized passage can seem to be very much a presentationalist idea. (And I will only be concerned with what is suggested by this specific passage. I will not enter further into Gibbard exegesis.) Some concepts are normative but the properties they stand for are not. However, first, Gibbard appears to arrive at the conclusion he states via the thesis that "a normative and a naturalistic concept might signify the very same property"—but even given this thesis, the property signified by both these concepts may well be a genuinely normative property (unless it is just assumed that a normative property could not be ascribed by a non-normative concept[37]). Further argument is needed to conclude that the property is not normative. Second, in the very next sentence, Gibbard does speak of properties as normative, in a way that suggests he does not mean to deny that some properties are normative but only to deny that properties are "distinctly" normative, whatever exactly that means. (Maybe he means: a property is not "distinctly" normative if it qualifies as normative simply by being a property ascribed by a normative concept?)

6.6 Parfit Against Naturalist Realism

Let me now turn to some arguments that Derek Parfit (2011) has mounted against naturalist realism. Parfit's work is an important one, but I believe his arguments depend on carelessness about the concept/property (or generally representation/represented) distinction that in various ways has been central to my discussion. Consideration of Parfit's argument brings out the relevance of presentationalism in yet another way.

I start with what Parfit labels the Triviality Objection. Consider the following Utilitarian Naturalist claims:

(A)   When some act would maximize happiness, this act is what we ought to do.

(C)   When some act would maximize happiness, this property of this act is the same as the property of being what we ought to do.[38]

Parfit argues:

(1)   (A) is a substantive normative claim, which might state a positive substantive normative fact,[39]

where a normative claim is *substantive* when it is "significant, because we might disagree with [it], or [it] might tell us something that we didn't already know," and a normative claim is positive when it states or implies that "when something has

---

[36] Gibbard (2006), p. 144; my italics.   [37] Recall that in Chapter 4, I criticized this assumption.
[38] Parfit (2011), p. 334; repeated p. 343.   [39] Ibid., p. 343.

certain natural properties, this thing has some other, different, normative property."[40] Parfit doesn't explicitly state what it is for a *fact*, as opposed to a *claim*, to be substantive and positive. It is not entirely routine to adapt Parfit's characterization so as to apply to facts. The claim that water is water and the claim that water is H_2O differ in substantiveness, but are often taken to state the same fact. Is the fact they state substantive or not?

Parfit goes on,

> (2)   If, impossibly, (C) were true, (A) could not state such a fact. (A) could not be used to imply that, when some act would maximize happiness, this act would have the different property of being what we ought to do, since (C) claims that there is no such different property. Though (A) and (C) have different meanings, (A) would be only another way of stating the trivial fact that when some act would maximize happiness, this act would maximize happiness.[41]

Parfit concludes that naturalism is not true.

I don't think this is a compelling argument. A first point regarding this argument can be stated briefly: While the Utilitarian Naturalist would want (A) to come out as a substantive claim, it is not immediately clear why she should even want it to come out as a positive claim in Parfit's sense, given her commitment to (C). Isn't it just her *view* that the normative property in question isn't a different property from the natural property in question?

What Parfit says under (2) can be seen as an objection to this: surely it can't be blithely accepted that (A) just states the "trivial fact" that Parfit there mentions? But here it matters that Parfit is carelessly going back and forth between talking about *claims* and talking about *facts*. His carefully explaining what it is for a claim to be substantive and positive while omitting to explain the corresponding thing for facts is a symptom of this. That water is water is a trivial claim; that water is H_2O is not. But these two claims, it is commonly held, correspond to the same fact. Is that *fact* trivial or not? That seems like a bad question. Compare here the remarks about being substantive and positive, a few paragraphs back.

Of course, a naturalist who responds to Parfit by appealing to the distinction between claims and facts would have to say something about just how claim (a), that when some act would maximize happiness, this act would maximize happiness, and claim (b), that when some act would maximize happiness, this act would be what we ought to do, differ even though they correspond to the same fact. But for anyone on board with the idea of claims differing in content corresponding to the same fact, this should seem like a research project rather than an immediately devastating problem. This simply parallels the question of how two concepts ascribing the same property can be such that one concept is normative and the other is non-normative. I argued

---

[40] Ibid., p. 342.   [41] Ibid., p. 343f.

in Chapter 4, using the "thgir" example, that all theorists, including non-naturalists, should agree that there can be non-normative predicates ascribing the same properties as normative predicates do. But if so, then the question of what distinguishes a normative and a non-normative concept ascribing the same property arises for theorists of all stripes.

Dowell and Sobel (forthcoming) discuss the Triviality Objection at some length. Their reading of Parfit's argument is in some ways more sympathetic than mine. I will not discuss the exegetical issue of who gets Parfit right. But let me discuss the argument of Dowell and Sobel's Parfit and explain why I don't think that argument works either. Dowell and Sobel's (henceforth: *D&S*) Parfit is on board with the general idea that different claims can state the same fact. But he is concerned with exactly how the different claims can differ in the case at hand. He is concerned with the naturalist's claim that a normative and a non-normative claim can state the same fact and asks wherein the claims can differ, for example such that one is normative and the other is not. He operates with an in some ways Fregean assumption to the effect that for two expressions to have different senses is for them to be conventionally associated with different properties. The problem he sees is that if all normative properties are descriptive properties, then one cannot explain how one expression is normative and the other is not by appeal to how one is conventionally associated with normative properties and the other is not.

A first remark is that the Fregeanism of D&S' Parfit is somewhat peculiar. One would have thought a consistent Fregean holds that every thought about an entity is sense-mediated; both thought about particulars and thought about properties. But then one cannot simply associate an expression with a property; at most what one can do is associate an expression with a property *under a mode of presentation*. (And whatever modes of presentation are, thinking of something under a mode of presentation is then not simply to again associate a property with it.) The reason why this is relevant to the argument of D&S' Parfit should be obvious. If one does not individuate senses simply by appeal to properties, then even if normative *properties* are all descriptive that does not entail, or even suggest, that there is no way to distinguish the *senses* of normative expressions from the senses of descriptive ones.

Second, the argument of D&S' Parfit seems to generalize broadly, in a way that should seem problematic. Consider any view according to which some intuitively higher-level A-facts are in fact identical to some intuitively lower-level B-facts, although A-claims are different in content from B-claims. Many philosophers hold such views, for example about the relations of various sorts of facts to physical facts. But the argument of D&S' Parfit generalizes. He can ask wherein the supposed difference between A-claims and B-claims consists, and he can find nothing better to say than that A-expressions are associated with A-properties. But since A-properties are identical to B-properties, that is no difference at all.

D&S propose to respond to the arguments of their Parfit by adopting a direct reference theory instead of a Fregean theory, and then say about the sorts of cases at hand what friends of direct reference theories generally say about cases where sentences that intuitively differ in meaning state the same fact. As per my first remark on D&S' Parfit, I don't think one needs to abandon a Fregean view to respond to his arguments. There is also something else that puzzles me about their response. The naturalist realist who is the target of Parfit's argument does operate with the idea that there is a distinction between normative and non-normative expressions, and between normative and non-normative claims. One possible naturalist response to Parfit might be to question the supposed distinction between the normative and the non-normative. That is not D&S' line. But I don't see how they propose to distinguish between normative and non-normative expressions or claims corresponding to the same properties or facts. In general, the direct reference theory might threaten to preclude the possibility of normative and non-normative expressions corresponding to the same property. Given a direct reference view, the ordinary meaning of an expression is a matter simply of what it stands for, so either expressions are determined to be normative by the normativity of what they stand for (but then if an expression is normative, any other expression which corefers with it is also normative), or one cannot speak of expressions that are normative (or non-normative) at all. D&S might in response say that what distinguishes the intuitively normative expressions has to do with their *metasemantics*; or they might appeal to some mechanism like conventional implicature and say that what distinguishes normative expressions from non-normative ones is a matter of what they conventionally implicate. Compare earlier remarks on referentialism, in Chapter 4.

Parfit's other main argument against naturalism, the Fact-Stating Argument, is as follows:

(1)   We make some irreducibly normative claims.
(2)   According to Non-Analytical Naturalists, when such claims are true, they state facts that are both normative and natural.
(3)   If such normative facts were also natural facts, any such fact could also be stated by some other non-normative, naturalistic claim.

Therefore,

(4)   Any such true normative claim would state some fact that is the same as some fact that could be stated by some other, non-normative claim.
(5)   If these two claims stated the same fact, they would give us the same information.
(6)   This non-normative claim could not state a normative fact.

Therefore,

If these two claims stated the same fact, by giving us the same information, this normative claim could not state a normative fact.

Therefore,

Such normative claims could not, as these Naturalists believe, state facts that are both normative and natural.[42]

Before discussing the details of this argument, it is worth noting that it seems to generalize. First, the argument seems to generalize widely, to other supposed theoretical identifications. Let me focus on the case of biology, although the point is completely general. One could consider any case where "higher-level" B-claims are supposed to state the same facts as "lower-level" A-claims.

(1*)   We make some irreducibly biological claims (i.e. biological claims as opposed to claims that pertain to physics).

(2*)   According to non analytic physicalists, when such claims are true, they state facts that are both biological and physical.

(3*)   If such biological facts were also physical facts, any such fact could also be stated by some other non-biological, physical claim.

Therefore,

(4*)   Any such true biological claim would state some fact that is the same as some fact that could be stated by some other, non-biological claim.

(5*)   If these two claims stated the same fact, they would give us the same information.

(6*)   This non-biological claim could not state a biological fact.

Therefore,

If these two claims stated the same fact, by giving us the same information, this biological claim could not state a biological fact.

Therefore,

Such biological claims could not, as these physicalists believe, state facts that are both biological and physical.

In cases like this, one would think that apart from the non-reductive physicalist view that biological facts are determined by but not identical to physical facts, and the eliminativist view that there are no biological facts but only physical ones, there is a coherent intermediate position according to which there are biological facts but they are identical to physical facts. What Parfit in effect offers is a very general argument, ruling out the intermediate position. It is problematic that the argument generalizes in the way it does.

The "thgir" example, introduced in Chapter 4, points to another problem with Parfit's argument. Points made in that earlier discussion together with moves made in Parfit's argument serve to rule out all realist views according to which some facts

---

[42] Parfit (2011), p. 338f.

are normative. (I use prime signs to indicate the premises that are modified from Parfit's original argument.)

(1)   We make some irreducibly normative claims.
(2′)   According to all normative realists, when such claims are true, they state facts that are normative.
(3′)   Any such fact could also be stated by some non-normative claim. [By the "thgir" argument earlier.]

The rest would be as before:

(4)   Any such true normative claim would state some fact that is the same as some fact that could be stated by some other, non-normative claim.
(5)   If these two claims stated the same fact, they would give us the same information.
(6)   This non-normative claim could not state a normative fact.

Therefore,

If these two claims stated the same fact, by giving us the same information, this normative claim could not state a normative fact.

Therefore,

Such normative claims could not, as these realists believe, state facts that are normative.

I take it that Parfit would try to resist this argument by rejecting (3′), trying to find a way to somehow block the "thgir" argument. I of course think the "thgir" argument is a good one. And while I don't think the conclusion of the argument just rehearsed is obviously false—indeed, it may well be true—it seems to me the conclusion is not something that can be arrived at this easily. So it seems something must be wrong with this argument, and if the fault does not lie with the "thgir" argument, the flaw in this argument lies in something it shares with Parfit's original argument.

Parfit's Fact-Stating Argument is in effect an argument that any purported naturalist realist must be a presentationalist, for she cannot in fact respect the idea that the facts stated by normative claims are themselves normative. I think there is at least some reason to share Parfit's suspicion that the naturalist realist ought really to be a presentationalist. But I don't think his argument to this effect works, since his reasoning by my lights can be generalized as indicated.

Saying that Parfit's argument must go wrong is not yet to indicate how it goes wrong. I am happy to accept (1) and (2). (3) is fine as well, except for conveying that if normative facts were non-natural, they could not be stated by non-normative claims. (4) follows from the preceding. Given (5) and (6), what follows is smooth sailing. But (5) sounds a bit mysterious: what does the information talk here amount to? There is a way of understanding "information" such that (5) is trivial: two claims give the same information iff they state the same fact. Might that be what Parfit has in mind? Moreover, as for (6), it sounds question-begging as it stands: wouldn't an opponent of Parfit be apt to think that a normative and a non-normative claim could state the same fact? But Parfit's idea may be that by (5), if two claims stated the same fact, they would give the same information, and this makes (6) reasonable to accept. For a non-normative claim to state a normative fact, it would have to give normative *information*, and that it does not do. But if "information" is understood as just suggested, this is still question-begging. And if we understand "information" in such a way that two claims which state the same fact can differ in what information they provide, (5) would be false.

6.7 A Problem for Presentationalism?

What problems might be raised for the presentationalist view? Certain examples prominently discussed in the literature, such as R.M. Hare's case of the missionary and the cannibal and Terence Horgan and Mark Timmons' Moral Twin Earth cases, can be used to spell trouble for presentationalism.[43] Recall the Moral Twin Earth thought experiment. Consider a different community speaking some version of English, using normative terms spelled and pronounced the way that our terms are, and having the same normative roles—where normative role is whichever kind of "role" for deliberation and decision-making normative predicates have which distinguishes them from merely descriptive predicates—as ours, but having determinately different conceptions of what falls under these terms. Intuitively, sameness of reference in this case goes with sameness of normative role. But it appears the presentationalist must say that the terms have different reference. The similarities between the terms have to do with normative role, and by the presentationalist's lights, normative role does not determine reference. On the additional element view, normative role is not even in the market to determine, pertaining instead to another aspect of meaning; on the imperfect satisfier view, other aspects determine reference given that there is no normativity in the world.

Even if this is a genuine problem for presentationalists, the presentationalist is not worse off than are friends of the most prominent forms of contemporary naturalist realism—the Moral Twin Earth argument, as Horgan and Timmons present it, is an argument against a number of views in this latter category, and seems as effective against them as it is against presentationalism.

The presentationalist, moreover, has some things she can say which accommodate the supposed Moral Twin Earth intuitions. The additional element theorist can emphasize that the intuition of shared content is due to the fact that the additional element of a normative term's meaning in fact is shared between our term and the corresponding Moral Twin Earth term. The imperfect satisfier theorist can appeal to similarities between the conceptions associated with the terms.

---

[43] See e.g. Hare (1952, pp. 148–9) and Horgan and Timmons (e.g. 1992a, 2009).

Which views *do* accord with the supposed Moral Twin Earth intuitions? Traditional expressivist views are arguably well placed to accord with these intuitions, since these views accord pride of place to normative role in their accounts of the meanings of normative expressions. But what broadly realist views—what views allowing that atomic normative sentences can be mind-independently true—can accord with them? Here is one thing worth stressing. Prominent among realist views that accord with these intuitions will be Alternative-unfriendly views according to which our normative predicates are referentially normative. Mere appeal to non-naturalism will not help, as the normative predicates of different communities that share normative role in principle compatibly with non-naturalism could ascribe different non-natural properties.[44]

One may think that one way to determine whether an Alternative-friendly view or an Alternative-friendly view is correct is by appeal to intuitions about Moral Twin Earth-style cases; about the possibility of scenarios like Alternative. As earlier mentioned, there are reasons to be cautious about an intuition-based strategy. Merli (2002) argues that the scenarios in question are underdescribed. Dunaway and McPherson (2016) note complications due to the possibility of reference magnetism. Dowell (2016) argues that the intuitions drawn upon in Moral Twin Earth cases aren't plausibly directly related to what makes for linguistic competence, and hence these intuitions do not have "probative value." I think Dowell overstates her case. Compare: the ability to make reliable intuitive judgments about whether, given a certain configuration on the board, white can checkmate black in *n* moves is hardly directly related to chess competence. One can be able to play the game of chess while being quite poor at making these judgments. But still, if a high proportion of competent chess players make the judgment that white can checkmate black in *n* moves, that is good evidence that white can indeed do so.

A different sort of reason for being skeptical of Moral Twin Earth intuitions in the present context is that the present concern is not with how our actual normative terms happen to work but with what possible normative terms there are; and Moral Twin Earth thought experiments tend to be used to elicit intuitions about our ordinary terms. That said, facts about what is actual can be relevant to issues about what is possible: most obviously because actuality entails possibility. However, I will now turn to an argument for (some modest) skepticism about reliance on intuitions in this type of case.

Appeal to broadly speaking linguistic intuitions is the least controversial when it is a given that there are two different meanings a word could have, and the intuitions speak to the question of which meaning a given actual word has. If, for example, the question is whether a Gettier case counts as knowledge, there is no principled

---

[44] I do not say that appeal to referential normativity is the *only* thing that could help secure accord with the supposed Moral Twin Earth intuitions. One could, for example, appeal to reference magnetism instead. See Edwards (2013) and Dunaway and McPherson (2016).

problem. For it is not in serious doubt that there are possible meanings for the string of symbols "knows" such that Gettier cases count as "knowledge" in that sense (for example, it is *possible* to use "X knows that p" such that this is true already if X has a justified true belief that p) and also possible meanings such that Gettier cases don't count as knowledge in those senses. (Pick just about any purported analysis of knowledge designed to respect the Gettier intuitions. Even if that analysis doesn't get the actual meaning of "knows" right, it is not to be doubted that the analysis describes a possible meaning for a word.) Moreover, radical skepticism aside, it is not really in doubt that these different meanings are non-defective: different words "knows" with these meanings are non-empty, they are not radically indeterminate in extension, etc. For each of these notions of knowledge, there is "knowledge" in the sense at issue. But in the case we are concerned with, there is a live question as to whether any words could have, so to speak, non-defective Alternative-unfriendly meanings. It is not in question whether a community could have—so to speak— Alternative-unfriendly *semantic intentions*: to have the (implicit) semantic intentions to use words that function as the Alternative-unfriendly theorist says the thinnest words function. But if there simply are no properties that satisfy the criterion I have proposed for being normative, then these intentions can't be satisfied. In some way the relevant words would be defective. One needn't get into what form the defect-iveness would take. Unless the world fulfills its part of the bargain and provides a property of the right kind, then there won't be non-defective words of the kind the Alternative-unfriendly theorist believes in.

Compare: we might have a word, "gidplissing," and a debate between those who think the word is simply true of those things around us that we tend to describe as gidplissing (or stand in the right causal relation to our tokenings of our concept *gidplissing*, or satisfy the non-theistic descriptions we associate with "gidplissing"), whether or not there is a divine entity, God, such that those things please this entity, and those who think that it is a condition for x to be gidplissing that x pleases such an entity. Let's say that those in the former group understand "gidplissing" as *gidplissing1* and those in the latter group understand "gidplissing" as *gidplissing2*. It cannot be in serious doubt that there are such possible meanings as *gidplissing1* and *gidplissing2*. But since it is a live possibility that God does not exist, it is in doubt whether there is a possible meaning *gidplissing2* which is non-defective. Suppose now, parallel to the Moral Twin Earth case, that there is another community with a word "gidplissing*." They tend to describe other things as "gidplissing*" than we describe as "gidplissing" (or other things stand in the right causal relations to their use of "gidplissing," or they associate different non-theistic descriptions with "gidplissing" than we do). There is among them a debate about "gidplissing*" parallel to our debate about "gidplissing," with the same two types of contenders.

It may be no secret where this is going. We can imagine there being intuitions to the effect that "gidplissing" and "gidplissing*" (non-defectively) corefer. Someone who believes in God and is in the second camp can be presumed to have such intuitions. But the correctness of such intuitions is dependent upon there being a God, and one ought to be careful about relying on them. Whatever in the end to say about matters religious, these intuitions about "gidplissing"/"gidplissing*" are importantly different from, for example, intuitions about Gettier cases, and they are not as clearly to be relied upon.

It is straightforward to apply this to the case of Alternative-unfriendliness. To believe that some normative predicates have non-defective, Alternative-unfriendly meanings is relevantly analogous to believing that there is a God. I don't mean, of course, that believing there is normativity in the world is bound up with there being a divine being. What I do mean is that like in the case of consideration of what is "gidplissing," the correctness of the intuition that two otherwise disparate predicates with the same normative role are coextensive is hostage to metaphysical fortune.

I certainly don't mean to say that intuitions hostage to metaphysical fortune are worth nothing. Such a claim would be, well, rash, to put it mildly. For example, it is a natural and reasonable view, whatever in the end its fate, that analytic metaphysics is a rather successful enterprise which relies on intuitions, and these intuitions are obviously hostage to metaphysical fortune. But such intuitions still have a different, less secure standing than do linguistic intuitions that are not so hostage. Even if use of such intuition can be legitimized, their probative value should be regarded as lesser than that of ordinary linguistic intuitions. Ordinary linguistic intuitions are if not constitutive of their subject matter then at least akin to being so.[45] If we didn't make the judgments we make and use our expressions and concepts the way we do, then we would be using expressions and concepts with different meaning and content. The same thing cannot be said for metaphysically laden intuitions.

Now, as I have described matters, the question of Alternative-friendliness is a question of how to decide between two types of broadly realist theories. But also expressivists sometimes rely on Moral Twin Earth scenarios. This might be thought relevant to the question of how to evaluate intuitions about these scenarios. The intuition that the two communities are talking about the same thing in cases of the kind considered is not straightforwardly an intuition in favor of a certain kind of realism, but can be used also to support different kinds of theories. It is then, it may be suspected, misleading to compare them to the coreference intuitions in the "gidplissing"/"gidplissing*" case.

However, the "gidplissing"/"gidplissing*" case is relevant also to how expressivists use Moral Twin Earth scenarios. Suppose in that case the intuitions of the language users are overwhelmingly that "gidplissing" and "gidplissing*" are coreferring, and that these intuitions depend on the belief that there is a God. Then suppose further that someone then were to say that even if there isn't a God, we ought still to respect these coreference intuitions, and if an expressivist account of the talk of what is

---

[45] See further Eklund (2015).

"gidplissing" and "gidplissing*" can respect these intuitions, the intuitions support an expressivist account. I don't think this would be persuasive. If the intuitions in question are due to a false belief in this way, the intuitions do not support expressivism. Correspondingly for Moral Twin Earth scenarios.

If one cannot reasonably adjudicate between Alternative-friendly and Alternative-unfriendly theories by appealing to Moral Twin Earth intuitions, how else might one try to adjudicate the dispute? One may wish to apply the following train of thought: On independent grounds, naturalism is plausible. There are certainly Alternative-friendly theories compatible with naturalism, but it is not immediately clear that there are Alternative-unfriendly theories compatible with naturalism. To settle whether there are, one would need to get clearer on what normative roles are than I have managed to be. So the relevant research project would be that of getting clearer on normative role, and on whether Alternative-unfriendliness requires non-naturalism.[46]

The naturalist may think: if Alternative-unfriendliness does not in fact require non-naturalism, then it avoids the metaphysical and epistemological puzzles associated with non-naturalism. (How can we respectably include non-natural properties in our metaphysics while remaining scientifically respectable? And how can we know of these non-natural properties?) But this is not exactly right. Epistemological puzzles remain for any Alternative-unfriendly view. Suppose we can convince ourselves that ordinary naturalistic properties are what normative concepts ascribe, even given an Alternative-unfriendly view. Then there may be no great mystery concerning how we can know *of these properties* what they are and what things instantiate them. But for all that it can still be completely unclear how we could be justified in any beliefs concerning which properties are picked out by our normative concepts, it can still be

---

[46] Here is an argument to the effect that naturalism surely can accommodate Alternative-unfriendliness, and more generally that Alternative-unfriendliness need not be very metaphysically demanding. It is adapted from Williams (forthcoming).

Suppose that an interpretationist theory of meaning is correct: what the expressions of some language mean and refer to is a matter of what an ideal interpreter would take these expressions to mean and refer to. Then note that charity is plausibly an important constraint on good interpretation. But charity sufficiently broadly understood can enjoin that I should interpret someone as meaning wrong by "wrong" and right by "right," despite certain radical differences between her uses of these words and mine, because any other interpretation would be uncharitable. Any other interpretation would depict her as shaping her emotions and deliberation on irrelevant grounds—on grounds not having to do with wrongness and rightness. So given the underlying view on meaning, I should interpret her as meaning wrong by "wrong," and since no metaphysics is wheeled in, this is all consistent with naturalism.

There is a lot to say about this line of reasoning. But let me just say this. Even assuming that, interpretationism plus plausible principles of interpretation yield that our normative concepts and an alternative community's concepts with the same normative role would have the same reference. Even so, there would remain questions of whether these concepts would have determinate and in other ways non-defective reference. It is part of the set-up that we and they associate different descriptive beliefs with the concepts. If the reference of our concept and theirs is the same and it is non-defective, it has to be determined by something that is shared between the concepts; that is, the normative role. So in the end this appeal to interpretationism and charity does not suffice to show that the naturalist can be Alternative-unfriendly.

completely unclear how we can be justified in any belief about what normative concepts apply to. (Compare perhaps: Let's call a property *goddy* if it is God's favorite naturalistic property. Then whichever property is goddy, this property is such that we can have knowledge of it through the same means that we can have knowledge of other naturalistic properties. But supposed knowledge *that this property is goddy* can for all that present distinctive problems.)

7

Being Against What Is Plainly Right

Chapter 6 dealt with serious objections to the idea that one can appeal to Alternative-unfriendliness to vindicate ardent realism. While the objections are not knock-down, no compelling responses were given. For all that I wish or can say, it is an open question what in the end to say about them.

In this chapter I will turn to something different. I will simply be concerned with an application of what has come up so far to a different type of issue. Antimoralism or immoralism, sometimes associated with Marx and Nietzsche (though I will not attempt any scholarly discussion), is sometimes brought up as a theoretical option. Some of the theoretical options that have come up in the discussion can serve as bases for different forms of antimoralism or immoralism. To relate to the title of the present chapter: they point to ways in which one might be against what is plainly right.

7.1 Antimoralism

An *antimoralist* or *immoralist* purports to somehow be against morality itself. Marx and Nietzsche are often mentioned as examples of antimoralists. But what might it be to reject morality as such? What sort of thesis might that be? The reason this fits in with the discussion in the rest of the book is that the theoretical map I have provided helps highlight some important but perhaps easily overlooked ways in which one might, in some sense, be an antimoralist.

Let me start by providing a list of some very disparate ways, familiar from the literature, in which one might, for good reasons or bad, classify as an antimoralist. Having provided this list I will indicate how the kind or kinds of antimoralism I will focus on differ from the ideas listed. (I will not take a stand as to the appropriateness with which the label "antimoralism" is applied to the ideas in this list. I mention them primarily to set them aside as ideas I will not myself be concerned with.)

(a) When someone indicates that she is "against morality," it may seem natural to take her to really mean that she is against what is commonly regarded as morally good and morally right. When someone like Nietzsche seems to speak out against morality, then it can seem that the proper way to state what is going on is that he rejects moral values ordinarily taken as fundamental, so fundamental that they can seem constitutive of morality, but the correct way to state his view is that what is really morally right isn't what is regarded as morally right.

(b) Commonly discussed alternatives to ordinary realism about morality can be seen as fodder for antimoralism. Take for example the simplest forms of expressivism, according to which to call things good or bad is little more than to say "Hooray!" or "Boo!" to these things.[1] This can be seen to have antimoralist implications: "You attach so much weight to moral truth—but once we have seen the truth of Boo/Hooray expressivism, we can see that there is no truth of the kind you so cherish." Moreover, a moral relativist saying that moral claims can never be absolutely true but can only be true relative to this or that framework can make much the same speech.

(c) One can emphasize the distinction between what is *morally* good or right and what is good or right *simpliciter*, or *all things considered*. It is relatively commonplace to say that there is a conceptual distinction there: that one can meaningfully raise the question "I know φ-ing is morally right, but is it right?". The antimoralist can take this further, insisting that what is morally right needn't be right at all; moral rightness does not even provide pro tanto support for rightness. One way she might do that is to assimilate the concept of being specifically morally right, and generally the specifically moral concepts, to thick concepts—the restriction to what is moral introduces the "thickness"—and she can say that since thick concepts can generally be objectionable, moral concepts can be objectionable. (One might compare being specifically *morally* right to being right according to some specific code of conduct; specifically one to which we harbor deep-seated objections. Say, "fascistically right.")

(d) A less radical way in which one might be "anti-moral" is that one can hold that while something's being morally right always is a consideration in favor of it being right, moral considerations can sometimes or often be *outweighed* by other considerations.[2] Moral considerations carry less weight than they are otherwise commonly taken to do.

(e) A different kind of critique of morality is that our moral beliefs are simply the products of, say, social and economic circumstances, and/or that moral beliefs actually play only a negligible role in the explanation of action—how we act

---

[1] For example, a non-cognitivism much like that of Ayer (1936).
[2] See e.g. Williams (1981, 1985) and Wolf (1982).

depends on other factors.[3] More generally, one can think that moral considerations are for one reason or other explanatorily inefficacious.[4]

(f) The sorts of historical circumstances that give rise to the problems that morality is meant to solve—our having different interests, and there not being enough resources for all interests to be satisfied—is not in fact inherent in the human condition. So the concerns of morality are more parochial than might otherwise be assumed.[5]

The different forms of "antimoralism" (if the label is appropriate in all cases) just listed are of course all potentially significant. But I will not discuss them further here.

Some forms of antimoralism listed here are just forms of traditional antirealism. The pros and cons of such views are of course widely discussed. I want to focus on subtler views: views that tend to get overlooked.

Some of the forms of antimoralism listed trade on the distinction between what is, specifically, morally good and right and what is good and right simpliciter. Such antimoralist views might of course be quite significant. But I wish to consider more grand views—views that take aim at goodness and rightness simpliciter.

---

[3] Compare here the following passages from Marx:

> [What opinion] should we have of a chemist, who, instead of studying the actual laws of the molecular changes in the composition and decomposition of matter, and on that foundation solving definite problems, claimed to regulate the composition and decomposition of matter by means of "eternal ideas", of "*naturalité*" and "*affinité*"? Do we really know any more about "usury" when we say it contradicts "*justice éternelle*", "*équité éternelle*", "*mutualité éternelle*", and other "*vérités éternelles*" than the fathers of the church did when they said it was incompatible with "*grace éternelle*", "*foi éternelle*" and "*la volonté éternelle de Dieu*"? (Marx 1867, pp. 84–5; italics in the original)
>
> ...this "moral" shows how little Maine understands of the matter; so far as these influences (economical before everything else) possess [a] moral modus of existence, this is always derived, secondary modus and never the prius. (Marx 1880–2, p. 329)

And here is Richard Miller (1984) expounding on one aspect of Marx's thought:

> As a basis for self-sacrifice to bring about social change, morality is less effective, for most people, than concern for a group with whom one shares common enemies and with whom one frequently cooperates on the basis of real and growing reciprocity. In part [Marx] seeks to make this idea more compelling, as it applies to contemporary societies, by pointing out its good fit with contemporary events, above all, the revolutions of 1848–49. In his accounts of those revolutions (and, later, the Paris commune), he constantly contrasts the heroism of those taking part in relatively class-conscious worker-led uprisings with the timidity of their liberal bourgeois compatriots, whose moral concern was engaged but whose class interest was ambiguous. (p. 67)

[4] Here is Engels:

> While in everyday life, in view of the simplicity of the relations discussed, expressions like right, wrong and sense of right are accepted without misunderstanding even with reference to social matters, they create, as we have seen, the same hopeless confusion in any scientific investigation of economic relations as would be created, for instance, in modern chemistry if the terminology of the phlogiston theory were to be retained. *The confusion becomes still worse if one, like Proudhon, believes in this social phlogiston, "justice".* (Engels 1872–3, pp. 624–5; italics mine)

[5] See Lukes (1985), pp. 33–5 on when the "conditions of *Recht*" are and are not fulfilled.

Generally, what I am after is a view that focuses on what is right simpliciter, does not take issue with the thesis that some things objectively are right simpliciter, and yet says something more fundamental and radical than the antimoralist theses presented in (d)–(f) do. It will be useful to have a label for the kind of antimoralist view I am getting at. Call an antimoralist view satisfying these desiderata a *subtle antinormativist* view. (Given that the focus is on the good and right, etc., *simpliciter* rather than specifically on the *morally* good and right, "normativism" is more apt than "moralism.")

The reason for focusing on subtle antinormativist views is that they cut rather more deeply than views that simply concern the moral or are about downplaying to some extent the significance of some normative thought, along the lines of (d)–(f), and they are rather more subtle than traditional antirealist views, and thereby more easily overlooked.

Suppose someone were to say "φ-ing is right, but I am against φ-ing!." What kind of statement might this be? It could of course amount to the speaker's owning up to some personal flaw. But suppose this isn't stated as an admission but is affirmed proudly. The speaker could use "right" to mean morally right, and hold that what is morally right is not always all-things-considered right. But suppose the speaker specifies that by "right" she means *plainly* or *all-things-considered* right. The speaker could use "right" in a so-called inverted-commas sense, to stand for what is generally considered right, so what she actually asserts is that φ-ing is *generally considered* "right" but still she is against φ-ing. But suppose she insists that she does not mean to use "right" in an inverted-commas sense. Is there any way that her speech can be made good sense of? Yes, if a subtle antinormativist view is true.

A number of suggestions that have come up earlier in the discussion can serve as bases for subtle antinormativist views.

Consider first *hyperdescriptivism*. The hyperdescriptivist view is that sentences are not themselves normative. Some sentences tend to be used normatively but that is a different matter. The hyperdescriptivist can allow that there is such a thing as what is right simpliciter and such a thing as what is good simpliciter, and that some things are right simpliciter and good simpliciter. But for the hyperdescriptivist, "good" and "right," even when used with their all-things-considered senses, are just words among others. It is natural for the hyperdescriptivist to say that while we do tend to attach special importance to what is good or right simpliciter, there is nothing special about the meanings of the words "good" or "right" or about what they stand for that provides any kind of ulterior justification for this. If someone instead attaches the same importance to some clearly descriptive, non-normative property F, how could any hyperdescriptivist reasonably fault her? (Consider the possible objection, "but what is F isn't always good." To this, someone valuing what is F might equally reasonably reply: "but one might equally say, what is good isn't always F!".)

Similar remarks apply to the *presentationalist*. In fact, the presentationalist can add something to what the hyperdescriptivist says. She can say that positive normative words like "good" and "right" as a conventional matter present the properties they stand for in a positive light, but that this is treacherous for the association is arbitrary: quite different properties could have been presented in the same positive way, and there is nothing in the order of things that make the properties that "good" and "right" stand for especially apt to be thus presented.[6] (There will be natural psychological and historical reasons why we have picked out these properties by these positive words. But the presentationalist might emphasize that this is metaphysically no different from how there are natural historical reasons for why certain racist communities and societies have the kinds of negative words they do for minority groups.)

More generally, similar remarks apply, mutatis mutandis, to all Alternative-friendly views that do not allow that there is a Further Question of the kind discussed in Chapter 2. A main point of the whole discussion of the scenario I called Alternative was to emphasize that for theorists of this kind, there is nothing objective to support our concern with the properties we happen to ascribe by our normative words, including the thinnest ones.

It may be useful to consider, in this connection, what I will refer to as the *semantic conspiracy theory*: a certain theory concerning the history of our normative terms. According to the semantic conspiracy theory, a group of people (the aristocracy, say) together decided that certain properties were to have labels that presented them in a positive light and certain other properties were to have labels that presented them in a negative light. They got the rest of the people to use these labels, but in ignorance of the true history of them—and believing that the properties deserved these labels because of normative features of these properties. The semantic conspiracy theory as just sketched is of course too simple to be taken seriously. But it helps put in a stark light the sort of antinormativism that naturally goes with presentationalism. And even if what the semantic conspiracy theory states is not an actuality, particular group interests can have affected how we have ended up designating the properties normatively positively or negatively in the way we have. And more generally, if presentationalism is right, there is something metaphysically arbitrary about any way of designating properties normatively positively or negatively, given that there is no normativity in the world—nothing about the properties in and of themselves that is normatively positive or negative.

While it is important to stress how views of the kinds discussed—hyperdescriptivism, presentationalism, Alternative-friendly views generally—allow for a certain kind of

---

[6] Allen Wood says about Marx, "For Marx, justice is the property a transaction possesses when it stands in a functional relationship to the mode of production in which it takes place. It is a separate question whether, when, and from whose point of view just transactions are something valuable" (1979, p. 269). Of course the claim of Wood's Marx concerns only justice and not the moral generally—and still less the normative generally. But it is still a striking remark, and it is worth pausing on. What Wood's Marx in the first instance insists upon is that the property of justice is not itself a normative property. This is compatible with both hyperdescriptivist and presentationalist views (specifically on justice), for he might go on to say different things about the *concept* of justice consistently with what he says about the property.

antinormativism even while being fundamentally different from traditional antireal-ist views, none of this should be particularly surprising given what has gone on earlier. I have kept emphasizing how these views in different ways fall short of giving one everything one might have wished for in terms of normativity in the world.

But consider now an Alternative-friendly view that allows that there is a Further Question (whether "effable" or not—see again Chapter 2). Such a view obviously allows for subtle antinormativism. It can be that what falls under "right" and "good" is, in some sense, not what we *ought* to value. As in Chapter 2 when I discussed views of this kind, the specter of ineffability arises: isn't the "ought" used here *our* "ought"—and is it not a trivial truth that we ought to value what is right and good? To get around these worries, let me for ease of exposition temporarily adopt a view according to which the Further Question is effable: Sider's view, discussed in Chapter 2, according to which there is an issue of whether some normative terms are more elite than their counterparts. In Siderian terms, what might be the case is that what our words "right" and "good" ascribe are not elite, but some alternative concepts of what is right and what is good are. Again there is room for subtle antinormativism. There are facts about what is good and what is right, and some things are objectively good and objectively right, but our attachment to what is good and what is right is misplaced.

So far I have only considered how things look from the perspective of Alternative-friendly views of various kinds. Let me now consider whether Alternative-unfriendly views too can allow for subtle antinormativism. If our "thinnest" normative words function as, for example, the friend of a Wedgwood-style theory says they do, then there is something about the world as it is in itself that privileges some properties as the referents of our thinnest normative words. But still there are ways to combine a Wedgwood-style theory with subtle antinormativism. One must distinguish between, on the one hand, the claim that a Wedgwood-style theory is true of the thinnest possible normative expressions, and on the other, the claim that a Wedgwood-style theory is true of *our actual* thinnest expressions. Our thinnest expressions need not be the thinnest possible expressions. If so, then even if the thinnest possible norma-tive expressions cannot fail to ascribe something genuinely normatively relevant, an antinormativist stance on our thinnest actual expressions can be correct. Here is a quick sketch of how this can come to be the case. At first, a predicate F has a maximally thin meaning. But firm beliefs are formed concerning what is and isn't F and this becomes so ingrained in F's use that the contents of beliefs become conventionally associated with F. F is no longer maximally thin: its conceptual role in practical reason no longer exhausts its meaning. F has, so to speak, become descriptively contaminated.

Suppose lastly that there is no good response to the embarrassment of riches objection discussed in Chapter 3, so even if an Alternative-unfriendly theory is true, there are in a relevant sense alternative normative concepts, much as given an Alternative-friendly theory. Then the situation is like that which obtains given an Alternative-friendly theory. One could adopt a deflationary view, saying there are these alternative normative concepts and that is that, or one could insist that there is an (ineffable) Further Question.

Attention to the possibility of subtle antinormativist views is important. Ethical inquiries are often not conducted in a self-consciously concept-critical way: our actual concepts are employed and without attention to the fact that these concepts have formed under particular historical circumstances, in such a way that it cannot be blithely assumed that these concepts do not carry with them important ideological assumptions.

It is possible to use traditional forms of antirealism for the purposes of radical critiques of morality. ("When you say that __ is just, you are just saying hooray for __"; or "When you say that ___ is just, you are just saying that ___ is just relative to such-and-such standards.") But subtle antinormativism provides less obvious ways to substantiate such critiques.

Suppose that one initially wants to motivate radical politics by appeal to what is right, and one wants to claim that the actual order of things is not right. One enters a debate about rightness. But the debate, conducted in the way philosophical debates are standardly conducted, shows that the actual order of things is in fact right. Considerations about, e.g., judgments about possible cases and what we would judge to be "right" in those cases provide strong support for the view that the actual order of things is the right order of things, and the correct conclusion is indeed that the actual order of things is the right order of things. Is everything lost for the would-be radical? Not necessarily. The spirit of her view can still be defended. She might argue, e.g., that our moral and political inclinations or beliefs have affected the meaning and reference of our actual "right" and what concept of rightness we use. There are other possible normative concepts regulating the sorts of things that "right" is used to regulate, and those normative concepts are the ones we ought to employ. The radical taking this line can agree that the capitalist system is "right" but insist that we not take this as speaking in favor of the capitalist system. Compare objectionable thick concepts. If objectionable thick concepts are non-empty, even someone who finds concepts pertaining to sexual morality like *lewd*, *chaste*, and *perverted* objectionable ought to agree that behaviors paradigmatically regarded as lewd, chaste, or perverted indeed are lewd, chaste, and perverted—but she would disavow the evaluations associated with these claims.[7]

---

[7] As discussed in Chapter 4, Allan Gibbard (1992) uses "lewd" as an example of an objectionable thick term. At one point he turns to the following objection to his account:

> ...although I may condemn many acts that others would call lewd, I do not condemn them as lewd. People have objected this disclaimer, to my "leaving the term to the prudes". We should object to harassment, they say, and to causing undue offence. Sexual displays are one way of doing these things. We need some standards, then, for what behaviours constitute harassment or offensiveness. (For simplicity, let me just speak of harassment.) The

A radical adopting hyperdescriptivism could hold that to say that the capitalist system is "right" is really only to describe it in a particular way, and nothing more. Adopting presentationalism, she could say that "right" presents the property it refers to in a favorable light but would warn against drawing conclusions about the normativity of the property itself from this. Or, allowing that there is a Further Question of the kind earlier discussed, she might say that it is another notion of what is right—right*, not coextensive with what our "right" stands for—that is more elite. Or she can accept Wedgwood's view on the thinnest normative concepts and hold that our "right" is, in the terminology earlier introduced, contaminated. In the sense of an uncontaminated "right," the actions condoned by capitalism are not right.

7.2 Boyd on the Divine Right of Kings

In Chapter 2, I discussed what Richard Boyd said in response to a certain possible objection to his theory, an objection to the effect that the property that causally regulates our use of a normative term like "right" may fail to be something that ought to be valued in the way that we value rightness. In connection with the discussion of antinormativism, I now want to discuss this matter more fully. Let me start by quoting Boyd more extensively than earlier:

The second objection I want to consider represents a criticism of moral realism often attributed to Marx.... The objection goes like this: The moral realist—in the guise of the homeostatic consequentialist, say—holds that what regulate the use of moral terms are facts about human well-being. But this is simply not so. Consider, for example, sixteenth-century discussions of rights. One widely acknowledged "right" was the divine right of kings. Something surely regulated the use of the language of rights in the sixteenth century, but it clearly wasn't human well-being construed in the way the moral realist intends. Instead, it was the well-being of kings and of the aristocratic class of which they were a part. I agree with the analysis of the origin of the doctrine of the divine right of kings; indeed, I believe that such class determination of moral beliefs is a commonplace phenomenon. But I do not believe that this analysis undermines the claim that moral terms refer to aspects of human well-being. Consider, for example, the psychology of thinking and intelligence. It is extremely well documented...that the content of much of the literature in this area is determined by class interests rather than by the facts. Nevertheless, the psychological terms occurring in the most egregiously prejudiced papers refer to real features of human psychology; this is so because, in other contexts, their use is relevantly regulated by such features. Indeed—and this is the important point—if there were not such an epistemic (and thus referential) connection to

> reactions of alleged victims are not the last word: a person might feel harassed by perfectly innocent actions, actions people should feel free to perform. We need to work out standards, then, for when sexual display constitutes harassment. A good term for such behaviour is "lewd". (p. 281)

Gibbard responds (sensibly, to my mind) by saying that while the policy described, not leaving the term to the prudes, might be sensible, it involves changing the meaning of the word. One might add that overlooking that actually used words can be objectionable can lead one to fail to notice how the meanings of the words used can lead users astray.

real psychological phenomena, the ideological rationalization of class structures represented by the class-distorted literature would be ineffective. It's only when people come to believe, for example, that Blacks lack a trait, *familiar in other contexts as "intelligence"*, that racist theories can serve to rationalize the socioeconomic role to which Blacks are largely confined. Similarly, I argue, in order for the doctrine of the divine right of kings to serve a class function, it had to be the case that moral language was often enough connected to issues regarding the satisfaction of real human needs. Otherwise, an appeal to such a supposed right would be ideologically ineffective. Only when rights-talk has *some* real connection to the satisfaction of the needs of nonaristocrats could this instance of rights-talk be useful to kings and their allies.[8]

Although Boyd discusses the objection he brings up as an objection to moral realism generally, it ought to be clear from the nature of the objection that it specifically is an objection to versions of moral realism that, like Boyd's, in some way or other are Alternative-friendly.[9] An Alternative-unfriendly realist can raise this objection to Boyd as much as an antirealist can. Such a realist could believe that there is a normative property that is especially well suited to play the role of rightness, and she might naturally also hold that this is the property ascribed by our "right"—and her objection to Boyd might be that given Boyd's metasemantics, our "right" does not ascribe this property. Furthermore, the objection Boyd mentions is an objection one can envisage an antinormativist making. While it is possible to raise the objection as an objection to Boyd's theory of the semantics of normative terms, it is possible to raise it not as an objection to that theory, but as an objection to the idea that, given that theory, we are justified in being concerned with what is right and good and ought to be done in the way that we are.

As mentioned earlier, Boyd's response is—roughly—to say that despite doctrines like the divine right of kings, normative terms really refer to properties that it is proper to value in the ways associated with the terms. If they didn't, then considerations about what is right and wrong, etc., would not have the force they do. But comparing the cases of objectionable thick terms and of slurs casts doubt on Boyd's claims here. The racist's or bigot's calling someone a "nigger" or a "faggot" might still have force, as might calling someone "lewd," "perverted," or "slutty."

Moreover, Boyd's formulations are equivocal in a way that is relevant. He says, for example, "such class determination of moral beliefs is a commonplace phenomenon" and adds: "I do not believe that this analysis undermines the claim that moral terms refer to aspects of human well-being." Later in the same passage he says, "in order for the doctrine of the divine right of kings to serve a class function, it had to be the case that moral language was often enough connected to issues regarding the satisfaction of real human needs." Focus on the last of these statements and the "often enough."

---

[8] Boyd (1988), p. 337 (emphasis in original).
[9] Boyd does speak about the moral and not about the normative generally. But compare earlier remarks in Chapter 2 about generalizing from the moral to the normative.
   Boyd defends a kind of causal theory of reference-determination. Beliefs are not as straightforwardly reference-determining as they are according to common descriptivist theories. But our beliefs enter the story also given Boyd's account; they enter as part of the story about causal regulation.

A term can be connected to issues relating to the satisfaction of real human needs "often enough" for its use to be able to influence opinion even while, so to speak, the term is such that its employment is objectionable. There may—to relate back to how many seemingly objectionable thick terms pertain to sexual morality—be a negative thick term used to condemn certain types of sexual behavior that really are very much worthy of condemnation, but this negative term is also true of sexual behaviors that do not deserve such condemnation. If so, then complacently continuing to use the term for the purposes of evaluation is not in order. (Perhaps "sexually perverted" is like that. Some prominent examples of sexual perversion—those including the harming of innocents—are deserving of condemnation. But some unusual sexual practices arguably falling under the label are not so deserving.) Moreover, considering the whole plethora of normative terms, it is not obvious that a normative term needs to have any real connection to the satisfaction of human needs at all for it to have the sort of usefulness Boyd is talking about—witness paradigmatic examples of slurs.

Given the way Boyd himself talks about this, he makes it sound as if the problem, even assuming it is real, is not very serious. If the concept *right* is often but not always connected to the "satisfaction of real human needs," then we can easily improve the way we think and talk about the normative by simply replacing the actual concept *right* with some alternative normative concept that is more reliably connected to the satisfaction of real human needs. But there would appear to be lots of possible concepts that are in some way or other reliably connected to the satisfaction of human needs. One concept might, so to speak, weigh different needs one way, while another concept weighs them another way; one is generally concerned with the maximization of human needs, one takes more seriously the "separateness of persons" and cares more about how the satisfaction of needs is distributed among persons, etc. Which one ought we to employ?

Again, to stress something that has come up earlier in the discussion: There is a strong temptation to here simply say, "we settle what concept we ought to employ simply by engaging in normative theorizing"—that is, we do that which we are already engaged in qua normative theorists.[10] But to respond in this way is to fail to realize the seriousness of the challenge. For if there are these possible concepts, right1 and right2, let us call them, then those normative theorists who employ right1 will arrive at truths about what one right1 to do and not, and those who employ right2 will arrive at truths about what one right2 to do and not. One will naturally want to ask whether one ought to use right1 or right2 in normative thinking. But the question is problematic. What about the "ought" used in the question itself? Those who use "ought" to mean *ought1* will ask one question, whether one ought1 to be concerned with what is right1 or what is right2, whereas those who use "ought" to mean *ought2* will ask another, whether one ought2 to be concerned with what is right1 or what is right2.

---

[10] Compare the discussion of this objection in Chapter 3.

8

Connections

What I have been concerned with in this book is to call attention to a number of metaethical, or more generally metanormative, questions that arise when we pay attention to how the normative concepts we have are just some of the possible normative concepts there are. I have used this to problematize what it takes to vindicate ardent realism, and to raise questions regarding what it takes for there to be normativity in the world. While these obviously are central concerns in the literature, my approach to them is rather special. In this chapter I will explore connections with what I have brought up and other discussions in the literature. The chapter will inevitably have a somewhat listlike character. I will relate what I have been concerned with to the issue of normative indeterminacy (section 8.1), Scanlon's quietist realism (section 8.2), whether the sorts of issues I have raised for ardent realism arise also for some theories that are not (or are not obviously) versions of metaphysical realism (section 8.3), a prominent objection to non-naturalism (section 8.4), the problem of "creeping minimalism" (section 8.5), and, lastly, the characterization of normative concepts as essentially contestable (section 8.6).

8.1 Normative Indeterminacy

Let me begin by considering some recent discussions relating to normative indeterminacy. Consider first what Tom Dougherty (2014) says when bringing up meta-normative problems relating to indeterminacy:

Analogously, a [semantic indecision] theorist about "permissible" would say ... that this term is associated with multiple precise extensions. Some of these include the destruction of the nineteen week fetus; other extensions do not. But for none of these extensions is it the case that the term determinately refers to this extension. No extension stands out with a special ethical glow (although their intersection arguably does have a special ethical significance). Rather there is a multiplicity of ethically relevant extensions here. I suspect that many metaethicists will find this consequence an interesting ethical result in itself.[1]

Dougherty doesn't say explicitly exactly *why* this "ethical result" would be an interesting one, but what I take it he must have in mind is this. Suppose that under

---

[1] Dougherty (2014), p. 370f.

one precisification "permissible" ascribes property F1 and under another it ascribes property F2, and a certain action has F1 but not F2. What then should be our attitude toward performing this action? I take it that for Dougherty "permissible" is just one example of a thin normative term, and that indeterminacy in other thin terms would present the same sort of theoretical problem. There is something interesting and puzzling about this. But what exactly is it? I suggest that Dougherty's puzzle concerning normative indeterminacy is very similar to the puzzle regarding alternative normative concepts that I discussed in Chapter 2. In each case we in some sense have different "candidates" for being what a given thin term stands for, and in each case we have that given the plethora of candidates one wants to ask the question of which one of these candidates should be picked. (With noted problems regarding how to understand the "should" here.) In fact, I don't think Dougherty's "interesting ethical result" is essentially bound up with semantic indeterminacy. Given the similarity between Dougherty's puzzle and the one I have earlier discussed, indeterminacy is not necessary for the general problem to arise. What about sufficiency? In some sense, indeterminacy is sufficient for the puzzle to arise: already given indeterminacy, Dougherty's question can be *raised*. But there are assumptions given which Dougherty's question appears to have a rather straightforward answer, and doesn't quite deserve the label "puzzle." For example, if a supposed thin normative term is semantically indeterminate but there are independent reasons for thinking that one precisification is normatively privileged over the others, we don't really have a genuine puzzle on our hands. There would clearly be such independent reasons if the term in question somehow were indeterminate as between a merely descriptive precisification and a normative one. By contrast, there is a serious puzzle if the term is associated with a determinate normative role but that role does not suffice to determine a unique referent—the term is semantically indeterminate as between a number of different referents and they all have equal claim to normative relevance.

In the passage from Dougherty, the issue of whether there is semantic indeterminacy in "permissible" is run together with the thought that no candidate referent for "permissible" possesses, in Dougherty's terms, ethical glow. The notion of ethical glow—or as I will talk about it, since the present focus is on normativity generally, *normative* glow—is of course very impressionistic. But even so, it should be clear that there are different ways in which these things can come apart. It can be that exactly one of the precisifications possesses normative glow. An expression can be indeterminate in reference as between a number of different candidates, even while one of these candidates is in some sense privileged over the others and is the one we in some sense *ought* to be primarily concerned with.[2]

Dougherty says in the parenthetical remark that "their intersection [the intersection of the different extensions] arguably does have a special ethical significance."

---

[2] Dougherty also speaks of what is "ethically relevant," but seems to presuppose that each precisification has a claim to ethical relevance.

This point corresponds to the point, discussed in Chapter 3, that one can want to appeal to what is "superright"—what falls under "right" and all of its normative counterparts—to get around problems having to do with "right" having non-coextensional normative counterparts. But it is arguably only plausible that the intersection does have a special ethical, or normative, significance if each of the precisifications does have some kind of normative significance, and that is not a given. What is more, to repeat a point from the earlier discussion of superrightness, even should all the precisifications have significance it could still be that super-rightness is in any way privileged when it comes to playing the rightness role. It can, for example, be that no predicate associated with the rightness role is coextensive with superrightness. In the case of "permissible," Dougherty's example, the issue stands out especially starkly. Something is superpermissible iff it is in the extension of every concept with the same normative role as the concept of permissibility. To adopt superpermissibility as one's notion of permissibility would be to adopt a particular, very strict line on what is permissible and not.

When talking about the possibility of semantic indeterminacy in normative expressions, Dougherty mentions some theories that are especially amenable to there being such indeterminacy. He brings up the causal theory and neo-descriptivism. I don't think it is a coincidence that the theories he brings up are paradigmatic Alternative-friendly theories. On those theories, the reference of normative terms is determined the same way that the reference of descriptive terms are determined, and straightforwardly semantic indeterminacy promises to arise in the way it does in the descriptive case. (Though one can certainly have semantic indeterminacy given Alternative-unfriendly views as well. For example, semantic indeterminacy can arise through it being indeterminate just which normative role is associated with a given term.)

In his (2000) review of Jackson (1998), where a version of descriptivism is defended, Stephen Yablo says:

A second option is to deny that … any descriptive property is such that "reasonable" stands for it as opposed to some other descriptive property…. It's compatible with [Jackson's points about supervenience] that there are and will continue to be many candidates, so that there is no particular descriptive property that deserves to be called "the" property of reasonableness. And now someone might say: Why should it make our blood race if "reasonable"—and by implication "right"—is determined to mark some descriptive line or other, if the question of the word's application to particular actions remains as contestable as ever? A finding of truth-aptitude begins to seem like a pretty superficial victory for the cognitivist. He is right about the technical semantical point: each evaluative predicate stands for a descriptive property. But when it comes to the larger issue of whether there is a truth of the matter about what is right (reasonable), matters are more or less as described by the non-cognitivist.[3]

---

[3] Yablo (2000), p. 17.

I take it that when talking about the many candidates, Yablo is talking about semantic indeterminacy. His point is that even if "reasonable" is determined to ascribe some descriptive property, there are many candidates for being the descriptive property that "reasonable" ascribes. And Yablo is right that on Jackson's descriptivist view there will likely be semantic indeterminacy. As noted, Dougherty makes the same point. (There seems, however, to be a slide in the passage from the point that there will be some indeterminacy to the claim that matters will be more or less as described by the non-cognitivist. The latter claim seems to require that the indeterminacy be rather massive.)

But why does the semantic indeterminacy matter to whether our blood should race? Suppose, contrary to what seems plausible, that given Jackson's descriptivist view, there is a particular descriptive property that deserves to be called the property of reasonableness (to stick with that example). So long as we, the folk, easily could have had a different (mature) folk morality, one can think: why should it make our blood race if "reasonable" is determined to mark this particular descriptive line?

Semantic indeterminacy in itself is not the source of the problems that Yablo is talking about. The real concern is that there is something *arbitrary* in what our normative terms ascribe. This arbitrariness is also the concern underlying some of the problems pressed earlier for Alternative-friendly theories. If there are non-coextensive normative concepts associated with the same normative role, then the question arises of which of these concepts to use for normative purposes. If there is no Further Question about what normative concepts are normatively privileged—recall the ineffability worry—then it seems there is an arbitrariness in which ones of these concepts one opts for.

If there is normativity in the world, as I have characterized such normativity—if there are properties ascribed by non-defectively referentially normative predicates—there is some reason to think that the arbitrariness is avoided. But that hinges on the workability of the notion of sameness of normative role.

In his (2012), Ryan Wasserman says the following about moral realism, in the context of a discussion of vagueness and indeterminacy:

on the epistemicist picture, moral predicates are more like "bald" than "gold". And I think that a moral realist—a *serious* moral realist—should resist this conclusion. For the serious moral realist, moral terms pick out *metaphysically important properties*. The property of *being morally obligatory*, for example, is more like the property of *being gold*, than *being bald*. So, the semantics of moral terms should be more like the semantics of natural kind terms. So, moral terms are not semantically plastic. So, the epistemicist response must be denied.[4]

Intuitively, a term is semantically plastic when it could easily have referred to or ascribed something different from that which it actually refers to or ascribes.

---

[4] Wasserman (2012), p. 78.

I think the views on moral realism to which Wasserman here gives expression are widespread. But they are problematic. Consider first the claim that for the serious moral realist, moral terms pick out "metaphysically important properties." Note first that moral realism is standardly characterized in such a way that the objective truth of some (atomic) moral statements is sufficient for moral realism.[5] This is what I have earlier called broad realism. Metaphysical importance of the properties is neither here nor there. But perhaps the "serious" is there to take care of that: we are not talking about any old moral realism but *serious* moral realism. Wasserman does not explain his use of "serious." Second, even accepting Wasserman's claim about what "serious" moral realism demands, one may be suspicious of the inference from the claim that the *property* of being morally obligatory is in some crucial respect ("metaphysical importance") like the *property* of being gold to the conclusion that the *semantics* (or metasemantics) of the terms "morally obligatory" and "gold" must be importantly analogous. Third, there is of course the point I have earlier sought to stress: on prominent construals of "metaphysical importance"—construals of metaphysical importance as eliteness—the metaphysical importance of the properties ascribed by moral predicates seems orthogonal to the question of ardent moral realism. It is not a given, of course, that Wasserman's "serious" moral realist corresponds to my "ardent" moral realist. Perhaps given what Wasserman means by "serious," to be a serious moral realist just is to be a realist who thinks moral predicates ascribe metaphysically important properties. However, this invites the question of what is interesting regarding serious moral realism thus construed.

Thus far I have been making points critical of Wasserman. But there is also a fourth point to make, one that is friendlier to what Wasserman is driving at. There is *something* to the sense that normative realism (or, better: serious normative realism, or, maybe better still: ardent normative realism) demands that normative terms not be semantically plastic, and this is illustrated by the scenarios involving different communities that I have brought up: if thin normative terms are semantically plastic then there can be different communities using semantically different thin normative terms in the way described. That seems to present a problem for ardent normative realism, as I have discussed. But to the extent that this is what underlies the sense that ardent normative realism is incompatible with semantic plasticity, the upshot may be somewhat more subtle. It is one thing to say that small differences in associated folk theories or in relevant causal relations—generally, the sorts of things that determine reference according to Alternative-friendly theories—ought not to matter to the reference of a normative term, and another to say that small differences in something directly normatively relevant like normative role ought not to matter to the reference of a normative term. Considerations having to do with Alternative in the first instance only support the former claim.

---

[5] See for example Sayre-McCord (2011).

8.2 Scanlon's Quietism

In recent work, for example his (2014), T.M. Scanlon has defended a certain kind of quietistic realism about the normative. The quietistic aspect is a matter of, for philosophical reasons, refusing to address questions about how normative properties and facts relate to other properties and facts. Here is a representative passage:

the way of thinking about these matters that makes the most sense is a view that does not privilege science but takes as basic a range of domains, including mathematics, science, and moral and practical reasoning. It holds that statements within all of these domains are capable of truth and falsity, and that the truth values of statements about one domain, insofar as they do not conflict with statements of some other domain, are properly settled by the standards of the domain that they are about. Mathematical questions, including questions about numbers and sets are settled by mathematical reasoning, scientific questions including questions about the existence of bosons, by scientific reasoning, normative questions by normative reasoning, and so on.[6]

Where others might tackle questions of normative metaphysics by figuring out how normative facts and properties might relate to other kinds of facts and properties, Scanlon thinks that we should remain within the realm of normative reasoning itself. The general idea is one that can be evocatively stated using Carnap's (1950a) distinction between *external* and *internal* questions. Issues about the truth of normative claims are to be settled using "internal" means. To ask the "external" question about how normative properties and facts relate to non-normative ones is to engage in illegitimate metaphysics.[7] Scanlon proposes to dispose of objections like Mackie's queerness objection by saying that the objectors try to raise external questions.

   Scanlon brings up the following objection to his view:

David Enoch argues that my account of the normative domain is deficient in this way by considering the possibility of people who treat as reasons for action considerations that we would not regard as reasons. He argues that since their reasoning about these "counter-reasons" satisfies the internal standards that they accept, just as our reasoning about reasons satisfies standards internal to the normative domain as we understand it, I am committed to

---

[6] Scanlon (2014), p. 19.

[7] This is of course only a brief summary of Scanlon's view. An immediate objection to Scanlon's view as described is whether he would not by the same token have to allow for the truth of statements about the existence of witches made within witch discourse. But in response Scanlon insists that some claims of witch discourse "conflict with claims of physics and other empirical sciences, and this conflict provides decisive reason to reject the idea that there are witches and spirits" (p. 21). A supposedly crucial difference between normative discourse and witch discourse is that the claims of normative discourse do not conflict with scientific claims. (Of course one may wonder what justifies Scanlon in maintaining that when witch discourse and scientific discourse conflict, scientific discourse trumps witch discourse. Must he not engage in "external" theorizing to arrive at this verdict?)

   Incidentally, it shouldn't be assumed that the usage of "external" and "internal" here captures what Carnap meant. Nor does Scanlon insist otherwise.

the conclusion that these "counter-reasons" exist just as much as our reasons do, and that my view is therefore unable to give sense to the idea that our conclusions are correct and theirs mistaken.

This problem seems to me illusory. These imagined conclusions about "counter-reasons" conflict with our conclusions about reasons only insofar as they are interpreted as conclusions about reasons. So the question of which of us is correct is a normative question, which can be answered only through normative reasoning. It is a question about the content of the best account of the normative domain—the realm of reasons.[8]

While this may not be immediately evident, I think what is at issue here is precisely the question of whether normative role in this case determines reference. Can there be people with a notion of "counter-reason" such that counter-reasons aren't reasons but that a different community could use a notion of counter-reason for the same purpose, or, dare I say it, with the same normative role, that we use the notion of reason for? Scanlon replies to Enoch, "These imagined conclusions about 'counter-reasons' conflict with our conclusions about reasons only insofar as they are interpreted as conclusions about reasons." Well, maybe. Either the normative role associated with our concept reason is reference-determining or it is not. If it is, then counter-reasons are different from reasons only if the normative role associated with the concept of counter-reasons is different: and Scanlon can insist that if the normative role is different then counter-reasons just are not relevant. If it is not, then counter-reasons do present a problem, contrary to what Scanlon suggests. The problem is the same as the problem for Alternative-friendly theories that has been the focus of my discussion.

Of course, in saying what I am saying I am going far beyond what is explicitly found in Scanlon's text. But consider Scanlon's "These imagined conclusions about 'counter-reasons' conflict with our conclusions about reasons only insofar as they are interpreted as conclusions about reasons." If counter-reasons are different from but in normative competition with reasons—if the other community's concept counter-reason is associated with the same normative role as our concept reason, but is not coextensive—then I don't see how Scanlon could reasonably dismiss these worries. But if counter-reasons can be different from reasons only by failing to be in normative competition with them, Scanlon's reply is appropriate.[9]

What this indicates is that the viability of Scanlon's outlook depends on issues in the theory of reference-determination. This is relevant, for a main theme in Scanlon's discussions of the metaphysics of the normative is to emphasize a certain kind of discourse pluralism. In brief, the line is that familiar problems concerning moral realism only arise if we try to assimilate all discourses instead of simply judging them

---

[8] Scanlon (2014), p. 29. Enoch's discussion is in Enoch (2011), pp. 122–33. In his (2011), Tristram McPherson brings up an objection similar to Enoch's, talking about "schmeasons."

[9] Qualification: The complications brought up under the heading of the embarrassment of riches problem come up here too.

on their own terms: it is only then that we are tempted to ask questions about how normative properties relate to, e.g., physical properties. But if the tenability of Scanlon's overall view depends on claims about what sorts of discourses there can be—can there be counter-reasons discourse in addition to reasons discourse?—then the tenability of his view depends at least on issues in philosophy of language, and issues about the normative aren't quite as autonomous from other issues in philosophy as Scanlon's rhetoric can make them out to be. So long as the dependence is only on how things turn out in philosophy of language, one can say that this was or should have been evident all along, as Scanlon's discourse pluralism is a thesis in philosophy of language. But one can say more. Whether counter-reasons discourse is reasons discourse—whether "counter-reason" as used by the community imagined turns out to corefer with "reason"—arguably depends on properly metaphysical matters. It depends on whether there is any possible semantic value for "counter-reason" and "reason" that so to speak is especially fit to be picked out by an expression with the normative role shared by these expressions. We are doing metaphysics anyway, despite Scanlon's intentions to the contrary.

There are three replies to this that I can foresee on Scanlon's behalf. Since my main concern isn't with Scanlon's view but with the potential relevance of the distinctions I am concerned with, let me just describe these possible replies rather briefly and not enter into any discussion about their viability.

One reply would be to say that we are indeed doing straightforward metaphysics, but we are still not forced to say how normative properties relate to non-normative properties. All we are required to weigh in on is the question of how different properties ascribed by normative predicates relate to each other. The metaphysics we are forced to engage in does not vitiate Scanlon's claims to the effect that one need not take seriously metaphysical questions about the relation between normative properties and a supposed reduction base.

A second reply would be to endorse a more radical or thoroughgoing discourse pluralism than that espoused by Scanlon. It would be to simply accept that there is counter-reason discourse alongside reasons discourse but insist that to accept this point about the space of discourses does not significantly affect anything: there just are no external standards by which to judge reasons discourse. From within reasons discourse one can just dismiss counter-reasons as not being reasons. The resulting view is something that, for obvious reasons, would not satisfy an ardent realist: for someone using counter-reasons discourse can from within that discourse just dismiss reasons as not being counter-reasons.

A third reply would be to say the sort of thing that expressivists like Blackburn and Gibbard say in different but similar contexts. Claims about whether "counter-reason" and "reason" corefer are, despite appearances, themselves normative claims, and should be seen as made within reasons discourse. This would involve treating normative discourse, and the semantics of normative discourse, in a quite different way from that in which descriptive discourse is standardly treated.

8.3 Ardent Non-Realists?

Ardent realism has been a recurrent theme in the present discussion. I brought up the view by saying: spot the realist everything, when it comes to discussions in the literature. Can it not still be that a certain kind of motivation often underlying moral realism can fail to be satisfied? There can still be alternative normative concepts, and it can be that there is no Further Question as to whether to use our normative concepts or some alternative concepts recommending importantly differ-ent types of action. While this is an in some ways useful way to frame the discussion, it narrows focus to theories that are in other respects realist. But there are of course many metaethical theories that are not realist theories, and one can wonder whether the possibility of alternative normative concepts does not present problems also for some such theories.

Scanlon's quietism, just discussed, can perhaps be regarded as a case in point. Scanlon is sometimes regarded as a non-naturalist realist, but his opposition to external questions may justify putting him in a different camp—he can be regarded as a quietist where this is seen as something different from realism. Of course any discussion of this can threaten to degenerate into a discussion of how to use various "ism"-labels. But my point for present purposes is that even if he is a "quietist," Scanlon can—in principle, and whether or not in the end reasonably—be concerned about alternative normative concepts in just the way that the ardent realist is. For example, he can be concerned about what privileges reasons over counter-reasons. Perhaps any worries about privilege on his part are in the end unprincipled—is he perhaps trying to raise an external question of the kind he officially disavows? However that may be, it is intelligible enough that a theorist could wish to combine a quietist refusal to entertain external questions with a concern about alternative normative concepts.

Moreover, some non-cognitivists, from Hare onwards, have wanted to combine their non-cognitivism with saying that moral judgment is in some way objective. The simplest illustration is Hare's own appeal to the universalizability of moral judgments, and the kind of consequentialism he took to be justified by this. A non-cognitivist in this way concerned to defend the objectivity of moral judgment can in principle be concerned about alternative normative concepts. Even if our concept *right* works in such a way that everyone employing it is compelled to accept *that ϕ-ing is right*, some alternative concept of rightness right* can work in such a way that everyone employing it is compelled to accept *that ϕ-ing is not right**, and that is all there is to it. And the non-cognitivist concerned to defend objectivity can feel dissatisfied: Bad Guy can simply be employing the alternative rightness concept.

In recent work, Huw Price and Joshua Gert have wanted to defend a broadly pragmatist account of truth in the normative realm.[10] Normative judgments are apt

---

[10] See e.g. Price (2013) and ch. 1 of Gert (2012).

for truth, but truth is not understood as realist correspondence but as something constructed out of practice. (Needless to say, I am painting with very broad brush strokes here. Since I will only make general remarks about the sort of view Price and Gert defend, there is no need to get into the details.) Someone saying that truth is constructed out of practice can in principle be very amenable to a kind of relativism: there are different practices, and different truths constructed out of these practices. But Gert prominently brings up the example of astrology, and talks about how astrology can be mistaken in its ontological presuppositions—so it is not as if anything goes.[11] One can raise the same question about Price's and Gert's pragmatism as about different views: can there not be alternative normative concepts—alternative discourses, alternative practices? And can the pragmatist really help herself to saying that all other normative discourses besides ours would rest on false presuppositions? And if not, might she not worry about that—about, for example, whether there is any sense in which some discourse may be privileged over others?

There has been lots of hedging in the last few paragraphs: occurrences of "can," "might," and the like. This is because the theorists concerned, the quietist, the objectivity-defending cognitivists, and the pragmatists, *need* not worry about the possibility of there being alternative concepts. Just like a realist (in the broad sense) who is not an ardent realist, she can say that so long as there is not anything internal to our practice of using the normative concepts we have that is problematic, we can stick to these concepts whether or not there are possible alternatives. There is nothing that I would want to argue that could force her to abandon that position.

But equally clearly, her motivations behind defending her view can be such that she is reasonably worried about alternative normative concepts. A Scanlonian quietist can be as concerned as any other sort of realist to show that there is something in the nature of things that underlies Bad Guy's being mistaken, and she can appeal to a Carnapian internal/external distinction primarily to ward off concerns about the moral facts she posits. If this is her motivation, alternative normative concepts are relevant in the way indicated. Similarly, a non-cognitivist defending some sort of objectivity of moral judgment can be as concerned as the ardent realist to show something about where our Bad Guy goes wrong: it is only that she does not wish to appeal to some moral facts to show this but instead to something about the nature of moral judgment. If this is her motivation, then again the possibility of alternative normative concepts is relevant. And a pragmatist of Price's or Gert's kind can be like the non-cognitivist in this regard.

For any theorist such that her motivations lead her to be worried about alternative concepts, the question will arise of whether her theory of reference-determination allows her to be Alternative-unfriendly. Can normative role determine reference on

---

[11] If a discourse can be flawed because of its ontological presuppositions, this can be the case also for normative discourse. Gert is well aware of this and seeks to address this worry. Since the details of Gert's position are not my present concern, I will not get into this.

her conception? Or, well, if she does not think that normative expressions refer or ascribe to begin with, then the question does not arise in exactly this form. But the question will arise in some form or other.

Will it be easier or harder for a theorist of one of the kinds to defend Alternative-unfriendliness than it is for an ardent realist to defend Alternative-unfriendliness? This will depend on the details from case to case. But maybe it will be easier for a non-cognitivist to be Alternative-unfriendly, since it will be natural for her to insist that normative role is the only semantically relevant feature.

Even if Alternative-unfriendliness can be defended, there remains the embarrass-ment of riches objection—the objection from there being possible expressions with slightly different normative roles and yet in normative conflict. When discussing the embarrassment of riches objection I suggested, on the ardent realist's behalf, the sparseness reply: even if there are many possible expressions associated with slightly different normative roles, maybe there are normative properties corresponding to only some of these roles. It may be that the various non-realists may be in a worse position to advert to the sparseness reply: that they are in a worse position to claim that the world simply fails to supply the worldly relata of the different normative expressions. It is the normative realist who thinks of the worldly relata as independ-ently constituted who can say that as a metaphysical matter of fact these relata may simply fail to exist.

8.4 On an Objection to Non-Naturalism

Appeal to Alternative-unfriendliness view can help a would-be non-naturalist reply to some regularly voiced objections to non-naturalism.

Consider a familiar objection to the effect that positing non-natural properties does not help with the puzzles of normativity. Here is Ridge (2014a) presenting this objection:

it is not clear how cognizing some non-natural property could rationally commit someone to acting in a certain way. "So giving all my money to charity has this irreducible non-natural property whose nature cannot be further elucidated; what is that to me?" seems like an intelligible thought. To this extent, the move away from naturalism seems unlikely to help solve the problem which motivated it.[12]

There is one point made here which simply should be conceded. No property in itself can reasonably be held to be such that cognition of it in itself can serve to rationally commit to action. But nor does the non-naturalist have to hold that some property is like that. There would be a problem for non-naturalism if the only way to cash talk of irreducibly normative properties were as properties such that cognition of them in itself rationally commits in that way. But the present appeal to Alternative-unfriendliness

[12] Ridge (2014a), p. 4.

provides an alternative. Even given this appeal to Alternative-unfriendliness, the thought "So giving all my money to charity has this irreducible non-natural property whose nature cannot be further elucidated; what is that to me?" certainly makes reasonable sense. But even if merely judging, of some irreducible non-natural property, that giving to charity has this property does not have the consequences in question, a suitable normative concept, C, of this property can be such that judging that giving to charity is C does rationally commit and one cannot reasonably go on to ask "what is that to me"; and independent considerations (such as to the effect that C is referentially normative) yield that C ascribes a non-natural property.[13] Concept C could be like this if its normative role determines its reference.

As is clear from Ridge's statement of the objection, it concerns how judging (or cognizing) something can rationally commit to action. There appears to be an implicit assumption behind the objection as stated, namely that the realist, at least the non-naturalist realist, should seek to explain how cognizing a property can by itself rationally commit to action. (The assumption in question may not be one that Ridge himself in the end accepts.) But it is fine for a realist to say that whether there is rational commitment to action depends on how—under what guise, or mode of presentation, or description—the property is cognized. Cognition of the property need not in and of itself be what is committing.

8.5 Creeping Minimalism

The problem of *creeping minimalism* (introduced under that name in Dreier 2004) is a certain problem concerning how to distinguish a realist position from a sophisticated antirealism. Even an expressivist can allow that normative judgments are true, by using a so-called deflationist or "minimalist" view on truth, on which to call a truth-bearer p true more or less just is to say: p. Such an expressivist can also mimic the realist's talk of, e.g., facts, adopting a corresponding minimalist construal of facts-talk. (It is a fact that p if and only if p.) A corresponding minimalism can also be proposed concerning talk of properties and propositions. It can be proposed that the schema

"S" expresses the proposition that S

provides a full theory of proposition-expression (where for "S" any declarative sentence of the language can be substituted), and that the schema

x has the property of being F iff x is F

---

[13] Well, there is a complication. Ridge seems to bring up two different things in the passage quoted. One, seemingly, is whether cognition of the supposed property in question rationally commits. The other is whether one can cognize the property but go on to ask "what is it to me?". This latter issue *sounds* like it is about whether cognition of the property serves to motivate. That is different from whether cognition of the property rationally commits. I briefly discussed the supposed connection between normativity and motivation in Chapter 5. I suspect, given the context, that the "what is it to me?" is not supposed to be about motivation, and at any rate, in the present discussion in the main text I don't intend to discuss motivation.

provides a full theory of properties (where for "F" any meaningful predicate of the language can be substituted).[14] Minimalism can further be defended concerning assertion and belief: any ordinary utterance of a declarative sentence counts as an assertion, and belief is related analytically to assertion through the principle that if someone sincerely makes an assertion then she has a belief that can be expressed by the sentence used.

If indeed minimalism can be defended regarding all these notions, then the problem arises of how to distinguish expressivism from realism. Helping herself to minimalism, the would-be expressivist can say that normative sentences are truth-apt and express propositions, that normative predicates stand for properties, that ordinary utterances of normative sentences are assertions, and that these sentences express beliefs. But what then distinguishes her from a realist?

The discussion of creeping minimalism in some ways parallels some main themes in this book. In each case we have a standard kind of characterization of realism; in each case we have some considerations that seem to suggest that for some purposes the characterization does not state a sufficient condition. I have been concerned to show that mere realism does not suffice for the truth of ardent realism. The challenge of creeping minimalism is that also a quasi-realist can accept the statements ordinarily used to characterize realism.

But although the issues are analogous, they are different. A solution to the problem of creeping minimalism is not immediately a solution to the present problem. In outline, a solution to the creeping minimalism problem would be to provide a distinction between mere minimal notions of truth and reference and more substantive notions of truth and reference, and then characterize realism in terms of substantive truth. But even if the creeping minimalism problem could be solved that way, the present problems remain. This is easily seen from the fact that even if we stipulate a distinction between minimal and more substantive notions of truth and reference, and that normative statements are apt for substantive truth (and some atomic ones are substantively true), that is not enough to vindicate ardent realism. Bad Guy's statements, about what is right* and wrong*, can likewise be substantively true. Nor does a solution to the present problems immediately help with the problem of creeping minimalism. I am helping myself to the talk of reference-determination, without pretending that I have anything to say that meets the challenge of appropriately distinguishing between minimal and more substantive notions of reference.

What is more serious, the sort of theory that I have argued the ardent realist does best to adopt—an Alternative-unfriendly theory—presents problems for important purported solutions to the problem of creeping minimalism. Let me explain.

---

[14] There is more to be said about the proper formulation of the schemata, and whether there even is an acceptable formulation. For my purposes I will simply take for granted that there is some appropriate formulation available to the minimalist.

Dreier's own suggested solution to the problem of creeping minimalism is to appeal to explanation; specifically, what to appeal to explains our beliefs and judgments. By "explanation," Dreier here does not mean causal explanation or etiology. Instead he is concerned with what is sometimes called "metaphysical" explanation: what does the fact that you believe that such-and-such *consist in*. Dreier suggests that

expressivists are distinguished by their claim that there is nothing to making a normative judgment over and above being in a state that plays a certain "non-cognitive" psychological role, a role more like desire than it is like factual belief.

He immediately goes on, "to explain what it is to make a moral judgment, we need not mention any normative properties."[15] What Dreier suggests in these two passages is by no means obviously equivalent. In the former passage, he appeals to a distinction between psychological roles; in the latter, he talks about the need to mention (normative) properties. The suggestions are equivalent given the assumption that if a state has the role of a factual belief, then in an explanation of what it is to be in that state, some property it is about must be mentioned.

Why would there be a need to mention a property a state is about for that state to be a factual belief? Dreier does not say. One possibility is that there is some sort of content externalism in the background. Maybe for the state to be what it is, there needs to be the right sort of causal link between properties in the world and the state obtaining? A problem regarding this diagnosis of what is going on in Dreier is that content externalism is general, and would seem to apply to all contentful states, whether factual beliefs or not.

But suppose I have the following view on a class of mental states. These states are factual beliefs with content. But what makes these states factual beliefs is the fact that they have the (narrow or internal) cognitive roles that they do. When one of these states is about a property, this is so because the property stands in the right relation to the cognitive role in question. Compare the conceptual-role view on the logical connectives. What makes it true that a speaker uses the concept conjunction is that she has a concept with the right sort of (narrow) cognitive role, and the explanation of why this concept has the semantic value it has, the conjunction operation, is that this operation stands in the right relation to the cognitive role. For example, if the concept has this semantic value then the inferences we are disposed to make are truth-preserving.

This sort of view, whatever in the end its fate, is prima facie a coherent view. But it does not seem to be a view on which the properties the states are about figure in a metaphysical explanation of what it is to be in that state. The explanation need only advert to the cognitive role in question. It may be that, necessarily, the state is about

---

[15]   Dreier (2004), p. 39.

what property it is about by virtue of the cognitive role. But even so, one need not mention the property in an account of the nature of the state. So Dreier would seem to have to deny that this view is coherent.

One reason why this sort of problem case is relevant is that the kind of view just described is like the view concerning the normative that I have proposed the ardent realist does best to adopt. On this view on the normative, normative beliefs are factual and about certain normative properties, but he defends a kind of cognitive role view on the content of normative expressions and concepts.

A friend of this view could in principle still sign off on everything Dreier says when describing the expressivist's stance, to repeat:

expressivists are distinguished by their claim that there is nothing to making a normative judgment over and above being in a state that plays a certain "non-cognitive" psychological role, a role more like desire than it is like factual belief

and "to explain what it is to make a moral judgment, we need not mention any normative properties."[16]

Overall, then, the kinds of views I have called attention to help problematize the creeping minimalism worry (again, insofar as this worry is worth taking seriously to begin with). Far from solving that problem, they exacerbate it.[17]

---

[16] There is a discussion in the literature of the relationship between Wedgwood's view—which I have presented as a paradigm of the kind of view that the ardent realist does well to adopt—and Gibbard's expressivist view. Both Wedgwood and Gibbard assign a central role to normative role in their theories of the contents of normative expressions and concepts, and they both allow that normative sentences are truth-apt. How then can they be distinguished? Blackburn and Sinclair (2006) suggest the following:

> The difference between Gibbard's view and those that more commonly go under the label "descriptivist" is in their explanation of our practice of making normative judgements. Descriptivists hold that some part of the explanation of that practice must involve seeing normative judgements as tracking or attempting to track some sort of property, natural or non-natural. Expressivists deny that the explanation of the practice will involve any such component. This, Gibbard agrees, is the essence of expressivism. (p. 703f)

The talk of "tracking" properties is not very helpful absent further elaboration. Given minimalism about property talk, Gibbard too can say that normative judgments are *about* properties, and he can say, for example, that the judgment that φ-ing is right is true iff φ-ing has the property of being right. It is not obvious that "tracking" a property needs to come to more than this. Maybe the talk of "tracking" properties can be taken to amount to more, but it would need to be said just what this something more might be. As for Blackburn and Sinclair's talk of "explanation of the practice," the same remarks apply as applied to Dreier's appeal to explanation talk. Cannot also Wedgwood say that the explanation of the practice of making normative judgments need not involve talk of properties tracked? Properties are indeed tracked on a Wedgwood-style view, but it is not clear that this carries any load in the *explanation* of the practice of making normative judgments: this practice can be explained simply by appeal to how we form preferences.

[17] There are other potential problems regarding the suggestion that one can distinguish between the realist and the quasirealist by appeal to explanation. It intuitively does not seem necessary to hold that normative properties have explanatory roles to be a realist. Can I not be a realist while holding that normative properties are all Compare the philosophy of mind. Epiphenomenalist dualism faces its share of problems. But it can hardly reasonably be suggested that the dualist in question fails to be realist about the mental because of her insistence that mental properties are epiphenomenal.

Dreier presents the creeping minimalism worry as a serious problem, and the problem is generally regarded as serious. It is not clear to me that this assessment of the problem is correct. It is by no means clear that there are minimalist notions of truth, propositions, properties, assertion, and belief that capture these phenomena to the extent that there is nothing that can be said to distinguish substantive notions of truth, or propositions, or . . . from their minimalist counterparts; and the problem only arises on the supposition that they do capture this. There is a risk that the debate over creeping minimalism devolves into something less than interesting. If one theorist says, "Spotting the minimalist expressivist that there can be minimalist notions of A, B, and C, can one distinguish between minimalist expressivism and realism," and another one responds that one can state the distinction in terms of notion D, the first can in principle say "but what if one also spots the minimalist expressivist that there can be a minimalist notion of D"—and the game can go on.

Attention to Alternative-unfriendly views presents problems also for other kinds of attempts to characterize the theoretical map. Ridge (2014a) says that expressivism is better seen as a *metasemantic* thesis than as a semantic thesis (where a semantic theory characterizes meanings and a metasemantic theory is about that in virtue of which expressions have the meanings they do). But a problem for Ridge's proposal is that as far as metasemantics is concerned, Alternative-unfriendly theories do seem more akin to expressivist theories than to other kinds of purportedly realist theories. They emphasize normative role, and the role of normative role in the determination of other semantic properties, in a way otherwise associated with expressivist theories.

8.6 Essential Contestability

Ever since W.B. Gallie (1956) introduced it into the literature, the notion of essential contestability has held some appeal for those theorizing about the normative.[18] Their thought is that somehow essential contestability characterizes the realm of the normative. There arguably is a clear intuition that the normative somehow characteristically admits of substantive disagreement, even if the specific normative

---

[18] Gallie actually spoke of what is essentially *contested*. But like most contributors to the literature post-Gallie, I take the liberty of instead speaking of the essentially contest*able*.

Among authors who appeal to essential contestability to help characterize the normative (or "evalu-ative") are Roberts (2013) who takes essential contestability to be a necessary for being normative, Wiggins (1987) (pp. 198–9, 207) who describes normative language generally by appealing to essential contestability (p. 207 of book version), and Dancy (1996) who tentatively claims that *only* the normative is essentially contestable (he says that the "natural" cannot be, and context indicates that by the "natural" he means the non-normative). MacIntyre (1973): "Normative debate is ineliminable from the question of how the concept of education is to be applied. The concept, like those of political parties or science—or for that matter of bourgeoisie or of tragic drama—turns out to be essentially contestable, an expression I borrow from Professor W. B. Gallie" (p. 7). For further references, see Väyrynen (2014).

Of course, one can in principle take essential contestability to be an important notion without seeing it as helpful in characterizing the realm of the normative.

concepts that Gallie and many after him have described as essentially contestable are thick concepts.

In this section I will talk about the idea of essential contestability and the idea that the realm of the normative can be characterized in terms of this. Much of what I have to say will be negative. But toward the end of the section I will relate back to the views that have been highlighted earlier in the book, and outline how the intuitive sense that there is something to Gallie's idea of essential contestability can be accommodated in the present framework.

Gallie not only introduced the general notion of essential contestability but also presented some supposed conditions for when a concept is an essentially contestable concept (an ECC):

(G-I)   it must be appraisive in the sense that it signifies or accredits some kind of valued achievement.

(G-II)   This achievement must be of an internally complex character, for all that its worth is attributed to it as a whole.

(G-III)   Any explanation of its worth must therefore include reference to the respective contributions of its various parts or features; yet prior to experimentation there is nothing absurd or contradictory in any one of a number of possible rival descriptions of its total worth, one such description setting its component parts or features in one order of importance, a second setting them in a second order, and so on. In fine, the accredited achievement is initially variously describable.

(G-IV)   The accredited achievement must be of a kind that admits of considerable modification in the light of changing circumstances; and such modification cannot be prescribed or predicted in advance. For convenience I shall call the concept of any such achievement "open" in character.[19]

Gallie describes these conditions as "the four most important necessary conditions to which any essentially contested concept must comply."[20] Gallie adds three more conditions, but I will focus on the four just mentioned. In focusing on these conditions, I follow the lead of Pekka Väyrynen's recent discussion of essential contestability (2014).[21]

---

[19] Gallie (1956), p. 171f.   [20] Ibid., p. 172.
[21] However, Evnine (2014) stresses the importance for Gallie of the conditions I don't bring up in the main text, while noting that those conditions tend to be downplayed (p. 122fn5). Evnine may have a point about Gallie's specific view, but the reason the conditions mentioned in the main text tend to be emphasized is that they are more reasonably thought to be closely tied to the general intuition.
  Gallie's fifth condition is that "each party recognizes the fact that its own use of it is contested by those of other parties, and ... each party must have at least some appreciation of the different criteria in the light of which the other parties claim to be applying the concept in question. More simply, to use an essentially contested concept means to use it against other uses and to recognize that one's own use of it has to be maintained against these other uses. Still more simply, to use an essentially contested concept means to use it both aggressively and defensively" (p. 172). The sixth condition is that an essentially contestable concept must be derived "from an original exemplar whose authority is acknowledged by all the contestant users of the concept" (p. 180). The seventh condition is that it be probable or plausible "that the continuous

Much of the discussion of essential contestability has tended not to focus much on Gallie's specific criteria. (Väyrynen's recent discussion is one important exception.) And it is important to distinguish between the intuitive motivation behind essential contestability and the specific criteria proposed by Gallie. The intuitive motivation has to do with the sense that normative concepts give rise to disputes that are for general reasons hard or impossible to settle. One way to spell out the intuition is to appeal to something like what has come to be called faultless disagreements, and say that where C is a normative concept, there can be faultless disagreement over whether something is C. A case of faultless disagreement in the sense at issue is a case where there is disagreement but neither party is guilty of a mistake, where a party is guilty of a mistake, in the relevant sense, already if what she maintains is false (it does not matter if she is epistemically justified). This is the stronger way to spell out the intuition. On a weaker way to spell out the intuition, the intuition is simply that it is really hard, perhaps in practice impossible, to settle the dispute in question.

Let us call a concept which is essentially contestable in the intuitive sense EC-intuitive, and let us call a concept which satisfies Gallie's conditions EC-Gallie. There are then three questions we can distinguish between: What is the relation between a concept's being normative and its being EC-intuitive? What is the relation between a concept's being normative and its being EC-Gallie? What is the relation between a concept's being EC-intuitive and its being EC-Gallie?

Start with the last question. On the face of it, satisfaction of (G-IV) plausibly entails being EC-intuitive: if a concept satisfies (G-IV) it permits of intractable disagreements. But (G-IV), as well as the intuitive understanding of essential contestability, admits of stronger and weaker interpretations. On a stronger understanding of (G-IV) it is in principle impossible to say exactly what the "achievement" must be like. On a weaker understanding, (G-IV) speaks only of what is in practice impossible. A similar distinction can be drawn with respect to EC-intuitive: on the strong interpretation (the one I gave voice to in the previous paragraph), normative concepts are supposed to give rise to in principle intractable disagreements; on a weaker interpretation, the disagreements are merely in practice intractable and are not faultless in the sense indicated. For the claim about the entailment to hold, one must not understand (G-IV) weakly but EC-intuitive strongly. Since (G-II) and (G-III) state preconditions for (G-IV), anything that satisfies (G-IV) satisfies these conditions too. But why would being EC-intuitive have to entail any of the complexity mentioned in (G-II)–(G-IV)? Questions about what is the right thing to do seem to give rise to intractable disagreements as much as questions about what is democracy do (to mention one example of a concept sometimes mentioned as essentially contestable), so it is as attractive to think that thin normative concepts are EC-intuitive as it is to think that thick normative concepts are. But the thinnest concepts

competition for acknowledgement as between the contestant users of the concept, enables the original exemplar's achievement to be sustained and/or developed in optimum fashion" (p. 180).

don't appear to have the complexity that characterizes concepts such as concepts like democracy; instead they are frequently said to be simple and indefinable.[22]

Turn now to the relation between being EC-Gallie and being normative. As noted, some theorists take essential contestability to somehow characterize the realm of the normative. I take it that by "concept C is appraisive" Gallie means that concept C is normative (as a matter of content), so (G-I) alone ensures that there is a connection but it does so by brute force. (G-I) seems rather disconnected from the other conditions, and satisfaction of (G-II)–(G-IV) does not seem to be sufficient for being normative. Other complex concepts too seem to give rise to faultless disagreement. By what I said in the previous paragraph, satisfaction of (G-II)–(G-IV) is hardly necessary for being normative.

As for the relation between being EC-intuitive and being normative, what I have to say about that is clear already from the above. Maybe it is plausible that normative concepts are the source of intractable disagreements. But why couldn't non-normative concepts too give rise to such intractable disagreements? Moreover, even if some normative concepts do indeed give rise to intractable disagreements, reasons to doubt that they *all* do have prominently been discussed in the literature. For example, Philippa Foot (1958) famously uses thick concepts (her example is the concept *rude*) to argue that moral arguments are not always liable to breakdown. (I will criticize Foot's reasoning in Chapter 9.) To be sure, Foot's argument is precisely only to the effect that moral arguments are not always liable to breakdown, but it might be natural for a friend of Foot's line of reasoning to think that at least thick normative concepts are not more prone to give rise to intractable disagreements than other types of concept are.

In his (2014), Väyrynen at some length develops concerns related to some concerns I mentioned above relating to EC-Gallie, and with close attention to how Gallie actually reasons. Väyrynen notes that Gallie takes (G-II)–(G-IV) to secure (G-I). Gallie says, "my suspicion is that no purely naturalistic concept will be found conforming" to (G-I)–(G-IV), and the context strongly suggests that he is using "naturalistic" to mean non-normative: he contrasts being "naturalistic" with being "appraisive."[23] In response, Väyrynen argues that many terms or concepts that satisfy (G-II)–(G-IV) aren't normative. Väyrynen focuses on gradable expressions that are multidimensional and whose dimensions admit of different relative weightings in the interpretation of the expression. "Painful" is the example he mostly focuses on.[24]

---

[22] As the example of democracy illustrates, some concepts that have been prominently argued to be essentially contestable are not uncontroversially normative. Given independent argument that all essentially contestable concepts are normative, one can argue that a concept is normative by arguing that it is essentially contestable. But the fact that some prominent examples are not clearly normative problematizes any case that could be made for linking essential contestability to normativity.

[23] Gallie (1956), p. 174fn2.

[24] It can be objected that perhaps "painful" is normative (and perhaps even its supposed essential contestability shows it to be so). Väyrynen adduces some purported reasons for thinking that it isn't, and

As Väyrynen notes, such gradable expressions satisfy (G-II) and (G-III). It is not immediately guaranteed that they satisfy (G-IV), but Väyrynen says that when one of these terms "is context-sensitive, it will be particularly clear that the relative weightings may be modified in ways that cannot be predicted or prescribed in advance; this will secure (G-IV)."[25] Given that these gradable expressions aren't normative, it is then clear that (G-II)–(G-IV) can be satisfied without (G-I) being so.

I am inclined to believe, with Väyrynen, that one can construct counterexamples to Gallie's claim. But a possible response on Gallie's behalf is to query whether (G-IV) really is satisfied in the case Väyrynen describes. What does the talk of "cannot be prescribed or predicted in advance" in the statement of (G-IV) mean? As I have mentioned, this talk admits of a weaker and a stronger interpretation. Given the weak interpretation, the gradable expressions Väyrynen focuses on arguably do satisfy (G-IV). Given the strong interpretation, they arguably do not, and Väyrynen does not have a counterexample. On the other hand, (G-IV) strongly interpreted is considerably more controversial. Väyrynen can just reformulate his case. He can say: given the weak interpretation of (G-IV), (G-IV) does not state anything which plausibly sets the normative apart from the non-normative; given the strong interpretation, (G-IV) is hardly plausible even in the case of the normative.

The distinction between the weak and the strong interpretation also relates to something I said above. I stated above that satisfaction of (G-IV) entails being EC-intuitive. But that is correct only given what I have now called the strong interpretation.

While the thinnest normative concepts don't seem to have the conceptual complexity that might characterize some or all thick concepts—they don't seem to possess complex analyses—there are in some sense different *criteria*, considerations with evidential weight, that weigh against each other when we decide whether something is good or right. It could be insisted that this is all that the talk of internal complexity in concepts should be taken to amount to in the context. (In support of this it should be noted that in the literature on thick concepts, many authors take thick concepts to be unanalyzable—the descriptive and normative elements cannot be disentangled.[26] If such unanalyzability precluded being essentially contestable in the sense given by Gallie's specific conditions, thick concepts would not be essentially contestable in that sense either.) I don't think that this by itself salvages the idea that (G-II)–(G-IV) state a necessary condition on normativity. For the thesis that they amount to such a necessary condition demands that they hold of *all* normative concepts, and the thesis would demand for its truth that no *possible* normative concept fails to be complex.

---

mentions other possible examples, "is the same species as" and "money," should the specific example "painful" be found wanting (p. 477f).

[25] Väyrynen (2014), p. 475.

[26] See e.g. McDowell (1979, 1981), Williams (1985), Dancy (1996), Roberts (2011, 2013b) and Kirchin (2010, 2013b).

In a recent discussion, Debbie Roberts says that concepts that are essentially contestable "*characteristically*, rather than just conceivably, admit of substantive disagreement."[27] I am not sure exactly what Roberts means by "characteristically" in the context, but will not pause on the matter. (If our community became more homogeneous so many normative disputes no longer arose, would that on Roberts' view mean that some relevant concepts had ceased to be essentially contestable?) The disagreements are not just disagreements about what the concepts apply to but the disagreements concern "competing conceptions of the content of the concept."[28] Roberts further says, "what is essentially contestable in the case of essentially contestable concepts is whether a particular set of lower-level features give rise to the real similarity or essence of the property in question."[29] And in connection with this, she emphasizes that "it seems possible that evaluative disagreement can persist even if the disputants agree on all relevant non-evaluative features present in a particular case."[30] If essential contestability is cashed out in this latter way, then it appears that there will be essential contestability also outside the normative realm. In many cases where one has higher-level and lower-level discourse (say, psychological and physical discourse), disagreements stated in terms of the higher-level discourse can rationally persist given agreement on the lower-level facts. Roberts is well aware of this. Although she appeals to essential contestability in the context of a discussion of what characterizes the normative (or the evaluative, in her terminology), she only speaks of essential contestability as a necessary condition for being normative. However, the point about how essential contestability, in Roberts' sense, generalizes beyond the normative also indicates how Roberts' way of cashing out the notion fails to get at the intuitive motivation behind it. Surely to speak of something as essentially contestable is somehow to say that it cannot be settled; but saying that it cannot be settled whether p on the basis of facts at a lower level is itself a far cry from saying that p cannot be settled full stop.

Generally, I doubt that there is any way to rescue the conception of essential contestability handed down to us by Gallie. I have despaired over how best to cash the general essential contestability intuition while it still plausibly characterizes the normative, and I have presented problems regarding the specific conditions (G-I)–(G-IV) that Gallie presented. But several of the views that have come up in discussion earlier go some way toward respecting intuitions underlying thinking of normative concepts as, in some intuitive sense, essentially contestable. Moreover, the normative comes out special so that the "contestability" as cashed out is not, for example, unknowability as may be found in other discourses as well.[31]

---

[27] Roberts (2013), p. 89.   [28] Roberts (2013a), p. 89.   [29] Ibid., p. 90.
[30] Ibid., p. 90. Roberts uses "evaluative" where I here use "normative."
[31] Even if, contrary to what I have argued, normativity of concepts could be elucidated by appeal to the notion of essential contestable concepts, the question of what makes a property normative would remain. The idea would have to be that normative properties would have to be such that no matter how they are conceptualized, claims about what instantiate them will be essentially contestable.

Even though I am skeptical of Gallie's claims about essential contestability, and about the idea that the normative can be characterized by appeal to the notion of essential contestability, there is something intuitively plausible about the idea that the normative has a special connection to essential contestability. And several of the views that have been characterized throughout the course of this book can to some extent make good on this. Let me briefly outline how.

Recall first the deflationary view I discussed back in Chapter 2. This is a view according to which an Alternative-friendly view is true, and there moreover is no Further Question of any kind. There are only facts about what is "right" in one sense, "right" in another sense, etc. Given a deflationary view, a certain kind of "essential contestability" phenomenon arises. There is nothing to suggest that it is essentially contestable what is "right" in any given sense. But it will be—in one intuitive sense—essentially contestable which "right" to use. Suppose first that two communities using different notions of "right" come into contact with one another. Given the practical significance of judgments about what is "right" (in either sense), the communities may well not rest content with the fact that they employ different notions of "right": there is still the question of which notion of rightness is to guide one's actions. And this dispute will, if there is no Further Question, be intractable in a distinctive fashion. There will simply be no fact by virtue of which one disputant wins.

Now, maybe there are not actually different linguistic communities like this. But on the deflationary view, there will be many different possible notions of "right" and given the fact that there is diversity of normative views in our society, it is reasonable to speculate that it is to some extent semantically indeterminate which notion of right *our* "right" expresses. It is then also natural to speculate that disputes about what is right are to some extent questions about how to precisify our actual "right." But if there is no Further Question, then it will be right1 to precisify "right" one way, right2 to precisify it another way, etc., *and that is all there is to it.*

Suppose now instead that there is a Further Question which is ineffable. More fully, the supposition is that an Alternative-friendly view is correct, and there is a Further Question about which "right" to use—but this Further Question is ineffable. On this view, too, a kind of essential contestability intuition is respected. For what users of different notions of "right" disagree about is then something that cannot even be properly stated. By virtue of that, this disagreement differs from other disagreements over what is unknowable, or even where there is no fact of the matter. The situation in relevant respects is much like it is under the deflationary view, for while there is a Further Question it cannot be stated.

Suppose lastly that an Alternative-unfriendly theory is true. This is a different scenario but one can still capture something in the vicinity of the essential contestability intuition. Above I noted that there are stronger and weaker claims here. The stronger claim amounts to a faultless disagreement claim. The weaker claim is just a claim to the effect that it is in some ways especially hard to settle disputes of the relevant kind. Compare here Roberts, who insists that agreement over the lower-level facts is not sufficient to establish agreement over normative facts. Above I said that what Roberts points to is not something that is peculiar to the normative case, but she only points to something that happens in many cases where one is dealing with higher- and lower-level facts. But if an Alternative-unfriendly view is correct, then the relation between the normative and the non-normative is more problematic than in other cases: for given such a metasemantically radical view, the reference of normative terms and concepts is determined in a different way from the way in which the reference of descriptive terms and concepts is determined.[32]

---

[32] Compare here the remarks on the open-question argument in footnote 42 of Chapter 2. The thought there too was that the conceptual gap seems more serious in a particular way in the case of the normative versus the descriptive, because there are significant metasemantic differences between these terms.

9

Thick Concepts

I have been concerned with the nature of normative concepts and the nature of normative properties. Throughout the discussion I have in appropriate places brought up slurs and thick concepts, although the focus has tended to be on thin concepts and the properties they ascribe. In this chapter I will discuss a number of issues relating to thick concepts. According to one rough characterization of the thick—I will shortly discuss serious problems with the characterization—thick concepts are value concepts with significant descriptive content. According to another rough characterization, thick concepts are more specific than thin ones. While one can see how these characterizations might end up equivalent, I think it is also clear how they might come apart.

Consideration of thick concepts is relevant to present concerns in part because an adequate characterization of normativity ought to be general enough to cover normative concepts and properties of all kinds. However, there are of course many different kinds of normative concepts and I obviously will not seek to address all the different cases. One reason why thick concepts are especially relevant to consider in the present context is the following. What I have been concerned with when talking about alternative normative concepts has been, in part, that our actual thinnest normative concepts may be such that it is not they but some counterparts that we ought[1] to use in our normative thinking. In the case of the thin normative concepts, the concern is somewhat abstract. But in the case of the thick, there do seem to be actual examples of objectionable concepts—in Chapter 4, I mentioned *lewd*, *perverted*, and *chaste* as examples that have come up in the literature. While one can expect the cases of the thin and the thick to be different, comparison of the thick may prove instructive.

9.1 What are Thick Concepts?

Much of the discussion in this chapter will be centered on the question of how to characterize what it is for a concept to be thick. I will first address this question without relating much to the main themes in the book; later in the chapter I will relate back to these main themes.

---

[1] As before: yes, there are problems about how to express this.

To see that there are problems regarding how best to characterize thickness, consider how certain characterizations given in the literature fail. Here, first, is Allan Gibbard's informal characterization:

(T1)   A term stands for a thick concept if it praises or condemns an action as having a certain property.[2]

This is unsatisfactory. One may be uneasy already about the talk of terms (as opposed to users thereof) praising or condemning actions; and one may be thus uneasy even if one allows that some terms are in and of themselves normative. But take such talk on board. After all, it may be taken to be simply a colorful way of saying that certain terms are conventional means for speakers to praise or condemn actions. There is still a problem. There is as much reason to think that paradigmatic thin terms satisfy the condition stated as there is to think that a term like "courageous" does. "Right" stands for the property of being right. And doesn't this term praise actions as having this property, just as "courageous" praises actions for being courageous? On a non-cognitivist view it can be in principle be denied that "right" stands for a property. But it is clear that Gibbard does not mean his characterization only to be acceptable to a non-cognitivist.

It may be suggested that by "property," Gibbard must have something more specific in mind. What he really suggests is something of the form:

(T1′)   A term stands for a thick concept if it praises or condemns an action as having a certain ___ property.

But what can we put for ___ here? A first thought is: *descriptive*. But what is it for a property to be descriptive? The following may be a natural suggestion. Suppose we can rely on a distinction between descriptive and normative *expressions* (and since we are talking about properties, we can focus on predicates). Then a descriptive property can be said to be one that can be ascribed by a purely descriptive predicate.[3] But with descriptive understood this way, (T1′) faces problems. On, for example, many naturalist theories it is happily embraced that the properties ascribed by thin concepts can also be ascribed by descriptive concepts. What is more, the "thgir" example introduced in Chapter 4 shows that on any metaethical view, all normative properties are descriptive in this sense. What Gibbard would need is a genuine restriction on the properties in question. We get such a restriction on any view on which not all properties are normative. What one puts for ___ can then simply be: *non-normative*. But this faces a different problem. What kind of reason is there to think that every thick concept stands for a property that is non-normative in this

[2] Gibbard (1992), p. 268f. This is the rough, informal characterization Gibbard starts out with. Later in his article he discusses more specific positive proposals. See my (2011a) for discussion of those parts of Gibbard's discussion.
[3] Compare the discussion of (P1) in Chapter 5.

sense? Why could not also thick concepts, and not only thin ones, stand for normative properties? This depends on what normative properties are. The matter was discussed in Chapter 5. I suggested that a normative property is one ascribed by some possible referentially normative predicate. The question then becomes: can some thick normative predicates be referentially normative, assuming some (thin) normative ones are? I return to this later. For now, only note that (T1′) construed as suggested just *assumes* that thick predicates could not ascribe normative properties.

Below I will return to accounts of thick concepts aimed at getting around these problems. But first let me indicate how the problems I have presented for Gibbard's informal characterization arise also for other characterizations of thick concepts, like the ones given by Jonathan Dancy and Bernard Williams. On Dancy's view on thick concepts, a thick concept is, somehow, associated with both a property and an attitude, and these are not in any way separable elements of the concepts, since "the property is best described as that of meriting the attitude, and the attitude is best characterized as the appropriate one given the presence of the property."[4] This is hardly satisfactory. First, Dancy indicates that it is peculiar to thick concepts that they are associated with both a property and an attitude. But as already stressed, on all natural views even thin moral concepts are associated with properties. Nor do the other constraints Dancy mentions avoid the problem. Consider the properties standardly held to be ascribed by *good* and *right*: the property of being good and of being right. It is far from obvious that these properties are not best described as that of meriting the relevant attitude. Or take the relevant attitudes: it is far from obvious that the attitude is not best described as the attitudes it is appropriate to adopt toward what is good and what is right, respectively. Both these speculations can be doubted. Some theorists will think that they have a better description of the property or the attitude. But the point I wish to make is only that it is no less antecedently plausible that Dancy's characterization is satisfied by the concept expressed by "good" than that it is satisfied by thick concepts.

Williams says of thick concepts that they are "world-guided," meaning that their application "is determined by what the world is like."[5] Thin concepts, by contrast, are supposed to have more of a purely action-guiding role. This faces the same type of problem as the characterizations offered by Gibbard and Dancy. Isn't also the application of the concept good determined by what the world is like? One might try to get around this objection by saying that what is special about thick concepts is determined by what the world is like *in descriptive respects*. But this again faces problems we have already seen: specifically, doesn't this too go also for the concept *good*?

Return also to the characterization of thick concepts as being different from thin ones in having *descriptive content*. The idea would be that while thin concepts are purely normative, thick concepts are normative concepts that in addition have descriptive

---

[4] Dancy (1996), p. 268.   [5] Williams (1985), p. 129.

content. But what is it to have descriptive content? If standing for some property or other is sufficient for having descriptive content, then unless some form of traditional antirealism is true, then all normative concepts have descriptive content. If the condition is that of standing for some non-normative property or other, then thick concepts have descriptive content only if the properties they ascribe are not normative. One may instead think that a normative concept's having descriptive content is a matter of having conceptual connections to concepts that are purely descriptive. Worth noting is that a characterization of thickness in these terms is only available to those who believe there are conceptual connections of the requisite kind, contra both followers of Quine and the more recent arguments due to Williamson (e.g. 2007). A different concern is that if there are these conceptual connections at all, it may reasonably be thought that also thin concepts are conceptually linked to the descriptive. Maybe "ought" conceptually implies "can." One would then have to conceive of the difference between the thin and the thick in terms of how substantive the conceptual links to the descriptive are.

As illustrated, it is far from easy to say what distinguishes thick concepts, and one central puzzle concerning the thick is: *what distinguishes thick normative concepts as such?*

Sometimes in the literature, the thin/thick distinction is discussed not as a distinction between different classes of *concepts* but as a distinction between different classes of *properties*. See, for example, Dancy (1993) and McNaughton and Rawling (2000). What might thick properties be? This will be properly discussed only later in the chapter. For now, simply note that several of the proposals we have seen for how to understand what thick concepts are even promise to help make sense of the idea of thick properties. If, along the lines of what Gibbard proposed, what makes a concept thick is that it somehow combines a property and an attitude, then the thickness has nothing to do with the property itself. Nor do I see even how to begin applying Williams' characterization in the case of properties. Dancy's characterization is different in this regard. If acceptable, it could perhaps serve also to show what it is for a property to be thick: a thick property is one best described as meriting a particular attitude.

9.2 Sufficiency and Emptiness

There are also other puzzles regarding thick concepts. Thick concepts are sometimes used in arguments to the effect that some normative sentences can be analytically entailed by descriptive sentences, contrary to a common belief (that no "ought" can ever be analytically or conceptually entailed by an "is"). One well-known argument of this kind is found in Philippa Foot's classic "Moral Arguments" (1958). In that article, Foot sets out to argue against what she calls the "breakdown theory" in ethics, according to which disputes about the applicability of an ethical concept are always liable to breakdown, in that there is no objective way of settling ethical arguments.

Foot's example is the concept expressed by "rude"—a concept that would be classed as thick given the thin/thick distinction. She notes first that "it expresses disapproval, is meant to be used when an action is to be discouraged, implies that other things being equal the behaviour to which it is applied will be avoided by the speaker, and so on."[6] The concept expressed by "rude" is *normative* (recall, yet again, that I am using "normative" in a broad sense). It is a value concept; specifically a negative value concept. But the concept also has descriptive conditions associated with it. In Foot's words, "it can only be used where certain descriptions apply."[7] She goes on, "The right account of the situation in which it is correct to say that a piece of behaviour is rude is, I think, that this kind of behaviour causes offense by indicating lack of respect."[8]

Since Foot says that "rude" can *only* be used where certain descriptions apply, it may be thought that her point is only that satisfaction of those descriptions is *necessary* for the applicability of the word "rude." But from the discussion that follows it is clear that she regards satisfaction of the descriptive conditions in question as *sufficient* for the applicability of "rude":

Given that reference to offence is to be included in any account of the concept of rudeness, we may ask what the relation is between the assertion that these conditions of offence are fulfilled—let us call it O—and the statement that a piece of behaviour is rude—let us call it R. Can someone who accepts the proposition O (that this kind of offence is caused) deny the proposition R (that the behaviour is rude)? I should have thought that this was just what he could not do, for if he says that it is not rude, we shall stare, and ask him what sort of behavior is rude, and what is he to say?[9]

On Foot's view, the concept expressed by "rude" is such that as a conceptual matter, anything that satisfies certain associated descriptive conditions falls under it; and since the concept is normative, we can conclude that if something falls under it, then it is bad, and is to be disapproved of. This is what allows Foot to argue against the breakdown theory in ethics. Notice incidentally that if Foot's argument here works, Foot also provides a promising solution to the problem of what distinguishes thick concepts from thin ones: if C is a thick concept then there is some substantive descriptive concept D such that "X is C" follows analytically from "x is D." (The "substantive" is there to rule out concepts like *is not self-identical*. Maybe important problems are skirted here.) Notice that this is an account of thickness that crucially relates thick concepts to descriptive concepts, not descriptive properties.

There is something intuitively attractive about Foot's outlook. But it is still clear that it must be rejected. As has come up in earlier chapters (Chapters 1 and 4), some

---

[6] Foot (1958), p. 102. [7] Ibid.

[8] Ibid. Even unclarity to the side, one may reasonably doubt whether Foot here has found an analytically sufficient purely descriptive condition for the applicability of "rude." Here is one worry. Does "causes offense by indicating lack of respect" mean *actually causes offense* or *would cause justifiable offense*? If the latter, then the condition is not descriptive. If the former, it fails to be extensionally adequate.

[9] Foot (1958), p. 103.

thick concepts are, somehow, *objectionable*. Somehow these concepts seem to pre-suppose or embody values that ought not really to be endorsed. Gibbard (1992) mentions *lewd* as an example: he does not agree on the view on sexuality which underlies the employment of this concept. Although the topic is not explicitly thick concepts, Graham Priest (1997) in effect argues that *sexually perverted* is an objec-tionable thick concept. While the examples can reasonably be doubted, I do not think that the phenomenon of objectionable thick concepts can be.[10]

The existence of objectionable thick concepts presents problems both for Foot's argument against the breakdown theory, and for the corresponding account of what makes a normative concept thick. Take *lewd*. Suppose the associated descriptive concept to be *is an overt display of sexuality*. (No doubt this is much simplified!) Then, by Foot's reasoning, it follows analytically from "x is an overt display of sexuality" that "x is lewd"; and since *lewd* is a negatively normative concept, it follows analytically from "x is lewd" that "x is (pro tanto) bad." Putting this together, we get that it follows analytically from "x is an overt display of sexuality" that "x is (pro tanto) bad." Someone who happily accepts that descriptive sentences can analytically entail normative ones will not immediately be put off by this. But when we are dealing with an objectionable thick concept, like *lewd*, this is plainly unacceptable. For if we think *lewd* is objectionable, we should also think that "x is (pro tanto) bad" does not follow—let alone analytically follow—from "x is an overt display of sexuality." The sample account of *lewd* is of course simplified. But the general point stands: in the case of objectionable thick concepts, we certainly don't want it to be the case that from "x is D," where x is the, or a, semantically associated description, "x is (pro tanto) bad" analytically follows.

So Foot's argument must go wrong. However, here is the puzzle. There is some-thing highly intuitive about what Foot is saying when she insists sometimes the satisfaction of certain purely descriptive conditions is sufficient for thick concepts to apply. How can this be accommodated, even while, in light of the problem of objectionable thick concepts, we cannot actually accept either Foot's argument against the breakdown theory or the corresponding account of what distinguishes thick concepts from thin ones? We might call this the puzzle of *seeming sufficiency*.

I should immediately further justify calling this a *puzzle*. Not everyone may be on board with the claim that it intuitively seems as though there are analytically sufficient conditions associated with thick concepts. After all, it is common, in discussions of thick concepts, to say that the descriptive element cannot be separated out.[11] But the point I am making can be made without commitment to what these theorists object to. The point is just that even if Foot's argument does not work, a satisfactory account

---

[10] If, as some writers do—see Elstein and Hurka (2009) and Blackburn (1984, 1992)—we include slurs among thick concepts, then it is even clearer that there are objectionable thick concepts.

[11] See e.g. McDowell (1979, 1981), Williams (1985), Dancy (1996), Roberts (2011, 2013b), and Kirchin (2010, 2013b).

of thick concepts should explain the intuitive attractiveness of the argument. Perhaps no notion of analyticity will in fact occur in the explanation. So objections to the idea of analyticity, or to the possibility of analytically separating out a descriptive element, are beside the point. (What is more, the claim that thick concepts are associated with analytically sufficient descriptive conditions does not entail the claim that there are necessary and sufficient descriptive conditions associated with these concepts.)

After having given the argument I summarized above, Foot somewhat qualifies her position:

> It is of course possible to admit O without asserting R, and this will not be like the refusal to say about prunes what one has already said about dried plums. Calling an action "rude" is a concept which a man might want to reject, rejecting the whole practice or praising and blaming embodied in such terms as "polite" and "rude". Such a man would refuse to discuss matters of etiquette, and arguments with him about what is rude would not so much break down as never begin.
>
> The only recourse of the man who refused to accept the things which counted in favour of a moral proposition as giving him reason to do certain things or take up a particular attitude, would be to leave the moral discussion and abjure altogether the use of moral terms.[12]

This is a kind of lack of nerve on Foot's part (even if, given what I have argued, this lack of nerve is appropriate). As mentioned above, Foot's purpose in bringing up the argument concerning *rude* is to argue against the so-called breakdown theory. But given what Foot here admits, she opens the door to a "second-order" breakdown theory: a breakdown theory concerning arguments over whether to engage in a particular practice of praising and blaming.[13]

There is a more damaging point to be made. If there is cause for lack of nerve, Foot's concession doesn't go far enough. If "x is D," for some descriptive concept D (perhaps *the conditions of offense are fulfilled*), really analytically entails "x is (pro tanto) bad" via analytically entailing "x is C" for some thick concept C (perhaps *rude*), my refusal to use the relevant thick concept only amounts to my refusing to give expression to certain truths—that from the fact that x is D it follows that x is (pro tanto) bad. The *facts* don't change!

Several other theorists aside from Foot who acknowledge the existence of objectionable thick concepts also take the route of saying that we simply should not employ them.[14] But this piece of advice, even if sound, leaves important issues unresolved. I've just mentioned the point that your not using a concept does not change what it applies to, nor what is entailed by the concept's applying to some given object. But the theoretical problem underlying this point is just that stressed earlier: where and how does Foot's reasoning go wrong?

---

[12] Foot (1958), p. 510.

[13] Glass (1973) makes this point, and the phrase "lack of nerve" is from him.

[14] See e.g. Priest (1997), Slote (1975), and Brandom (2000), pp. 69ff. Brandom, discussing the example "Boche" (originally from Dummett (1981)), does indicate that "Boche" is true of (some) Germans but otherwise does not get into what exactly "Boche" is true of or how that is determined.

There is another question in the vicinity. Are objectionable thick concepts empty or not? I think one cannot happily say that they are empty. If this is said about *lewd* or *sexually perverted*, just think about behaviors that would be regarded as paradigmatically lewd or paradigmatically sexually perverted. In these cases, modesty prevents me from bringing up really persuasive examples. But then consider "chaste"—and take someone who is a paradigm case of chastity. Is that person not chaste? Of course, if one finds *chaste* objectionable then one will be reluctant to *actually call* any behavior, no matter how paradigmatically chaste, "chaste." But that is a different matter from the question of whether claims to the effect that such behaviors are chaste would be *true*.

Moreover, the supposed emptiness of objectionable thick concepts would not explain the reluctance, on the part of those finding the concepts objectionable, not only to apply them to specific things but also to use these concepts in embedded contexts. Something else must be added to explain that. So the claim that objectionable thick concepts are empty is both intuitively implausible and unable to explain all the relevant data.

Third, I suspect that there is a sense that for C a positive (negative) thick concept, it is somehow part of the content of C that if something is C then it is thereby in that respect good (bad), and if a condition like that is part of the content of a concept, then anything falling under C will have to satisfy the condition. Since, for objectionable positive (negative) concept C, nothing is thereby in that respect good (bad), thick concepts will have to be empty. Talk of what is part of meaning or content is of course vague and impressionistic, and one can in principle decide to use the talk in such a way that the stated reasoning comes out correct. But on one intuitive reading of "part of meaning/content," what is semantically analytic is part of meaning—after all, it is something it is part of competence to be disposed to accept—and given that there can be untrue semantic analyticities, the stated reasoning comes out incorrect.

Based on the above considerations, I hold that the objectionable thick concepts are not empty. Belief to the effect that they are is due to various misconceptions.

Appeal to semantic analyticity also provides the key to an account of thick concepts that promises to solve the puzzles mentioned, and account for the features of thick concepts that have been discussed. Let me call it *the semantic analyticity account*.

Foot's (1958) discussion in effect suggested an account of thick concepts according to which C is a thick concept if and only if

(i)   there is some substantive descriptive concept D such that "x is D" analytically entails "x is C";

(ii)   if C is positive (negative), "x is C" analytically entails "x is (pro tanto) good" ("x is (pro tanto) bad").[15]

---

[15] As at some points earlier in the discussion, for example in Chapter 4, I am using "good" and "bad" as my sample thin notions in characterizations. Alternative formulations using "right" and "wrong", or "ought" or "reason," could be employed instead as far as I am concerned.

This account does not work, as illustrated e.g. by the discussion of objectionable thick concepts. But one gets around this specific problem if "analytically" in (i) and (ii) is understood to mean *semantically* analytically, as follows:

(i′)   there is some substantive descriptive concept D such that "x is D" semantically analytically entails "x is C";

(ii′)   if C is positive (negative), "x is C" semantically analytically entails "x is (pro tanto) good" ("x is (pro tanto) bad").[16]

Semantically analytic entailment is here understood on the model of semantic analyticity generally.

Intuitively: we are only saying that it is *somehow part of the content* of C that "x is C" is entailed by "x is D," and that it is *somehow part of the content* of C that "x is C" entails "x is (pro tanto) good" ("x is (pro tanto) bad"); we are not thereby saying that "x is C" *actually is entailed by* "x is D" and *actually entails* "x is (pro tanto) good" ("x is (pro tanto) bad").

Now recall the puzzles regarding thick concepts that have come up. One was how to account for what distinguishes thick concepts. Conditions (i′) and (ii′) jointly state what it is for a concept to be thick. Another puzzle was that of seeming sufficiency: it concerned how to accommodate the intuitiveness of the type of account suggested by Foot's discussion. The answer to this second puzzle is likewise straightforward. What is defended is a straightforward variant of the account suggested by Foot's discussion.

The friend of semantic analyticity further has a nice account of how there can be non-empty objectionable thick concepts. She can first say that a thick concept can be objectionable by virtue of there being some false but semantically analytic normative claim associated with the concept. As for the non-emptiness, the reference of an expression is what comes closest and close enough to satisfying the principles meaning-constitutive for the expression. A concept associated with a false semantically analytic claim can be non-empty so long as there is some non-empty referent that is close enough. Naturally, problematic questions can be raised with respect to this account of reference-determination. For example, the notion of closeness that is appealed to when it is said that the referent is the closest satisfier can be problematized. But the appeal to semantic analyticity does not give rise to any *new* problems; problems that do not arise for all versions of neo-descriptivism.

---

[16] Accepting also the claim about epistemic justification usually associated with epistemic analyticity would have some clearly counterintuitive consequences. Just by virtue of competence, one would be pro tanto justified in believing that if x is D then x is C, and that if C then x is (say) bad, even in the case of an objectionable thick concept. The best defense of this view on justification seems to me to be to bite the bullet and accept this consequence, but emphasize that pro tanto justification is cheap and that in every realistic case this pro tanto justification is defeated or overridden.

9.3 The Normative Role View and Thick Concepts

I defended the semantic analyticity account of thick concepts in my (2011a). I still think it might be right. But it is now clearer to me that its fate depends crucially on broader issues regarding the nature of normative concepts.

The view I defended in effect seeks to account for the normativity of thick concepts by relating them to the concepts of pro tanto goodness and badness. If one holds the minimalist view on what it is for a concept to be normative, one will be fine with this. But in Chapter 4, I gave reasons for thinking that we should not accept the minimalist view. One especially pertinent reason was that given an Alternative-friendly theory, there will be expressions with the same normative role as our "right" but different in meaning from that expression and not obviously standing in any conceptual entailment relations to it. Communities using such alternative expressions can use what intuitively are thick terms, but thick terms standing in conceptual entailment relations to the normative counterpart instead of to "right." These terms would then not be classed as thick given the current proposal.

A friend of the semantic analyticity account can in principle respond by holding on to (i') as an account of what makes a normative concept thick and say that one simply must revise (ii') as an account of what makes a concept normative in the first place. But suppose we favor a normative role view of what makes a concept normative, as I have argued (Chapter 4) that we should. Given this view, what makes a concept normative is its being associated with a given normative role, as a matter of content. Questions about what it is for a normative concept to be thick can then appear in a different light. This normative role view can in turn come in different flavors. The normative roles can, for example, be as coarse-grained as just being "positive" or "negative," or they can be regarded as considerably more fine-grained, in such a way that different normative concepts we employ will be associated with the same normative role only extremely rarely. The differences in content between different positive and negative normative concepts will then come from elsewhere. Given a coarse-grained version of the normative role view, one can think that differences in semantically analytic connections to descriptive notions make for the differences in content between thick concepts associated with the same (coarse-grained) normative role, and one can still appeal to conditions on the form of (i'). But if one thinks that differences between normative concepts are a matter of more subtle differences between their normative roles, as on a fine-grained view, one may find other views more natural. Then there will be further differences between normative roles, and one can hold that the differences between thin and thick concepts have to do with the kinds of normative roles they are associated with. This would be a rather different kind of view than that underlying appeal to (i') and (ii'). I will now turn to consider the prospects of such alternative views.

Ralph Wedgwood's account of the thick, provided in his (2001), is:

> [the rule for a thick concept] could be exactly like [Wedgwood's rule for a paradigmatic thin concept] except for employing a suitably restricted notion of *preference*. Suppose that this

restricted notion of preference is the idea of a preference-with-respect-to-a-certain-purpose: for example, one might prefer olive oil over sunflower oil for the purpose of making salad dressing, even if one prefers sunflower oil for the purpose of making mayonnaise. Then we could use this notion of a purpose-relative preference to give an account of some of the "thicker" moral terms, by appealing to some rule of the following form:

Acceptance of "x is better than y for purpose P" commits one to having a preference-with-respect-to-P for x over y.[17]

This account obviously fits nicely with Wedgwood's overall outlook. Thick concepts are characterized by their roles in practical reasoning. And this account is very natural for anyone who favors the kind of fine-grained normative role view on the normativity of expressions and concepts.

But there are some reasons for dissatisfaction with the view sketched. First, it provides no real answer to our second puzzle, the puzzle of seeming sufficiency. Second, it is hard to see how this allows for objectionable thick concepts. Of course, some purposes may be objectionable, but even if a given purpose is objectionable, there is not immediately anything problematic about talking about what is better than what for that purpose. Another possible concern about Wedgwood's account of the thick is that it appears to in a way drain the thick concepts of normativity. Just to say that something is good for purpose P isn't to positively evaluate it—or, more cautiously, is only to evaluate it *conditionally*—but to apply a positive thick concept to something is to do something stronger. If I were to call some behavior chaste, then I wouldn't merely say that for such-and-such purposes this behavior is good. Instead I would praise it, full stop. How does Wedgwood's account deal with that?

One thing a friend of Wedgwood's suggestion might suggest is that the relevant kind of talk can serve to *pragmatically* convey something normatively substantive: "why would the speaker assert that φ-ing would be right given such-and-such standards unless she favored those standards?". Finlay (2014) is a recent book-length defense of the view that this is how normative talk *always* works. Whatever

---

[17] Wedgwood (2001), p. 24f. Wedgwood goes on to discuss another type of account of thick terms within his general framework (p. 25):

> it is striking how many evaluative terms are derived from terms that describe a certain sort of attitude or response towards objects that satisfy that term: "desirable" is derived from "desire", "admirable" from "admire", and "tolerable" from "tolerate". There are many other examples: "laudable", "commendable", "honorable", "respectable", "despicable", "contemptible", "abominable", "detestable", "pitiable", and so on. Suppose that there is a state of mind of *endorsing an attitude*, such that one's endorsement of an attitude is susceptible to being guided by reasons, but is not just a matter of holding an evaluative belief about that attitude. Then we could explain the meaning of these evaluative terms by appealing to such rules as the following:
> Acceptance of "*x* is contemptible" commits one to endorsing an attitude of contempt towards *x*.

This may be a good account of "contemptible" and terms in the same category (the ones paradigmatically ending with "-able" and "-ible"). But this again fails to accommodate the possibility of objectionable thick terms.

the fate of a view as general as Finlay's, one may well hold that very often we convey outright recommendations (or disrecommendations) through pragmatic means: all we strictly *say* is that such-and-such is good for a given purpose; context indicates that the purpose is one of which we approve. But first, if the normative message is conveyed only pragmatically, in what sense are the expressions in question normative at all? (Although perhaps it can simply be denied that they are normative.) Second, there is the question of in what sense thick concepts can be objectionable, given this view.

Here is a different way to deal with thick concepts—or, generally, less than thin concepts—given a fine-grained normative role view. While Wedgwood's sample thin concept was governed by the rule

Acceptance of "B(x, y, me, t)" commits one to having a preference for doing x over doing y at time t,[18]

maybe a thick concept should be seen as governed by a rule of the form

Acceptance of "B*(x, y, me, t)" commits one to having a preference for doing x over doing y at time t on the ground that ____.

It is easy to see how B* could be objectionable. Maybe nothing actually does warrant preferring some course or other over another on exactly the ground ____ associated with B*. But given a sufficiently liberal metasemantics—given a theory of reference-determination allowing that a term can have an extension although nothing fully fits the conditions associated with the expression—B* could still manage to ascribe a non-trivial property: there can still be a property that comes closest and sufficiently close to fitting the role of B* that B* ascribes this property.

It remains to see how well this proposal regarding the thick deals with the three puzzles. The answer to the first puzzle would be that thick concepts are like B* rather than like B. The answer to the third puzzle would be provided by the liberal metasemantics. Unfortunately, the proposal leaves us without a satisfactory answer to the second puzzle. It is not explained why the seeming sufficiency phenomenon arises. The proposal does not provide even the hint of a suggestion in that regard.

To me that is a serious problem regarding taking B* to be a model of paradigmatic thick concepts. But I do not see what alternative informative characterization of the types of normative roles of thick concepts adequately deals with our three puzzles regarding thick concepts.

One could in principle go resolutely primitivist at this point and refuse to try to say anything informative about the types of normative roles thick concepts have such that thick concepts behave the way they do, simply insisting that the normative roles are such that thick concepts behave the way they do. For example, one can simply insist that the normative roles are such that the seeming sufficiency phenomenon arises, without seeking to explain how that is so.

---

[18] Wedgwood (2001), p. 15.

A different way to go would be to adopt a view modeled on the semantic analyticity account, simply revising clause (ii′) so that instead of speaking about conceptual entailment relations, one speaks of normative role. Instead of having "semantically analytically entails 'x is (pro tanto) good' ('x is (pro tanto) bad')," one could simply say: "is semantically associated with a particular normative role." But there is something unsatisfactory about giving this particular kind of dual-aspect account of thick concepts, with one clause, (i′), speaking to the concept's relations to descriptive concepts, and another clause being about having a normative role. Can these two aspects of a thick concepts vary independently of each other? If they cannot, that would stand in need of explanation. Why is it still appropriate to speak of two separate elements? If they can, then some other problematic questions arise. How do these two aspects relate when it comes to reference-determination? Take the normative role associated with the thick concept. Would it suffice to determine reference by itself? (If so, how does it interact with the other element of the thick concept?) Or does it somehow leave questions about reference open, and these questions then get settled by the descriptive element? I simply raise questions and have no knock-down arguments to offer, to the effect that the questions do not have satisfactory answers. But my own judgment is that the questions are hard to answer, and point to serious problems.

Yet another way of modifying the semantic analyticity account would be to revise

(ii′)   if C is positive (negative), "x is C" semantically analytically entails "x is (pro tanto) good" ("x is (pro tanto) bad"),

so that it instead reads

(ii″)   if C is positive (negative), "x is C" semantically analytically entails "x is (pro tanto) G," for some concept G with the same normative role as our concept good (/"x is (pro tanto) B," for some concept B with the same normative role as our concept bad).

or perhaps, in a more liberal version,

(ii‴)   if C is positive (negative), "x is C" semantically analytically entails "x is (pro tanto) G," for some concept G with a thin positive normative role (/"x is (pro tanto) B," for some concept B with a thin negative normative role).

These suggestions avoid objections raised so far. But they do have a somewhat ad hoc feel to them. Moreover, there is a concern that these formulations serve to highlight but that one might have had already with the original (ii′): even allowing that the requisite notion of semantic analyticity is in good standing, and allowing further that many thick concepts stand in conceptual entailment relations to thin concepts, why suppose that they *all* do? Maybe some thick concepts are understood independently of thin concepts.

However, while perhaps this concern has some force, it deserves stressing in the context that adherence to the claim that (ii′) or one of the modified versions now considered holds is not most reasonably or charitably construed as saying that all users of thick concepts must also possess thin concepts of the kind at issue. (Any more than conceptual connections between "bachelor" and "unmarried" show that one must possess the concept expressed by "bachelor" to possess the concept expressed by "unmarried.") A better construal is that the conceptual connection means that anyone who does possess both concepts must stand in the right cognitive relation to the entailment claim. Then (ii′) and its variants seem more plausible: for so long as thick concepts are either positively or negatively valenced, that valence is something it is arguably part of conceptual competence to appreciate, and seeing that a thick concept has a given valence can then further be held to be sufficient for being in a position to accept that some similarly valenced thin concept applies.

9.4 Defeasibility and Projectibility

I have brought up some important puzzles regarding thick concepts, to introduce the topic. Eventually I will bring up suggestions for how to solve these puzzles. But my main reason for discussing the topic here is not thick concepts per se. I am concerned with thick concepts only insofar as consideration of these concepts helps elucidate themes earlier brought up. From here on that is what I will focus on.

First I wish to make some points relating to Väyrynen's (2013) book-length defense of a *pragmatic* view on thick terms. According to this pragmatic view, thick terms are not normative (Väyrynen uses "evaluative") as a matter of their semantics; they are only pragmatically normative. Note that I here speak of terms rather than concepts. If thick terms are not semantically normative then the concepts they express are not normative as a matter of content. But it could still be that other concepts, not semantically expressed by thick terms, are normative as a matter of content and generally have the features normally ascribed to thick concepts.

Väyrynen's view can be expressed in one of two ways. Either one can say that there really are "thick terms" but they are not semantically normative, or one can say that since the terms in question aren't semantically normative, they are not thick but are only used thickly. Väyrynen himself speaks the former way. I find it more natural to speak the latter way. How to speak is just a matter of theoretical bookkeeping.

Väyrynen relies on two kinds of arguments. First, there are defeasibility arguments. Väyrynen emphasizes, for example, that it seems in order to say "whether or not Madonna's show is lewd, it's not bad in any way distinctive of explicit sexual display."[19] The thought is that if the evaluation were semantically associated with

---

[19] Väyrynen (2013), p. 70.

"lewd," it would not be in order to say this, any more than it would be in order to say "Sam is a bachelor, but Sam isn't a man."[20]

Second, there are projection arguments. Some people find some thick concepts objectionable. For example, some might find "lewd" objectionable, thinking its use in some way presupposes the prudes' way of thinking about sexuality (roughly, that its use presupposes that there is something bad about displays of sexuality). Following Väyrynen, call those with this view *lewd-objectors*. Lewd-objectors of course refuse to call things "lewd." They do not say, for instance, that "Madonna's show is lewd." What is more interesting, they would also (Väyrynen says) avoid using "lewd" in embedded contexts. Consider:

1a. Nuh uh, Madonna's show isn't lewd; it's sexually insinuating alright, but no private parts are exposed.
b. Is Madonna's show lewd?
c. Madonna's show might be lewd.
d. If Madonna's show is lewd, the tabloid press will go nuts.

The claim is that lewd-objectors would refrain from using 1a–1d. But this is something the semantic view cannot explain. If the evaluation were just part of the semantic content of "lewd," then the lewd-objector should have no problem at all with "Madonna's show isn't lewd." Some other account of the evaluation associated with "lewd" is needed. (I present Väyrynen's argument in a somewhat simplified way, as if it purported to be a demonstrative argument. Väyrynen himself rather presents his argument as an inference to the best explanation.)[21]

Focus first on the projection arguments. One immediate question is: cannot the same go for "good," even in its thinnest uses? Suppose you think that even in these uses "good" embodies a particular evaluative perspective, and this perspective is one you want to distance yourself from. You will then treat "good" the way the "lewd"-objector treats "lewd"; you are a "good"-objector. But is the situation with respect to "good" not then simply analogous to that of "lewd," so if projection considerations show that the latter is normative only as a matter of pragmatics, they show the same regarding the former?[22]

It is quite clear that one can have such a view on "good." Moreover, my discussion earlier in this book displays some ways in which this view can be undergirded. It might, for example, be that an Alternative-friendly view is correct, and one favors some alternative normative concepts over the ones we actually have.

---

[20] Well, it could be in order to say the latter in certain contexts. If Sam(antha) is female but behaves like a typical bachelor—fill in the details as you like—this is something one could convey by using this sentence. But then "bachelor" isn't used literally.

[21] In my summary of Väyrynen's main arguments I have stuck closely to Bedke's (2014) helpful way of characterizing them.

[22] Roberts (2015) makes a similar point about Väyrynen.

It may be tempting to argue as follows that the cases of "good" and "lewd" are not parallel. The "lewd"-objector as envisaged is not conceptually confused. But if someone thinks we should instead use notions of goodness* and badness*, not coextensive with the notions of goodness and badness, for evaluation, and refuses to use "good" and "bad," she is conceptually confused. The proper way for her to give voice to her view is by saying that in fact what is good is what is good* (perhaps contrary to common opinion about what is good).

This is a natural thing to think. But first, in connection with Väyrynen's use of projection arguments: how could it be properly *argued* that there really is this difference between "lewd" and "good"? Second, earlier (primarily in Chapter 2), I have discussed how on some views of the normative, there can be non-coextensive notions that are all in some sense normative counterparts of our "good." Given such a view, the "good"-objector's stance would seem to make perfect sense.

In connection with all this, let me make a few remarks on Blackburn's (1998, 2013) point that "thinking in terms of thick concepts ... discourages critique."[23] The argument, as stated in the later work, is this:

I have made this point before with the example of a group happy in the habit of appraising women as cute. We may want to say that there is something wrong with them, along the lines of this: they admire and respond excitedly (or perhaps enviously, if they are women) to the non-threatening, infantile, subservient selfpresentations that some women consciously or unconsciously adopt. Theirs is a group amongst whom women are successful by presenting themselves as there to be patronized, like pets or babies (which themselves are frequent terms of endearment). And that, we say, is bad.

Now this critique involved disentangling. It involved separating the features picked upon— the subservience and the rest—and the reactions of admiration and appreciation that they elicit from the group, and then finding it abhorrent that those features generated those reactions.[24]

As Chappell (2013) notes, there is an oddity in Blackburn's reasoning. For the criticism of the practice of appraising women as cute is by and large presented in thick terms, for example "infantile," "subservient," and "patronized." The conclusion is stated using the thin "bad," but that part could be excised without any obvious loss. But then Blackburn's own reasoning does not exemplify the need for thin terms, but rather indicates the opposite.

I think Chappell's criticism of Blackburn on this score is correct. But it may be thought that what Blackburn is really after is that thick terms, as opposed to thin terms, are such that their use might embody evaluative perspectives that ought not to be endorsed. Someone defending the spirit of Blackburn's remarks might say that while in practice we rely on the use of thick terms—and Blackburn's lapse clearly illustrates that—only the use of thin concepts can serve as a suitably neutral arbiter.

---

[23] Blackburn (2013), p. 123.   [24] Blackburn (2013), p. 123.

But of course, when the point is expressed that way, it is clear that it relies on substantive theoretical assumptions about how our thin terms work. In particular, it assumes that thin terms do not embody substantive assumptions as thick terms do, and that one's use of some thin terms does not itself constitute taking a stand on an in principle contestable issue.

Turn now to Väyrynen's defeasibility argument. The argument appears to rely on a particular assumption about what it is to be normative in the first place: Väyrynen seems to rely on an assumption along the lines of: a predicate F is normative iff "x is F" conceptually entails "x is good [bad] in some way." But one can well question the reasonableness of such an assumption, for reasons that came up in Chapter 4. If, for example, an Alternative-friendly view is correct and there are alternative normative concepts sharing normative roles with our normative concepts but not being coextensive with them, then these alternative concepts will not count as normative given this criterion. More generally, on either a metaphysical view on the concept question or the normative role view on the concept question that I prefer, it is far from immediate that what Väyrynen treats as necessary for evaluativeness really is so. Most obviously, a friend of the metaphysical view or the normative role view can eschew conceptual entailment talk altogether. She can say what is special about the normative without invoking conceptual entailment relations. This is important given the not uncommon skepticism about conceptual entailment.[25] The skeptic about conceptual entailment can, to be sure, also be skeptical of the suggestion that normative roles can be conventionally associated with concepts; but the issues are different and the skepticism about conceptual entailment does not obviously generalize.

9.5 Robust and Formal Normativity

There is another issue regarding normativity that raises some of the same issues as thick concepts. In the literature, there is some discussion of what is sometimes called *robust* versus merely *formal* normativity.[26] Given common glosses, what is robustly normative—paradigmatically, morality—has genuinely reason-giving force whereas what is merely formally normative—paradigmatically rules of etiquette, or chess—lacks such force.[27] But one can speak of reasons of etiquette; and someone seeing the position on a chess board can say, without speculating in any way about the aims of the players, "White has reason to move her queen to a safer position." Also the formally normative has some connection to reasons.

---

[25] See e.g. Williamson (2007).

[26] I take the terminology "robust" and "merely formal" from McPherson (2011).

[27] For some relevant discussions, see, apart from McPherson (2011), Joyce (2001, ch. 2) and Olson (2014, ch. 6).

A natural thing to say may then be that even given a distinction between what one plainly ought to do and what one morally ought to do, as a matter of fact, whenever one has moral reason to do something one thereby has some reason (plainly, simpliciter) to do this. This is what accounts for the robust normativity of morality. It is not the case that whenever one has reason of etiquette to do something one has reason (plainly, simpliciter) to do this. Hence etiquette is only formally normative.

My own view on robust versus formal normativity is a bit more complex. I want to draw a distinction analogous to the earlier distinction between the property question and the concept question. When one considers how to draw the (putative) distinction between the robustly and the formally normative, one can both ask how to draw this distinction within *normative language* and how to draw this distinction within *normative metaphysics*. Given the suggestion that the normative role of a less than perfectly thin predicate should be characterized conditionally in the way suggested a few paragraphs ago, it can in principle be maintained that there is no robust/formal distinction to be drawn between morality and etiquette at the level of representation: both saying that I have moral reason to φ and saying that I have reasons of etiquette to φ is saying something of the form: relative to such-and-such a standard or such-and-such aims, I have (plain) reason to φ. Talk of morality and talk of etiquette are classified in the same way, and both are different from all-things-considered normative talk. Even if there is a real and important distinction between the normativity of morality and the normativity of etiquette, that distinction shows up only at the level of metaphysics. It is here that it is relevant that moral reason to φ can as a matter of fact always (and metaphysically necessarily) be plain reason to φ while that does not go for reasons of etiquette. Someone who says that she has moral reason to φ but denies that she thereby has plain reason to φ may be mistaken and for general reasons, but she is not making a conceptual mistake. She is making a mistake about what normative reality is like.

A possible suggestion that emerges is that the normative role of every less than perfectly thin normative predicate "F" can be characterized conditionally: to say that something "is F" is to say that it is to be valued (/disvalued) given such-and-such aims, or relative to such-and-such standards, etc. This is like the suggestion from Wedgwood regarding thick concepts that was discussed in section 9.4. And it faces potential problems similar to those I raised concerning Wedgwood's suggestion. The suggestion appears to drain the relevant concepts of normativity. Merely to say that φ-ing is what would be right given such-and-such aims is not to say much. A speaker needn't agree with these aims at all; a remark to the effect that such-and-such is to be valued given such-and-such aims can be understood as merely descriptive.

The suggestion is, to stress, only tentative. I am stressing it in part just to highlight the uses of separating questions about language from questions about metaphysics. Someone can in principle agree that the distinction is a reasonable one to draw, and also hold that what is suggested regarding morality is a coherent option, while saying that as a matter of fact, "moral" functions in such a way that one is making a conceptual mistake if one does not accept that moral reasons are plain reasons. (A complication is that, as has come up in the earlier discussion, one understanding of talk of conceptual or analytic links is the semantic one characterized. But something can be semantically analytic without being true. It can be that competence with talk and thought of what is "moral" involves a disposition to accept that moral reasons are plain reasons, even though as a matter of fact, moral reasons are not always plain reasons.)

9.6 Epistemic Normativity

It may also be relevant to compare what is sometimes called epistemic normativity. We use what appear to be normative concept also in the epistemic realm: we speak of someone's belief as *justified*, or *known*. And the properties ascribed by these normative concepts can seem normative, just as much as the properties ascribed by moral concepts seem normative. Nothing I say in my discussion commits me either way on epistemic normativity, but it may anyway be useful to lay out what some of the options are, regarding what to say.

One possibility is just to deny the appearance of normativity. While we often do use "justified" (to express epistemic justification) and "knows" to appraise beliefs, the evaluation is only accidentally connected to the terms. A community of anti-intellectuals might say something of the form "S knows that p" and not see this as saying something positive about mental state, but perhaps even as something negative, while still using "knows" with the customary meaning. Compare, as earlier, "philosophy." In the philosophy department context, saying of something that it is "not philosophy" can be to condemn it, but when the physicist describes her colleague's work as "philosophy," that can be a form of condemnation—while still the philosophers and the physicists use "philosophy" with the same meaning. The word "philosophy" is not normative, even though some uses of it are.

To be sure, "justified" is in general a normative word. But "justified" has both epistemic and non-epistemic uses. One can ask whether my resentment of so-and-so is justified, without asking an epistemic question. I don't wish to make any claims about natural language semantics but one theoretical possibility, at any rate, is that the string of symbols "justified" in some uses expresses—semantically expresses—something normative, while when used to express epistemic justification it does not semantically express anything normative.

Another possibility is that the supposedly normative epistemic concepts indeed are normative, but their normativity is best understood conditionally, along the lines suggested in section 9.5. This would respect the seeming normativity of the epistemic concepts, even though the normativity is downplayed, as described.

But it is also possible to treat epistemic concepts as quite robustly normative within the present framework. One can say that these are normative concepts simply marked as epistemic by the kinds of normative roles they have, without their normativity being understood conditionally.

Needless to say, these remarks on epistemic normativity are sketchy. I do not have a particular view; I only distinguish salient possibilities.

A distinction I have earlier emphasized and which obviously is applicable also in the case of epistemic normativity concerns the normativity of concepts versus the normativity of properties. Various sorts of mixed views are possible. It can be that our actual epistemic concepts are normative only conditionally, but the properties they ascribe are robustly normative.

One reason why it is worth stressing the distinction between robust and formal normativity is that it crosscuts the distinction between categorical and hypothetical normativity in interesting ways. Despite not being robustly normative, the requirements of etiquette are categorical: they apply to an agent irrespective of her own goals and preferences.[28] One can think that something similar holds in the epistemic case. Let me illustrate. In his (2007), Terence Cuneo argues that antirealism about the moral generalizes to antirealism about the epistemic and that the latter is untenable. I will not discuss all the facets of Cuneo's case. But here is one point that is relevant. Cuneo devotes a chapter to discussing what he calls epistemic reductionism, the view that epistemic reasons as opposed to moral ones are only hypothetical. If epistemic reductionism were true, then the moral and epistemic cases would not be relevantly analogous, and Cuneo's argument would fail. As against this view, Cuneo brings up what seems to me a rather obvious, and obviously compelling, objection: differences in two thinkers' epistemic goals do not matter to how well epistemically justified they are in a given belief. (Cuneo argues this point by considering pairs of cases with thinkers in the same epistemic situations except for the possible differences that their epistemic goals differ.) But Cuneo fails to discuss what seems to me to be a more reasonable way to attempt to break the analogy between the moral and the epistemic case: suggesting that epistemic normativity but not the normativity associated with the moral is mere formal normativity. Above, I suggested that maybe moral concepts, as opposed to all-things-considered concepts, are merely formally normative. If this suggestion is correct, there of course still is no disanalogy between the moral and the epistemic. All I am concerned to do is to remark on the moves available to someone who wishes to resist Cuneo's argument; and the point of that in turn is to illustrate the theoretical map.

Hartry Field (2009) agrees with Cuneo that the case for antirealism about the moral generalizes to antirealism about epistemic normativity (but disagrees regarding this being any sort of reductio). He says for example:

basically, the same reasons that motivate antirealism about moral normativity, or about aesthetic goodness, extend to the epistemic case. (For instance, (i) the usual metaphysical (Humean) worry, that there seems no room for "straightforward normative facts" on a naturalistic world-view; (ii) the associated epistemological worry that access to them is

---

[28] Foot (1972), p. 308.

impossible (which is compounded by the fact that there is substantially greater disagreement about normative matters than about mathematical); (iii) the worry that the relation to norms is not only non-naturalistic, but "queer" in the sense that it's supposed to somehow motivate one to reason in a certain way.)[29]

But while a naturalistic worldview maybe cannot make room for robustly normative facts, merely *formally* normative facts are another matter altogether. What could fail to be naturalistically acceptable about facts about how well some actions or beliefs meet some given standard? What would be so difficult about access to such facts? The issue regarding motivation is different, but maybe the thing to say is there is only a rather indirect link between epistemic beliefs and motivation: epistemic beliefs do not by themselves motivate.

One can ask earlier questions about Alternative-friendliness specifically about epistemic concepts. Can there be alternative epistemic concepts, with the same (epistemic) normative roles as ours but differing in extension? As I stressed in Chapter 3, these questions cannot straightforwardly be raised in connection with all sorts of normative concepts. It is hard even to get a good intuitive grasp of what it is for a different concept to have the same normative role as our concept of being courageous but differ in other respects in a way that potentially matters to extension. The epistemic concepts seem to be like the thin normative concepts in this regard. Corresponding to different theories of what makes for justification or warrant, one can imagine different communities such that the epistemic practices of these communities are centered on the properties identified by these different theories—not only when it comes to the application of the expressions "justification" and "warrant" (in their epistemic uses) but in how they let their epistemic practices be guided by these properties—in terms of what they seek and in terms of what they epistemically praise and blame. One can then ask questions parallel to those I have asked regarding thin normative concepts. Are there epistemic normative roles that can determine reference?

9.7 Thick Properties

Thus far in this chapter I have, when speaking about the thick, spoken of thick terms and concepts. But as noted, some authors speak also of *thick properties*.[30] Sometimes I suspect that this is a mere mistake, and that authors who speak this way simply do not distinguish carefully between concepts and properties. But suppose we take the idea of thick properties, as opposed to thick concepts, seriously. How are we to understand it?

The account I have given of thickness of concepts obviously does not straightforwardly function as an account of the thickness of properties. For one thing, that account essentially appeals to semantically analytic entailments, and such entailments

---

[29] Field (2009), p. 354.   [30] See e.g. Dancy (1993) and McNaughton and Rawling (2000).

hold between items representing properties, not between properties themselves. So if one wants an account of what it is for a property to be thick, one will need to look elsewhere.

As mentioned early on in this chapter, thickness gets glossed in different ways. Sometimes thickness is understood as the merging of descriptive and normative aspects; sometimes it is understood as specificity. Let me consider each type of gloss in turn in connection with the idea of thick properties.

Consider first the idea that the thick somehow merges the descriptive and the normative. How is this merging to be understood in the case of properties? It may depend on what it is for a property to be descriptive in the first place. For example, if the descriptiveness of a property is identified with its non-normativity, then no property can be both normative and descriptive; but then, among other things, thick properties cannot be both normative and descriptive.

If the friend of the idea of thick properties holds that properties have some sort of *structure*, whereby they can have other properties as *constituents*, she can say that what is special about thick properties is that they have both descriptive and normative constituents.[31] But if she does not hold that properties are thus structured—and certainly the idea of structured properties is controversial (and should be controversial even if there are structured *predicates* and *concepts*)—she is forced to find some alternative account of descriptiveness.[32]

Here is one characterization that allows for this, brought up also earlier in this chapter: a descriptive property is one that can be ascribed by a purely descriptive predicate. In the first instance, this only pushes the problem back, as it relies on the notion of a descriptive predicate. But suppose that we understand a descriptive predicate to be one whose reference is determined in a way that it is not even partially referentially normative; that is, whose reference is not in any way determined by anything that makes the predicate normative. Then if we combine this with the characterization (P3),

---

[31] Although consider, for example, the putative structured property *is D and either N or not-N*, where D is a descriptive property and N is a normative property. If it is just a matter of logic that for every property P, everything is P or not-P, then this structured property should arguably be classified as descriptive despite having both descriptive and normative constituents.

[32] Some prominent authors who speak of the thick hold that while the thick in some sense has descriptive and normative elements, these elements cannot be "disentangled." See e.g. McDowell (1979, 1981), Williams (1985), Dancy (1996), Roberts (2011, 2013b), and Kirchin (2010, 2013b). I find this talk of what can and cannot be disentangled somewhat dark. But whatever it means, one may think that if thick properties have the kind of structure here envisaged, the descriptive and normative elements can be "disentangled" after all.

Incidentally, as we distinguish between the idea of thick concepts and thick properties, we should also distinguish between different possible entanglement theses. One entanglement thesis is that the descriptive and normative elements in thick concepts cannot be disentangled; another entanglement thesis is that the descriptive and normative elements in thick properties cannot be disentangled.

(P3)   A property is positively (negatively) normative iff it can be ascribed using a referentially normative predicate.

of what it is for a property to be normative, we allow for a property to be both descriptive and normative. But the suggested characterization of what it takes for a property to be descriptive is too liberal. Does any property fail to be descriptive, given this characterization? Recall "thgir." Even the property of rightness can be ascribed by a fully descriptive predicate.

Turn instead to the idea that the thick simply is more *specific* than the thin. In the case of concepts, this becomes something along the lines of:

(TC)   A positively (negatively) normative concept C is a thick concept just in case "__ is C" conceptually entails "__ is [to that extent] good" ("__ is [to that extent] bad"), but not vice versa.

Misevaluating objectionable thick concepts—non-empty objectionable thick concepts true of what is paradigmatically held to fall under them—are counterexamples to this principle. But appeal to specificity could for all that still help characterize what a thick normative *property* is. Maybe the following holds:

(TP)   A positively (negatively) normative property is thick if, necessarily, if __ is φ then __ is [to that extent] good (bad), but not vice versa.

(As in the discussion of suggestion (P2) regarding what makes a property normative, one might worry that this criterion is too permissive, and want to turn to a notion of essence to correct this.) An objectionable positive (negative) thick concept may then fail to ascribe a positively (negatively) normative thick property. But this can be seen as a welcome consequence: what is objectionable about some objectionable thick concepts might be precisely that they present properties that are not normative, or even normatively relevant, as normatively valenced a particular way.

Variant valence of properties, discussed in chapter 4, would present a problem for (TP). To repeat, the relevant variant valence thesis is:

(PV)   For some property that a thick concept ascribes, sometimes this property is a good-making (bad-making) feature of what has it and sometimes not.

If (PV) is true and some property which verifies it is normative, then (TP) is false. On the other hand, to relate to a consideration from the discussion of variant valence of concepts, if (PV) is true, then one may be skeptical of the idea that a property verifying it is normative, as opposed to, say, merely being a property which tends to have normatively significant consequences. With dismissive views on the property and concept questions a real option it cannot be blithely assumed that seemingly normative properties and concepts really are so.

(TP) might be acceptable as an account of thick properties. Another account of thick properties that might work takes its inspiration from the account of the necessary and sufficient conditions for a property to be normative that I have defended in Chapter 5. On that view, for a property to be normative is for it to be ascribed by some possible predicate whose reference is fully characterized by its normative role. Then assuming one can further classify some normative roles as thin and some as thick, one can suggest:

A thin normative property is one ascribed by a predicate whose reference is fully determined by some thin normative role.
A thick normative property is one ascribed by a predicate whose reference is fully determined by some thick normative role.

A thin normative role would be one like that of Wedgwood's "B(x, y, z, t)," which has to do with preference simpliciter, and a thick normative role could, for example, be like that of B* above, characterized also by more specific factors, like the ground of the preference. The characterization given in principle allows for some properties to be both thin and thick. If one is concerned to rule that out, one can, for example, add to the characterization of what it is to be a thick property that to be thick a property must not also satisfy the condition for thinness. Of course, I above presented some problems regarding taking B* to be our model of thick predicates. But the suggestion is general and can be applied so long as some sort of distinction between thin and thick normative roles can be drawn, and both thin and thick normative roles can determine reference.

10

Some Metaphilosophical Issues

10.1 Conceptual Engineering

On one traditionally common—and arguably still often implicitly adopted—way of looking at what much of philosophy is doing, we are studying *our ordinary concepts*: our concept of truth, our concept of knowledge, our concept of justice, and so on and so forth. Sometimes the "our" is not explicit: the target is described as *the* concepts of truth, of knowledge, of justice, etc. But these are our concepts. The topic of the study is these concepts and not some variant concepts we do not actually employ when describing and explaining the world.

Nowadays many would resist the talk of *concepts* in this connection—and there are many reasons to be unhappy with such talk—and instead say that what we study rather are truth, knowledge, justice, etc., and mean not the concepts concerned but the *properties* and *relations* they stand for: the property truth, the relation of knowledge that sometimes holds between thinkers and propositions, the property justice, etc. But when it comes to what I currently want to focus on, the reformulation is irrelevant. Even someone who insists that she rather is focused on properties and relations is focused on the properties and relations that the ordinary concepts stand for, and not the different properties and relations that some alternative concepts would stand for.

But already a little reflection shows how—what's the best way to put it?—*navel-gazing* this kind of study is. The concepts we have are the ones we have ended up with because of various biological and cultural factors. By some measure they have proven themselves, since we keep using them. But still, why should the concepts we actually have be the best conceptual tools for describing and theorizing about the relevant aspects of reality? Maybe philosophy should rather be concerned with *conceptual engineering*: it should study what concept best plays the theoretical role of our concept of truth and what features this concept has, what concept best plays the theoretical role of our concept of knowledge and what features this concept has, etc.[1]

---

[1] In an introduction to philosophy (1999), Simon Blackburn explicitly characterizes philosophy as conceptual engineering. Robert Brandom (2001) likewise uses this label. More recently (2011), David Chalmers has defended this conception of philosophy at some length but without using the "engineering" label. Alexis Burgess and David Plunkett (2013a, 2013b) characterize "conceptual ethics" as a research area, meaning by conceptual ethics normative questions about which concepts to employ. In a number of works, Sally Haslanger has discussed conceptual engineering for practical, political purposes (see her collection of essays (2012)).

It should also be engaged in other nearby issues such as what theoretical roles we want some concepts to play in the first place. Generally, we should be concerned with what concepts we should use when thinking and talking about the world.

When stating this alternative conception of what we should focus on, I have again slid into talking of philosophy as concerned with concepts. But again the point is easily restated in terms of properties and relations: why be concerned with the properties and relations that our ordinary concepts stand for rather than the most theoretically important properties and relations in the vicinity? I will, however, keep talking about concepts in this connection. There are two reasons for this choice. One is that this terminology has become entrenched: theorists talk about conceptual engineering and conceptual ethics. Another, more substantive, reason for the choice is that especially when normativity is our topic, we wish to distinguish between the question of whether some given property P is one such that we should employ expressions or concepts ascribing P in our theories of the world, and the question of whether to use expressions or concepts that present P in a particular way, for example as being valenced positively or negatively. For the statement of the second question, one needs to consider how P is represented.

It may be easiest to motivate the conception of philosophy as conceptual engineering by comparing how an opposing conception is motivated. Here is Antti Kauppinen (2007):

> Moral responsibility, for example, is not a technical notion, though some terms that philosophers use in explicating it may be. Indeed, why should anybody care about what philosophers do if they just argued about their own inventions? People want to know if they have moral responsibility or knowledge of other minds in the very sense in which they ordinarily talk about responsibility or knowledge, and to get at that sense one must work with the folk's own concepts. By and large, philosophers oblige; revisionism is a last resort, to be used only when one is convinced that the folk concept is hopelessly confused or too imprecise for one's purposes.[2]

Here is one point Kauppinen makes: the philosophical questions we start out with are questions that arise out of ordinary reflection, and are stated using ordinary concepts. We wonder about moral responsibility, not about (some feature picked out by) some related concept. But, first, it could be that although we state our concerns using a notion of moral responsibility, what we are at bottom concerned with would be better stated using some improved notion. Compare perhaps the development of physics, from rudimentary folk physics through today. Some of our original questions may have had to do with weight; but what we are at bottom concerned with is such that our concerns are better stated using more theoretically sophisticated notions. Second, even if Kauppinen is right in that we have a special kind of interest in questions best stated using ordinary concepts and not some related counterparts, it doesn't follow

---

[2] Kauppinen (2007), p. 96.

that the only, or the most, interesting philosophical questions in the vicinity are formulated using such concepts. Even if we do have some genuine interest in questions truly about *weight*, questions about mass, more attuned to the physical facts, are better to ask when our interest is with physical reality and not just our conception thereof.

I am not suggesting that the project of figuring out what our actual concepts are like and what they are true of (or what the properties they stand for are like and are instantiated by) should be dismissed as entirely devoid of theoretical interest: getting clear on the tools we have come to use to understand the world is *obviously* a worthwhile project. But distinguish between what we ought to focus on if our concern is *the relevant aspect of reality* and what we ought to focus on if our concern is *(human) thought about* the relevant aspect of reality. If our concern is the latter, of course there is a case for thinking about what our actual concepts are. Preference for philosophy as conceptual engineering relies on thinking of our concern as the former. Compare again the case of folk physics. If our concern is with the physical aspects of reality, as in physics, there is obviously no reason to stick with the folk concept of weight. Even if our main concern is the former one, there may still be some reason for dealing with the latter issue: attention to folk thought about a topic might be instrumental to arrive at questions about the topics itself, if only because it might help avoid some confusions.

Some friends of the idea of philosophy as conceptual engineering can tend to present the idea as something importantly new.[3] Care is needed here. First, it can reasonably be argued that conceptual improvement has in fact been a traditional concern of philosophy, and philosophers have de facto been concerned with technical concepts differing from their ordinary counterparts, even while they have not been explicit about this methodology and have not explicitly distinguished between what they have been concerned with and its ordinary counterpart. Second, some philosophers have been quite explicit about adopting a methodology like that currently being promoted under the name of conceptual engineering. Carnap's talk of explication comes to mind. And both Quine and latter-day Quineans are more concerned with what sorts of conceptual tools to employ than with what conceptual tools we happen to find ourselves with.[4]

Friends of conceptual engineering can also wish to discuss in general terms the principles that should guide conceptual engineering. But consistently with the case

---

[3] While Burgess and Plunkett (2013a) argue that "conceptual ethics" is an already existing research field, strikingly all their examples are of research of recent vintage.

[4] There are differences between contemporary friends of conceptual engineering on the one hand and Carnap and Quine on the other. For Carnap, the method of explication is bound up with replacing inexact concepts with more precise ones (he says in his (1950b)): "[t]he task of *explication* consists in transforming a given...inexact concept into an exact one or, rather, replacing the first by the second"), but this is no integral part of conceptual engineering. The Quinean disdain for questions about the exact nature of our ordinary concepts is bound up with the sense that there are no determinate facts of the matter as to how our concepts work; this is no integral part of conceptual engineering. See e.g. Carnap (1950b) for Carnap's approach. Quine's approach is discussed in his (1960), p. 258f.

that has been laid out here for philosophy as conceptual engineering, one can be skeptical of the prospects and fruitfulness of the search for such general principles.

Even while the reasons offered may—and I think should—make the conception of philosophy as conceptual engineering attractive, one may have the vague sense that somehow there must be important limits to conceptual engineering: that certain in some sense basic concepts cannot be replaced. Motivation for saying this might come from, say, Kantian philosophy, or a naturalistic philosophy according to which what is innate severely constrains which concepts we can use. I have nothing to say about those kinds of motivation. But there are other kinds of possible limitations to the conceptual engineering project. One possible limitation was discussed in Chapter 3, in connection with egalitarian pluralism about truth and reference. I there briefly presented an argument that one cannot make proper sense of the supposition that there is a community which employs a different concept of truth than we do. Another possible type of limitation has been illustrated by the discussion earlier in the book, and was discussed explicitly in this type of connection in Chapter 3. Suppose one tries to embark on the project of asking whether the thinnest concepts might be improved upon. How could one carry out that project? By asking whether it really is "ought," etc., that *ought* to be used for action-guiding purposes? The problem is one that has kept coming up throughout the book: we are using the "ought" we are trying to problematize in the very formulation of the question.

That the conceptual engineering project meets these obstacles when it comes to the thinnest normative concepts does not mean that we should not try to apply this kind of thinking in the case of the thinnest normative concepts. The guiding thought behind thinking of philosophy as conceptual engineering is that the concepts that we find ourselves with are only some among the possible concepts we could have and use. The concepts we have, we might have as a matter of historical accident. As I said above, in some measure they may have proven themselves by their usefulness. But that does not mean there are not more apt concepts for the theoretical and practical purposes that we have. It is crucial to be reminded of this, and perhaps especially so in the case of normative concepts, where our normative prejudices might have affected what concepts we have.

10.2 Contemporary Metaethics

Much contemporary work in metaethics makes heavy use of tools from philosophy of language and linguistics, and is based around sophisticated accounts of how our actual normative terms work. For example, there is much exciting work on deontic modals building on Angelika Kratzer's pioneering work on modals.[5] There is no denying the value in this work. But it is still limited in significance, insofar as it only

---

[5] See the essays in Kratzer (2012).

tells us about the nature of the linguistic tools we happen to have. Recall the Tragic community, from Chapter 1, whose normative terms fail to track the normatively significant properties. We might be in their situation. For that matter, our normative predicates might fail to ascribe normative properties at all—and they might fail to ascribe properties at all—even while there are normative properties.

I will illustrate the general concerns by considering Finlay's (2014) discussion of the semantics of normative terms, and the broader conclusions Finlay draws from what he arrives at regarding semantics. The work is a defense of Finlay's end-relational theory of such central normative words as "good," "ought," and "reason." In Finlay's view, these words "refer to probabilistic relations in which things stand to particular 'ends' or potential states of affairs that vary from context to context."[6] Roughly, to say of something e.g. that it is "good" is that it is likely to help bring about an end—and which end is at issue may differ between contexts. For example, if we are building something together and you point to a given tool and say "that is good," what you say is likely something along the following lines: use of that tool is likely to help bring about that we manage to build whatever we build. That *some* uses of "good" and other central normative words are like this is relatively uncontroversial and not very theoretically exciting. What is significant regarding what Finlay does is that he (a) manages to present a *unified* theory of all the different uses of the normative words in question, and in particular (b) that he rather persuasively argues what has just been sketched goes also for paradigmatic normative uses of these words of the kinds that the metaethics discussion has tended to focus on. To elaborate on the latter point: many theorists have held, and even simply implicitly assumed, that words like the ones Finlay focuses on have, so to speak, "plain" uses and that these uses are the most important ones. It can seem that one can ask oneself what one plainly ought to do (as opposed to what one ought to do to achieve this or that specific purpose), what plainly is good (as opposed to good for this or that other purpose), and what one plainly has reason to do (as opposed to reason to do for this or that other purpose). What Finlay argues is that even in the seemingly "plain" cases, one is really speaking end-relationally, appearances to the contrary.

Reflecting on the metaphysical significance of his theory of normative language, Finlay says: "So it would be fair to say that on the end-relational theory no properties or facts are normative per se (or absolutely), but only relative to agents or motivated perspectives."[7] But it surely cannot follow from the end-relational theory that no properties or facts are normative absolutely. The end-relational theory is only a theory about the normative language *we have.* The most that follows is that what we semantically express when using our normative vocabulary is never anything

---

[6] Finlay (2014), p. 1.
[7] Finlay (2014), p. 249f. Finlay only deals with *some* normative expressions, and his claim relies on the further, unargued assumption that all normative language can be dealt with in the way that he deals with the expressions he is concerned with. In the main text, I will abstract away from this (real) complication.

that is normative absolutely. This is compatible with some properties or facts being normative absolutely. One can perfectly consistently hold that Finlay is completely right about the normative language we do have, while there also are such possible predicates as those described by other theories. Insofar as Finlay's points regarding our normative language serve to argue against the view that some properties or facts are absolutely normative, it is only indirectly. For example, Finlay could argue that our belief that there is absolute normativity derives from misunderstandings of how our normative language works. Once we are clear on the workings of our language, that source of belief in absolute normativity should go away.[8]

Suppose that Finlay's theory of how our actual normative language works is right. Other accounts of the workings of normative language are still coherent accounts, describing possible languages. For example, G.E. Moore described how some possible normative vocabulary could work when talking about the nonanalyzability of "good." Wedgwood describes how some possible normative vocabulary works. This is so regardless of whether there are normative properties in the world answering to predicates like those that Moore and Wedgwood describe. It can, for example, be that Wedgwood's "B(x, y, z, t)" is meaningful yet fails to ascribe a relation and is true of nothing. If these other accounts describe possible languages, there is the question of which language we ought to use. (The awkwardness in framing that kind of question has of course been a theme throughout the book, but discussed primarily in Chapter 2.) I can envisage the response on Finlay's behalf that when we describe these supposed alternatives to actual normative language, we employ our own normative vocabulary: and if Finlay is right about how actual normative vocabulary works, then the descriptions of the supposed alternatives say something other than what those who put them forward tend to think they mean. But while I see that such a response may in principle be offered, it is hard for me to say something specific about unless it is spelled out in detail why this would be so. In the absence of such elaboration, I find it hard to say something more than: that just does not seem plausible to me.

It could further be insisted that although there are these other possible languages, questions about normativity are essentially questions about what gets expressed by the normative vocabulary of actual languages—that one simply changes the topic if one focuses on what is expressed by some in some sense corresponding vocabulary of some merely possible languages. One impatient response to is to say: who cares about whether the alternative vocabulary is "normative"? If it is not, then maybe *schmormative* questions are what we should focus on instead of strictly normative questions. Second, another response with which I am sympathetic is one in effect

---

[8] Compare too Wedgwood (2001): "[i]f the semantics of moral terms comes down in favor of [emotivism]...we should reject the very idea of moral properties" (p. 3). Not really: even if our actual moral terms do not refer to or ascribe moral properties, there might still be moral properties, and some possible terms could refer to or ascribe these properties.

presented by Guy Kahane (2013), albeit in a slightly different dialectical context. Kahane identifies what he calls the value role as "the role of setting a standard by which attitude and action can be made intelligible and justified, and in light of which we deliberate (in the first-person), and give advice or criticize (in the second- and third-person)." Kahane then notes that

we could identify the evaluative discourse of some utterly foreign culture without needing (or even being able) to determine whether its semantics is, say, response-dependent or not (this had better be true, given that we have trouble answering this semantic question about our *own* discourse!)

and uses this observation to argue that the value role can be played by discourses of all these kinds. Third, and most importantly, given the normative role view on the question of what makes expressions and concepts normative, plainly there can be normative expressions and concepts importantly different from those employed in our actual language: what makes an expression or concept normative is simply it being associated with some normative role.

10.3 Variance Theses

The sorts of philosophical and metaphilosophical issues that have come up throughout this book are usefully compared to some strands in the recent *metaontological* discussion. Let me first summarize these strands in their own right and then return to metaethics.

The contemporary metaontological discussion mainly concerns the status of the very enterprise of ontology, the branch of metaphysics concerned with what exists. Some find ontological questions genuine and deep; others have disdain for ontology and find the ontological questions discussed to be mere pseudoquestions or in some other way defective or shallow. In the contemporary discussion, Eli Hirsch has in a series of essays defended a certain kind of negative stance toward ontology. Hirsch is associated with two distinct but related metaontological theses: the doctrine of *quantifier variance*, and the idea that ontological disputes are *verbal*.[9]

The doctrine of quantifier variance (QV) is the view that "the world can be correctly described using a variety of concepts of 'the existence of something'" and that "different concepts of an 'object' might be employed in different conceptual schemes,

---

[9] The quick characterization of the doctrines found in the main text is somewhat quick. For a fuller discussion, see e.g. my (2011b). Two things are worth stressing. First, Hirsch does not defend either thesis in full generality, but only with respect to certain disputes regarding the ontology of physical objects. Second, I think it is pretty clear that Hirsch does not actually defend the thesis I call quantifier variance, even though some of his formulations suggest this and even though some of the literature in response to Hirsch has focused on this thesis. Note "the thesis I call quantifier variance." Hirsch defends a thesis he dubbed "quantifier variance," and the thesis I call quantifier variance corresponds to how that has sometimes been understood.

schemes that are all adequate for describing the world."[10] Using one concept of existence, one can truly say "tables exist"; using another concept, one can truly say "tables don't exist," etc. An integral part of this doctrine as presented is that no concept of existence is *metaphysically privileged*.[11] QV is then supposed to justify an antionto-logical stance as follows. If there simply are different equally good concepts of existence, then the interest of the claim that something "exists" in the sense of one or other of these concepts is deflated—this something can still fail to "exist" in the sense of others, and there is nothing privileging one of these concepts over others. The idea that there are different concepts of existence is pivotal to QV, and a crucial question regarding the doctrine is that of what it takes for something to be a concept of existence. An assumption underlying much of the discussion is the Quinean one that existential quantification expresses existence and we can say "there are Fs" to express that Fs exist, so the question becomes: what makes something an unrestricted exist-ential quantifier (or an existential quantifier meaning, or the type of concept expressed by an existential quantifier)?[12] And while that question perhaps has not received the attention it deserves, the type of answer usually found appeals to a conceptual, and more specifically inferential, role: what makes an expression express unrestricted existential quantification is that it obeys the standard inference rules—the standard introduction and elimination rules—associated with the existential quantifier.[13]

When talking about *verbal disputes* (VD), Hirsch says things like "I claim that the dispute between endurantists and perdurantists is verbal," where a verbal dispute is one where "each party ought to agree that the other party speaks the truth in its own language."[14] (There are many uses of the labels "endurantism" and "perdurantism" in the literature. On the way Hirsch uses these labels, the views differ primarily over what there is: the perdurantist believes in a strictly richer ontology as she believes in temporal parts and arbitrary sums thereof.) It would take us too far afield here to get into the details regarding this debate and what Hirsch says about it. The point is just that where friends of ontology take the disputants to be defending two importantly different theses about the nature of reality, Hirsch takes the disputants simply to be talking past each other. And the point is supposed to generalize to many other disputes regarding the ontology of physical objects. A main strand in Hirsch's argument for VD is that the *principle of charity* governs correct interpretation, and charity is especially important when it comes to certain classes of utterances, such as perceptual reports and utterances that concern what is regarded as a priori and necessary. VD is supposed to justify an antiontological stance in that if VD is true, many ontological disputes really just turn on the disputants' using language differ-ently, and do not concern anything deeper than that.

---

[10] Hirsch (2011), pp. 68, 139. In both places there are prominent references to Hilary Putnam as a friend of the view.
[11] Ibid., p. 84.   [12] See Quine (1948).
[13] See e.g. Hirsch (2011), p. 71, and Sider (2009), p. 393.   [14] Hirsch (2011), p. 229.

QV and VD, while related, are clearly in principle independent of each other. There can be a metaphysically privileged concept of existence even while different speakers employ different concepts of existence and thus speak past each other. Conversely, people with very different conceptions of what existence is can be employing one and the same concept even if no concept of existence is metaphysically privileged.

QV and VD obviously have possible counterparts in other parts of philosophy. For all sorts of different philosophical notions, X, one can ask whether there is a privileged concept of X; and one can ask whether disputes over "X" are in fact verbal and the disputants employ different concepts.

My own view is that QV and its counterpart theses in other areas of philosophy are of more principled philosophical significance than VD and its counterparts. If philosophers actually use different notions "X," that is of course a problem as far as debates as actually prosecuted are concerned. But so long as there is a privileged concept of X, one could in principle get around these concepts by debating what the privileged concept of X is, and then discussing what falls under this privileged concept X. Of course theses of VD's kind can serve an important critical purpose, showing that something is amiss with a debate as actually conducted. But conceived of as philosophical end results, verdicts on theses in the style of QV are of greater significance.[15]

(Meta)ethics is one domain where there are counterparts of QV and VD. The counterpart of VD would be that central disputes purporting to be about what is right, what is good, etc. are really only verbal disputes, with the disputants using "right," "good," etc. with different meanings. The counterpart of QV would be that there are different concepts of rightness, different concepts of goodness, etc., and none of these concepts are privileged over the others. In Chapter 2, I critically discussed the idea that debates over normative realism should be cast as debates over whether there are unique elite properties of rightness, goodness, etc., where "elite" is my term for what is sometimes otherwise called "natural," "fundamental," "joint-carving," etc. An upshot of this earlier discussion of Sider is that while one can speak of what is in some sense "privileged" both in the case of ontology and in the case of ethics, one should not assume that it is the same notion of privilege that is relevant in both cases. In the case of ontology, maybe being privileged can be understood as being elite.

The question of whether ethical disputes are merely verbal tends to come up in the literature, but indirectly. It is presupposed that ethical disputes, even fundamental ones, are not merely verbal, and this putative fact is put to theoretical work when particular theories of the workings of normative language are held to be inconsistent with this. This is, for example, a theme in the Moral Twin Earth literature.[16] It is generally a theme in the rich literature on moral disagreement.[17] What this literature

---

[15] See further Eklund (2016).

[16] See again Horgan and Timmons (1992a, 2009). I discussed some aspects of the Moral Twin Earth arguments in Chapters 2 and 6.

[17] See e.g. Björnsson (forthcoming), Plunkett and Sundell (2013), and Tersman (2006).

does not tend to bring up is whether there are *privileged* concepts of rightness, goodness, etc. While an analog of VD is prominent in the discussion, although seldom actually embraced, a counterpart of QV is hardly discussed.

As mentioned, one question that arises in connection with QV is what makes something a concept of existence to begin with. Analogous questions arise concerning the counterpart of QV in metaethics. What makes something a concept of rightness (goodness, etc.)? One answer to these questions is: playing the normative role associated with rightness (goodness, etc.). That is the answer that I have operated with. And that answer is somewhat analogous to the standard answer in the case of QV. What makes some expression express existence is its inferential role; what makes some expression express a concept of rightness is its normative role.[18]

There are further potential analogies. Return to the embarrassment of riches objection (Chapter 3). The concern was that even if normative role determines reference, so that all expressions semantically associated in the right way with the same normative role are guaranteed to have the same reference, expressions with slightly different normative roles can still differ in reference—and the problem presented by Alternative can be presented in new form, one where Bad Guy employs expressions and concepts differing slightly from ours in what normative roles they are associated with. Compare now what Sider says in the course of characterizing his "ontological realist" view on ontology:

Let's give the speakers of ordinary English "there exists"; let us henceforth conduct our debate using "∃". We hereby stipulate that "∃" is to express an austere relative of the ordinary English notion of existence. We hereby stipulate that although the meaning of "∃" is to obey the core inferential role of English quantifiers, ordinary, casual use of disputed sentences involving "there exists" (such as "Tables exist") are not to affect at all what we mean by "∃". We hereby stipulate that if there is a highly natural meaning that satisfies these constraints, then that is what we mean by "∃". Perhaps the resulting "∃" has no synonym in English. Fine—we hereby dub our new language Ontologese.[19]

Earlier in my discussion, I have used "elite" where Sider uses "natural," and I will continue doing so here, not wishing to tie my discussion to any specific conception of eliteness. The idea is that if there is a highly elite meaning that satisfies the constraints laid down, then threats to ontology as an enterprise are averted. Sider focuses on the following skeptical theses (PVI and DKL are here two ontological disputants whose initials happen to be those of Peter van Inwagen and David Lewis, the dispute over whether there are tables a suitable token of ontological dispute):

Equivocation PVI and DKL express different propositions with "There exist tables"; each makes claims that are true given what he means; so the debate is merely verbal.

---

[18] One should be careful not to overstate the analogy. One can speak of "role" in both cases, but it is not clear that in each case one speaks at the same level of abstraction.
[19] Sider (2009), p. 412.

Indeterminacy Neither PVI nor DKL expresses a unique proposition with "There exist tables"; in their mouths, this sentence is semantically indeterminate over various candidates, some of which make PVI's claims true, others of which make DKL's claims true. So the debate is ill-formulated.

Obviousness PVI and DKL express the same proposition with "There exist tables", but it is obvious by linguistic/conceptual reflection what its truth value is, so the debate is silly.[20]

Sider says that in Ontologese, "Equivocation, Obviousness, and Indeterminacy will all be false." What he means is that if the disputants both speak Ontologese, they won't speak past each other à la Equivocation, the answers to the questions formulated will not be obvious in the way described under Obviousness, and the questions will not lack answers because of semantic indeterminacy.[21] However, even if Sider is right about this, it remains that there are different existential quantifier meanings characterized by different inference rules. When Sider speaks of the core inferential role of English quantifiers, what he means are, he explains, the core inferential rules of quantification theory—by which he appears to mean the classical rules for the quantifier. But then consider the quantifier of some non-classical logic, governed by some different set of rules. Even if the classical rules pick out an elite meaning in the way Sider describes, it can in principle be that some non-classical rules in some analogous way pick out another fully elite meaning. Suppose "∃*" is an alternative quantifier governed by these non-classical rules. Then we can envisage some ontologists advocating that one should focus on what exists in the sense of "∃" and others advocating that one should focus on what exists in the sense of "∃*." Even if it is determinate what exists in each of these senses, this dispute remains unresolved.

All this said, there may be reasons not to be very concerned about this supposed problem in the case of ontology. Perhaps given independently plausible assumptions about the realm of the elite—say, concerning the non-redundancy of what is elite—there cannot be highly elite meanings corresponding to both these quantifiers. And what is more, perhaps one can adopt an ecumenical stance and say that if the meanings of both these quantifiers indeed are highly elite, we should simply be concerned *both* with what exists in the sense of "∃" and with what exists in the sense of "∃*."

The case of "∃" and "∃*" parallels the case motivating the embarrassment of riches objection in the case of metaethics, and that is one reason why it is interesting to bring it up. "∃" and "∃*" have different but only slightly different conceptual roles;

---

[20] Sider (2009), p. 386f.

[21] Perhaps it is worth pointing out that even if Sider is right about what happens when both disputants speak Ontologese, the specific features of Ontologese are irrelevant to some of the claims. Let L be any language L, whether particularly elite or not, without ambiguity or indeterminacy. Then under the assumption that the disputants both speak L, they will not speak past each other à la Equivocation, and the questions won't lack answers because of semantic indeterminacy. Likewise, there are ways of avoiding Obviousness that do not involve anything specific to Ontologese.

the embarrassment of riches objection concerns expressions with different but only slightly different normative roles. Recall, the embarrassment of riches objection was to the effect that even if normative role determines reference, it can be that different normative roles serve to determine reference in such a way that a version of the alternative concepts problem remains.

Neither of the two possible reasons mentioned for not worrying unduly about the case of "∃" and "∃*" has an immediate counterpart in the case of metaethics. I have argued that in the metaethics case one should not cash being privileged in terms of eliteness, in the sense of the metaphysical debate. This means that any general considerations pertaining to the non-redundancy of the realm of the elite will fail to carry over to the case of metaethics. And the ecumenical stance, whatever in the end to say about it, faces problems in the case of metaethics that it does not face in the case of ontology. Suppose there are two non-coreferential expressions, "right" and "right*," with different but only slightly different normative roles. And suppose some possible action that you might perform, and which is fraught with consequences, is "right*" but not "right." Thinking that one should be concerned both with what is "right" and with what is "right*" does not quite cut it. How does that help when you are faced with the question of whether to perform this action?

11

Concluding Remarks

Throughout most of this book I have been concerned with the distinction between theories according to which some possible predicates are referentially normative and theories that deny this. I have explored the distinction and its relevance for various issues in metaethics, emphasizing that under reasonable assumptions this is a crucial distinction in many ways. I will resist any temptation to repeat myself. If a reader has read all the way to here, she will anyway know what I am talking about.

One thing I have not done is to try to settle the issue of whether any possible predicates are referentially normative. In a way, this must be disappointing: I don't come down in favor of any particular view. But the reason I don't defend any view on this is that I don't know which view is correct.

One might have thought that one could settle the issue over referential normativity by appeal to linguistic evidence. But even if no actual predicates are referentially normative, some possible ones may well be (see Chapter 10 on the use of linguistic data concerning actual normative language). And even if our intuitions are to the effect that there is referential normativity, such intuitions should not be taken to carry as much weight as ordinary linguistic intuitions do (see Chapter 6, the discussion of "gidplissing"). One might think that reasons to favor naturalism are reasons to be suspicious of referential normativity—that any property that is intrinsically such that it is apt to be picked out by any non-defective predicate semantically associated with a certain normative role just could not be naturalistically acceptable. But even setting aside unclarity regarding exactly what naturalism is, it is not obvious to me why it would be so. Generally, any purported reason to think no naturalistic metaphysics could be up to the task is as much simply a reason to think that the property in question would have to be ~~really mysterious~~. One does not avoid the mystery by insisting that the property is non-natural; one merely labels it.

Sometimes I am even attracted to a ~~principled agnosticism~~ regarding whether there is any referential normativity. Perhaps there just is no way to settle the issue. But I don't have any argument in favor of this agnosticism apart from what I have already recounted: what might have seemed like reasonable strategies for settling the issue seem not to work very well.

The agnosticism so far professed concerns the existence of referential normativity. There is yet another big question about which I have no firm opinion. Throughout much of the book I have reasoned as if non-defective referential normativity suffices for the ardent realist's purposes. But a serious objection to such a claim—the embarrassment of riches objection—was presented and discussed in Chapter 3. The discussion was inconclusive. It was stressed that the most promising response to the objection ran into problems having to do with the possibility of embracing a certain kind of truth pluralism.

I have unequivocally claimed that ardent realism requires non-defective referential normativity, and that genuine normativity in the world requires the same. The open questions concern whether there can be non-defective referential normativity, and, as the embarrassment of riches objection brings up, just what else may be required for ardent realism.

References

Alm, David: 2000, "Moral Conditionals, Non-Cognitivism, and Meaning", *Southern Journal of Philosophy* 38: 355–77.

Anderson, Luvell and Ernest Lepore: 2013, "Slurring Words", *Noûs* 47: 25–48.

Ayer, A.J.: 1936, *Language, Truth and Logic*, Gollanz, London.

Baker, Derek: forthcoming, "The Varieties of Normativity", in McPherson and Plunkett (eds.) (forthcoming) *Routledge Handbook of Metaethics*, Routledge.

Barker, Stephen J.: 2000, "Is Value Content a Component of Conventional Implicature?", *Analysis* 60: 268–79.

Bar-On, Dorit and Matthew Chrisman: 2009, "Ethical Neo-Expressivism", *Oxford Studies in Metaethics* 4: 132–65.

Beall, Jc and Michael Glanzberg: 2011, "The Liar Paradox", in Edward N. Zalta (ed.), *Stanford Encyclopedia of Philosophy*. Available at http://plato.stanford.edu/entries/moral-non-naturalism.

Bedke, Matthew: 2009, "Moral Judgement Purposivism: Saving Internalism from Amoralism", *Philosophical Studies* 144: 189–209.

Bedke, Matthew: 2014, "Review of Pekka Väyrynen, *The Lewd, The Rude and the Nasty*", *Notre Dame Philosophical Reviews*. Available at http://ndpr.nd.edu/news/47974-the-lewd-the-rude-and-the-nasty.

Björnsson, Gunnar: forthcoming, "The Significance of Disagreement for Theories of Ethical Thought and Talk", in McPherson and Plunkett (eds.) (forthcoming) *Routledge Handbook of Metaethics*, Routledge.

Blackburn, Simon: 1984, *Spreading the Word*, Clarendon Press, Oxford.

Blackburn, Simon: 1992, "Morality and Thick Concepts II – Through Thick and Thin", *Proceedings of the Aristotelian Society*, suppl. vol. 66: 85–99.

Blackburn, Simon: 1993, *Essays in Quasi-Realism*, Oxford University Press, Oxford.

Blackburn, Simon: 1998, *Ruling Passions*, Oxford University Press, Oxford.

Blackburn, Simon: 1999, *Think*, Oxford University Press, Oxford.

Blackburn, Simon: 2013, "Disentangling Disentangling", in Simon Kirchin (ed.), *Thick Concepts*, Oxford University Press, Oxford, pp. 121–35.

Blackburn, Simon and Neil Sinclair: 2006, "Comments on Gibbard's *Thinking How to Live*", *Philosophy and Phenomenological Research* 72: 699–706.

Boghossian, Paul: 1996, "Analyticity Reconsidered", *Noûs* 30: 360–91.

Boghossian, Paul: 2003, "Blind Reasoning", *Proceedings of the Aristotelian Society*, suppl. vol. 78: 225–48.

Boisvert, Daniel: 2008, "Expressive-Assertivism", *Pacific Philosophical Quarterly* 89: 169–203.

Boyd, Richard: 1988, "How to be a Moral Realist", in Geoff Sayre-McCord (ed.), *Essays on Moral Realism*, Cornell University Press, Ithaca, New York, pp. 181–228.

Brandom, Robert: 2000, *Articulating Reasons*, Harvard University Press, Cambridge, Massachusetts.

Brandom, Robert: 2001, "Modality, Normativity, and Intentionality", *Philosophy and Phenomenological Research* 63: 587–609.

Brink, David: 1989, *Moral Realism and the Foundations of Ethics*, Cambridge University Press, Cambridge.

Brink, David: 2001, "Realism, Naturalism, and Moral Semantics", *Social Philosophy & Policy* 18: 154–76.

Burgess, Alexis and David Plunkett: 2013a, "Conceptual Ethics I", *Philosophy Compass* 8: 1091–101.

Burgess, Alexis and David Plunkett: 2013b, "Conceptual Ethics II", *Philosophy Compass* 8: 1102–110.

Carnap, Rudolf: 1950a, "Empiricism, Semantics and Ontology", *Revue Internationale de Philosophie* 4: 20–40. Reprinted with minor changes in *Meaning and Necessity: A Study in Semantics and Modal Logic*. Enlarged edition. Chicago: University of Chicago Press (1956).

Carnap, Rudolf: 1950b, *Logical Foundations of Probability*, University of Chicago Press, Chicago, Illinois.

Chalmers, David: 2011, "Verbal Disputes", *Philosophical Review* 120: 515–66.

Chappell, Sophie Grace: 2013, "There Are No Thin Concepts", in Simon Kirchin (ed.), *Thick Concepts*, Oxford University Press, Oxford, pp. 182–96. Published under the name Timothy Chappell.

Copp, David: 2000, "Explanation and Justification in Ethics", *Ethics* 100: 237–58.

Copp, David: 2001, "Realist-Expressivism: A Neglected Option for Moral Realism", *Social Philosophy & Policy* 18: 1–43.

Copp, David: 2004, "Moral Naturalism and Three Grades of Normativity", in Peter Schaber (ed.), *Normativity and Naturalism*, Ontos Verlag, Frankfurt, pp. 7–45.

Copp, David: 2009, "Realist-Expressivism and Conventional Implicature", *Oxford Studies in Metaethics* 4: 167–202.

Copp, David: 2013, "Normativity and Reasons: Five Arguments from Parfit Against Normative Naturalism", in Susana Nuccetelli and Gary Seay (eds.), *Ethical Naturalism: Current Debates*, Cambridge University Press, Cambridge, pp. 24–57.

Cuneo, Terence: 2007, *The Normative Web*, Oxford University Press, Oxford.

Dancy, Jonathan: 1993, *Moral Reasons*, Blackwell, Oxford.

Dancy, Jonathan: 1996, "In Defense of Thick Concepts", in Peter A. French, Theodore E. Uehling, Jr., and Howard K. Wettstein (eds.), *Moral Concepts*, Midwest Studies in Philosophy, Volume XX, University of Notre Dame Press, Notre Dame, Indiana, pp. 263–79.

Dancy, Jonathan: 2006, "Nonnaturalism", in David Copp (ed.), *The Oxford Handbook of Ethical Theory*, Oxford University Press, Oxford, pp. 122–45.

Daniels, Norman: 2011, "Reflective Equilibrium", in Edward N. Zalta (ed.), *Stanford Encyclopedia of Philosophy*. Available at http://plato.stanford.edu/entries/reflective-equilibrium.

Dougherty, Tom: 2014, "Vague Value", *Philosophy and Phenomenological Research* 89: 352–72.

Dowell, Janice: 2016, "The Metaethical Insignificance of Moral Twin Earth", *Oxford Studies in Metaethics* 11: 1–27.

Dowell, Janice and David Sobel: forthcoming, "Advice for Non-Analytic Naturalists", in Simon Kirchin (ed.), *Reading Parfit*, Routledge.

Dreier, Jamie: 1990, "Internalism and Speaker Relativism", *Ethics* 101: 6–26.

Dreier, Jamie: 2004, "Meta-Ethics and the Problem of Creeping Minimalism", *Philosophical Perspectives* 18: 23–44.

Dummett, Michael: 1981, *Frege: Philosophy of Language*, 2nd edn, Harvard University Press, Cambridge, Massachusetts.

Dummett, Michael: 1991, *The Logical Basis of Metaphysics*, Duckworth, London.

Dunaway, William and Tristram McPherson: 2016, "Reference Magnetism as a Solution to the Moral Twin Earth Problem", *Ergo* 3: 639–79.

Dworkin, Ronald: 2011, *Justice for Hedgehogs*, Harvard University Press, Cambridge, Massachusetts.

Edwards, Douglas: 2013, "The Eligibility of Ethical Naturalism", *Pacific Philosophical Quarterly* 94: 1–18.

Eklund, Matti: 2002a, "Inconsistent Languages", *Philosophy and Phenomenological Research* 64: 251–75.

Eklund, Matti: 2002b, "Deep Inconsistency", *Australasian Journal of Philosophy* 80: 321–31.

Eklund, Matti: 2005, "What Vagueness Consists In", *Philosophical Studies* 125: 27–60.

Eklund, Matti: 2010, "Vagueness and Second-Level Indeterminacy", in Richard Dietz and Sebastiano Moruzzi (eds.), *Cuts and Clouds*, Oxford University Press, Oxford, pp. 63–76.

Eklund, Matti: 2011a, "What are Thick Concepts?", *Canadian Journal of Philosophy* 41: 25–49.

Eklund, Matti: 2011b, "Review of Eli Hirsch, *Quantifier Variance and Realism*", *Notre Dame Philosophical Reviews*. Available at http://ndpr.nd.edu/news/24764-quantifier-variance-and-realism-essays-in-metaontology.

Eklund, Matti: 2012a, "Alternative Normative Concepts", *Analytic Philosophy* 53: 139–57.

Eklund, Matti: 2012b, "The Multitude View on Logic", in Greg Restall and Gillian Russell (eds.), *New Waves in Philosophical Logic*, Palgrave Macmillan, London, pp. 217–40.

Eklund, Matti: 2013, "Evaluative Language and Evaluative Reality", in Simon Kirchin (ed.), *Concepts*, Oxford University Press, Oxford, pp. 161–81.

Eklund, Matti: 2015, "Intuitions, Conceptual Engineering, and Conceptual Fixed Points", in Christopher Daly (ed.), *Palgrave Handbook of Philosophical Methods*, Palgrave MacMillan, London, pp. 363–85.

Eklund, Matti: 2016, "Carnap's Legacy for the Contemporary Ontological Debate", in Stephan Blatti and Sandra Lapointe (eds.), *Ontology After Carnap*, Oxford University Press, Oxford, pp. 165–89.

Elstein, Daniel and Thomas Hurka: 2009, "From Thick to Thin: Two Moral Reduction Plans", *Canadian Journal of Philosophy* 39: 515–35.

Engels, Friedrich: 1872–3, "The Housing Question", in Karl Marx and Friedrich Engels, *Selected Works*, Vol. I, Foreign Languages Publishing House, Moscow (1962).

Enoch, David: 2011, *Taking Morality Seriously*, Oxford University Press, Oxford.

Evnine, Simon: 2014, "Essentially Contested Concepts and Semantic Externalism", *Journal of the Philosophy of History* 8: 118–40.

Field, Hartry: 2009, "Pluralism in Logic", *Review of Symbolic Logic* 2: 342–59.

Fine, Kit: 1994, "Essence and Modality", *Philosophical Perspectives* 8: 1–16.

Finlay, Stephen: 2005, "Value and Implicature", *Philosophers' Imprint* 5: 1–20.

Finlay, Stephen: 2007, "Four Faces of Moral Realism", *Philosophy Compass* 2: 820–49.

Finlay, Stephen: 2010, "Recent Work on Normativity", *Analysis* 70:, 331–46.

Finlay, Stephen: 2014, *Confusion of Tongues*, Oxford University Press, Oxford.

FitzPatrick, William: 2008, "Robust Ethical Realism, Non-Naturalism and Normativity", *Oxford Studies in Metaethics* 3: 159–205.

FitzPatrick, William: 2009, "Recent Work on Ethical Realism", *Analysis* 69: 746–60.

FitzPatrick, William: 2011, "Ethical Non-Naturalism and Normative Properties", in Michael Brady (ed.), *New Waves in Metaethics*, Palgrave Macmillan, London, pp. 7–35.

FitzPatrick, William: 2014, "Skepticism About Naturalizing Normativity: In Defense of Ethical Nonnaturalism", *Res Philosophica* 91: 559–88.

Foot, Philippa: 1958, "Moral Arguments", *Mind* 67: 502–13. Reprinted in *Virtues and Vices*, Basil Blackwell, Oxford (1978), pp. 96–109.

Foot, Philippa: 1972, "Morality as a System of Hypothetical Imperatives", *Philosophical Review* 81: 305–16.

Frege, Gottlob: 1892, "On Concept and Object", *Vierteljahresschrift für wissenschaftliche Philosophie* 16: 192–205. Reprinted in Michael Beaney (ed.), *The Frege Reader*, Blackwell, Oxford, pp. 181–93.

Gallie, W.B.: 1956, "Essentially Contested Concepts", *Proceedings of the Aristotelian Society* 56: 167–98.

Geach, Peter: 1956, "Good and Evil", *Analysis* 17: 32–42.

Gert, Joshua: 2012, *Normative Bedrock: Response-Dependence, Rationality, and Reasons*, Oxford University Press, Oxford.

Gibbard, Allan: 1990, *Wise Choices, Apt Feelings*, Harvard University Press, Cambridge, Massachusetts.

Gibbard, Allan: 1992, "Morality and Thick Concepts (I) – Thick Concepts and Warrant for Feelings", *Proceedings of the Aristotelian Society*, suppl. vol. 66: 267–83.

Gibbard, Allan: 2003, *Thinking How to Live*, Harvard University Press, Cambridge, Massachusetts.

Gibbard, Allan: 2006, "Normative Properties", in Terry Horgan and Mark Timmons (eds.), *Metaethics After Moore*, Oxford University Press, Oxford, pp. 319–37.

Glass, Marvin: 1973, "Philippa Foot's Naturalism: A New Version of the Breakdown Theory in Ethics", *Mind* 82: 417–20.

Goodman, Nelson: 1955, *Fact, Fiction, and Forecast*, Harvard University Press, Cambridge, Massachusetts.

Hare, R.M.: 1952, *The Language of Morals*, Clarendon Press, Oxford.

Hare, R.M.: 1997, *Sorting Out Ethics*, Clarendon Press, Oxford.

Harman, Gilbert: 1986, "The Meaning of the Logical Constants", in Ernest Lepore (ed.), *Truth and Interpretation: Perspectives on the Philosophy of Donald Davidson*, Blackwell, Oxford, pp. 125–34.

Haslanger, Sally: 2012, *Resisting Reality*, Oxford University Press, Oxford.

Hawthorne, John: 2007, "Craziness and Metasemantics", *Philosophical Review* 116: 427–41.

Hay, Ryan: 2013, "Hybrid Expressivism and the Analogy Between Pejoratives and Moral Language", *European Journal of Philosophy* 21: 450–74.

Heathwood, Chris: 2015, "Irreducibly Normative Properties", *Oxford Studies in Metaethics* 10: 216–44.

Hirsch, Eli: 2011, *Quantifier Variance and Realism*, Oxford University Press, New York.

Hodes, Harold: 1984, "Logicism and the Ontological Commitments of Arithmetic", *Journal of Philosophy* 81: 123–49.

Hofweber, Thomas: 2006, "Inexpressible Properties and Propositions", in Dean Zimmerman (ed.), *Oxford Studies in Metaphysics*, vol. 2, Oxford University Press, Oxford, pp. 155–206.

Holton, Richard: 2010, "Comments on Ralph Wedgwood's *The Nature of Normativity*", *Philosophical Studies* 151: 449–57.

Hom, Christopher: 2008, "The Semantics of Racial Epithets", *Journal of Philosophy* 105: 406–40.

Hom, Christopher: 2010, "Pejoratives", *Philosophy Compass* 5: 164–85.

Horgan, Terence and Mark Timmons: 1992a, "Troubles for New Wave Moral Semantics: The 'Open Question Argument' Revived", *Philosophical Papers* 21: 153–75.

Horgan, Terence and Mark Timmons: 1992b, "Troubles on Moral Twin Earth: Moral Queerness Revived", *Synthese* 92: 221–60.

Horgan, Terence and Mark Timmons: 1996, "From Moral Realism to Moral Relativism in One Easy Step", *Crítica* 28: 3–39.

Horgan, Terence and Mark Timmons: 2000, "Copping Out on Moral Twin Earth", *Synthese* 124: 139–52.

Horgan, Terence and Mark Timmons: 2009, "Analytical Moral Functionalism Meets Moral Twin Earth", in Ian Ravenscroft (ed.), *Minds, Ethics and Conditionals*, Oxford University Press, Oxford, pp. 221–37.

Jackson, Frank: 1998, *From Metaphysics to Ethics*, Clarendon Press, Oxford.

Joyce, Richard: 2001, *The Myth of Morality*, Cambridge University Press, Cambridge.

Kahane, Guy: 2013, "Must Metaethical Realism Make a Semantic Claim", *Journal of Moral Philosophy* 10: 148–78.

Kauppinen, Antti: 2007, "The Rise and Fall of Experimental Philosophy", *Philosophical Explorations* 10: 95–118.

Kirchin, Simon: 2010, "The Shapelessness Hypothesis", *Philosophers' Imprint* 10: 1–28.

Kirchin, Simon (ed.): 2013a, *Thick Concepts*, Oxford University Press, Oxford.

Kirchin, Simon: 2013b, "Introduction: Thick and Thin Concepts", in Simon Kirchin (ed.), *Thick Concepts*, Oxford University Press, Oxford, pp. 1–19.

Kratzer, Angelika: 2012, *Modals and Conditionals*, Oxford University Press, Oxford.

Kripke, Saul: 1980, *Naming and Necessity*, Harvard University Press, Cambridge, Massachusetts.

Leiter, Brian: 2001, "Moral Facts and Best Explanations", in Ellen Frankel Paul, Fred Miller, and Jeffrey Paul (eds.), *Moral Knowledge*, Cambridge University Press, Cambridge, pp. 79–101.

Lewis, David: 1970, "How to Define Theoretical Terms", *Journal of Philosophy* 67: 427–46.

Lewis, David: 1972, "Psychophysical and Theoretical Identifications", *Australasian Journal of Philosophy* 50: 249–58.

Lewis, David: 1983, "New Work For a Theory of Universals", *Australasian Journal of Philosophy* 61: 343–77.

Lewis, David: 1984, "Putnam's Paradox", *Australasian Journal of Philosophy* 62: 221–36.

Lewis, David: 1997, "Naming the Colours", *Australasian Journal of Philosophy* 75: 325–42.

Lukes, Steven: 1985, *Marxism and Morality*, Clarendon Press, Oxford.

Lynch, Michael: 2009, *Truth as One and Many*, Oxford University Press, Oxford.

MacIntyre, Alasdair: 1973, "The Essential Contestability of Some Social Concepts", *Ethics* 84: 1–9.

Mackie, John: 1977, *Ethics: Inventing Right and Wrong*, Penguin, Harmondsworth.

Marx, Karl: 1867, *Capital* Vol. I, translation by Moore and Aveling, Foreign Languages Publishing House, Moscow (1959).

Marx, Karl: 1880–2, *The Ethnological Notebooks of Karl Marx*. (Studies of Morgan, Phear, Maine, Lubbock.) Translated and edited with an introduction by L. Krader, Van Gorcum, Assen (1972).

McCready, Eric: 2010, "Varieties of Conventional Implicature", *Semantics and Pragmatics* 3: 1–57.

McDowell, John: 1979, "Virtue and Reason", *Monist* 62: 331–50.

McDowell, John: 1981, "Non-Cognitivism and Rule-Following", in Steven Holtzman and Christopher Leich (eds.), *Wittgenstein: To Follow a Rule*, Routledge & Kegan Paul, London, pp. 141–62.

McNaughton, David and Piers Rawling: 2000, "Unprincipled Ethics", in Brad Hooker and Margaret Little (eds.) *Moral Particularism*, Oxford University Press, Oxford, pp. 256–75.

McPherson, Tristram: 2011, "Against Quietist Normative Realism", *Philosophical Studies* 154: 223–40.

McPherson, Tristram and David Plunkett (eds.): forthcoming, *Routledge Handbook of Metaethics*, Routledge, London.

Merli, David: 2002, "Return to Moral Twin Earth", *Canadian Journal of Philosophy* 32: 207–40.

Merli, David: 2009, "Possessing Moral Concepts", *Philosophia* 37: 535–56.

Miller, Alexander: 2003, *An Introduction to Contemporary Metaethics*, Polity Press, Cambridge.

Miller, Alexander: 2014, "Realism", in Edward N. Zalta (ed.), *Stanford Encyclopedia of Philosophy*. Available at http://plato.stanford.edu/entries/realism.

Miller, Richard: 1984, *Analyzing Marx*, Princeton University Press, Princeton.

Millgram, Elijah: 1995, "Inhaltsreiche ethische Begriffe und die Unterscheidund zwischen Tatsachen und Werten", in C. Fehige and G. Meggle (eds.), *Zum moralischen Denken*, Suhrkamp, Frankfurt, pp. 354–88.

Moore, G.E.: 1903, *Principia Ethica*, Cambridge University Press, Cambridge.

Moore, G.E.: 1942, "A Reply to my Critics", in P.A. Schilpp (ed.), *The Philosophy of G. E. Moore*, Northwestern University Press, Evanston, Illinois, pp. 535–677.

Morgan, Seiriol: 2006, "Naturalism and Normativity", *Philosophy and Phenomenological Research* 72: 319–44.

Oddie, Graham: 2005, *Value, Reality and Desire*, Clarendon Press, Oxford.

Olson, Jonas: 2014, *Moral Error Theory: History, Critique, Defence*, Oxford University Press, Oxford.

Parfit, Derek: 2006, "Normativity", *Oxford Studies in Metaethics* 1: 325–80.

Parfit, Derek: 2011, *On What Matters*, Oxford University Press, Oxford. (Vols I and II.)

Pautz, Adam: 2013, "Does Phenomenology Ground Mental Content?", in Uriah Kriegel (ed.), *Phenomenal Intentionality*, Oxford University Press, Oxford, pp. 194–234.

Peacocke, Christopher: 1987, "Understanding Logical Constants: A Realist's Account", *Proceedings of the British Academy* 63: 153–99.

Pedersen, Nikolaj and Cory Wright (eds.): 2013, *Truth and Pluralism: Current Debates*, Oxford University Press, Oxford.

Plunkett, David and Timothy Sundell: 2013, "Disagreement and the Semantics of Normative and Evaluative Terms", *Philosopher's Imprint* 13: 1–37.

Prawitz, Dag: 1979, "Proofs and the Meaning and Completeness of the Logical Constants," in Jaakko Hintikka, Ilkka Niiniluoto, and Esa Saarinen (eds.), *Essays on Mathematical and Philosophical Logic*, Reidel, Dordrecht, pp. 25–40.

Price, Huw: 2013, *Expressivism, Pragmatism and Representationalism*, Cambridge University Press, Cambridge.

Priest, Graham: 1997, "Sexual Perversion", *Australasian Journal of Philosophy* 75: 360–72.

Putnam, Hilary: 1975, "The Meaning of "Meaning"", in Keith Gunderson (ed.), *Language, Mind and Knowledge, Minnesota Studies in Philosophy of Science* 7, Minneapolis: University of Minnesota Press, pp. 131–93.

Quine, W.v.O.: 1948, "On What There Is", *Review of Metaphysics* 2: 21–38. Reprinted in *From a Logical Point of View*, Harvard University Press, Cambridge, Massachusetts (1980), pp. 1–19.

Quine, Willard v.O.: 1951, "Two Dogmas of Empiricism", *Philosophical Review* 60: 20–43.

Quine, Willard v.O.: 1960, *Word and Object*, MIT Press, Cambridge, Massachusetts.

Railton, Peter: 1986, "Moral Realism", *Philosophical Review* 95: 163–207.

Rawls, John: 1971, *A Theory of Justice*, Harvard University Press, Cambridge, Massachusetts.

Rayo, Agustín: 2013, *The Construction of Logical Space*, Oxford University Press, Oxford.

Raz, Joseph: 1999, "Explaining Normativity: On Rationality and the Justification of Reason", *Ratio* 12: 354–79.

Richard, Mark: 2008, *When Truth Gives Out*, Oxford University Press, Oxford.

Ridge, Michael: 2006, "Ecumenical Expressivism: Finessing Frege", *Ethics* 116: 302–36.

Ridge, Michael: 2007, "Ecumenical Expressivism: The Best of Both Worlds?", *Oxford Studies in Metaethics* 2: 51–76.

Ridge, Michael: 2012, "Supervenience and the Nature of Normativity", in Susana Nuccetelli and Gary Seay (eds.), *Ethical Naturalism: Current Debates*, Cambridge: Cambridge University Press, pp. 144–68.

Ridge, Michael: 2014a, *Impassioned Belief*, Oxford University Press, Oxford.

Ridge, Michael: 2014b, "Moral Non-Naturalism", in Edward N. Zalta (ed.), *Stanford Encyclopedia of Philosophy*. Available at http://plato.stanford.edu/entries/moral-non-naturalism.

Roberts, Debbie: 2011, "Shapelessness and the Thick", *Ethics* 121: 489–520.

Roberts, Debbie: 2013, "It's Evaluation, Only Thicker", in Simon Kirchin (ed.), *Thick Concepts*, Oxford University Press, Oxford, pp. 78–96.

Roberts, Debbie: 2015, "Review of Pekka Väyrynen, *The Lewd, the Rude and the Nasty*", *Ethics* 125: 910–15.

Sayre-McCord, Geoffrey: 2015, "Moral Realism", in Edward N. Zalta (ed.), *Stanford Encyclopedia of Philosophy*. Available at http://plato.stanford.edu/entries/moral-realism.

Scanlon, T.M.: 2003, "Thickness and Theory", *Journal of Philosophy* 100: 275–87.

Scanlon, T.M.: 2014, *Being Realistic About Reasons*, Oxford University Press, Oxford.

Schaffer, Jonathan: 2004, "Two Conceptions of Sparse Properties", *Pacific Philosophical Quarterly* 85: 92–102.

Scheffler, Samuel: 1987, "Morality Through Thick and Thin: A Critical Notice of *Ethics and the Limits of Philosophy*", *Philosophical Review* 96: 411–34.

Schiffer, Stephen: 2003, *The Things We Mean*, Oxford University Press, Oxford.

Schilpp, P.A.: 1942, *The Philosophy of G. E. Moore*, Open Court, La Salle, Illinois.

Schoenfield, Miriam: 2016, "Moral Vagueness is Ontic Vagueness", *Ethics* 126: 257–82.

Schroeder, Mark: 2007, *Slaves of the Passions*, Oxford University Press, Oxford.

Schroeder, Mark: 2008, "Review of Ralph Wedgwood, *The Nature of Normativity*", *Notre Dame Philosophical Reviews*. Available at https://ndpr.nd.edu/news/23382-the-nature-of-normativity.

Schroeder, Mark: 2009, "Hybrid Expressivism: Virtues and Vices", *Ethics* 119: 257–309.

Schroeter, Laura and Francois Schroeter: 2003, "A Slim Semantics for Thin Moral Terms?", *Australasian Journal of Philosophy* 81: 191–207.

Schroeter, Laura and Francois Schroeter: 2005, "Is Gibbard a Realist?", *Journal of Ethics & Social Philosophy* 1: 1–18.

Schroeter, Laura and Francois Schroeter: 2013, "Normative Realism: Co-Reference Without Convergence?", *Philosophers' Imprint* 13: 1–24.

Schwarz, Wolfgang: 2014, "Against Magnetism", *Australasian Journal of Philosophy* 92: 17–36.

Shafer-Landau, Russ: 2003, *Moral Realism: A Defense*, Oxford University Press, Oxford.

Sider, Theodore: 2009, "Ontological Realism", in David Chalmers, David Manley, and Ryan Wasserman (eds.), *Metametaphysics*, Oxford University Press, Oxford, pp. 384–423.

Sider, Theodore: 2011, *Writing the Book of the World*, Oxford University Press, Oxford.

Slote, Michael: 1975, "Inapplicable Concepts and Sexual Perversion", in Robert Baker and Frederick Elliston (eds.), *Philosophy & Sex*, Prometheus Books, Buffalo, New York, pp. 261–7.

Smith, Michael: 1994, *The Moral Problem*, Blackwell, Oxford.

Smith, Michael: 2013, "On the Nature and Significance of the Distinction between Thick and Thin Ethical Concepts", in Simon Kirchin (ed.), *Thick Concepts*, Oxford University Press, Oxford, pp. 97–120.

Sorensen, Roy: 2012, "Vagueness", in Edward N. Zalta (ed.), *Stanford Encyclopedia of Philosophy*. Available at http://plato.stanford.edu/entries/vagueness.

Stevenson, Charles L.: 1944, *Ethics and Language*, Yale University Press, New Haven.

Stich, Stephen: 1990, *The Fragmentation of Reason*, MIT Press, Cambridge, Massachusetts.

Strandberg, Caj: 2012, "A Dual-Aspect Account of Moral Language", *Philosophy and Phenomenological Research* 84: 87–122.

Streumer, Bart: 2011, "Are Normative Properties Descriptive Properties?", *Philosophical Studies* 154: 325–48.

Szabó, Zoltan: 2001, "Adjectives in Context", in Robert Harnish and István Kenesei (eds.), *Perspectives on Semantics, Pragmatics, and Discourse*, John Benjamins, Amsterdam, pp. 119–46.

Tappenden, Jamie: 1993a, "The Liar and Sorites Paradoxes: Toward a Unified Treatment", *Journal of Philosophy* 90: 550–77.

Tappenden, Jamie: 1993b, "Analytic Truth – It's Worse (or Perhaps Better) than You Thought", *Philosophical Topics* 21: 233–61.

Tersman, Folke: 2006, *Moral Disagreement*, Cambridge University Press, Cambridge.

Thomson, Judith Jarvis: 2008, *Normativity*, Open Court, La Salle, Illinois.

Tiffany, Evan: 2007, "Deflationary Normative Pluralism", *Canadian Journal of Philosophy*, suppl. vol. 33: 231–62.

Tresan, Jon: 2009, "The Challenge of Communal Internalism", *Journal of Value Inquiry* 43: 179–99.

van Roojen, Mark: 2006, "Knowing Enough to Disagree: A New Response to the Moral Twin Earth Argument", *Oxford Studies in Metaethics* 1: 161–94.

Väyrynen, Pekka: 2009, "Objectionable Thick Concepts in Denials", *Philosophical Perspectives* 23: 439–69.

Väyrynen, Pekka: 2013, *The Lewd, The Rude, and the Nasty*, Oxford University Press, Oxford.

Väyrynen, Pekka: 2014, "Essential Contestability and Evaluation", *Australasian Journal of Philosophy* 92: 371–88.

Wasserman, Ryan: 2012, "Personal Identity, Indeterminacy, and Obligation", in Georg Gasser and Matthias Stefan (eds.), *Personal Identity: Simple or Complex?*, Cambridge University Press, Cambridge, pp. 63–81.

Weatherson, Brian: 2012, "The Role of Naturalness in Lewis's Theory of Meaning", *Journal for the History of Analytical Philosophy* 1: 1–19.

Wedgwood, Ralph: 2001, "Conceptual Role Semantics for Moral Terms", *Philosophical Review* 110: 1–30.

Wedgwood, Ralph: 2007, *The Nature of Normativity*, Clarendon Press, Oxford.

Wedgwood, Ralph: 2010, "*The Nature of Normativity*: A Reply to Holton, Railton, and Lenman", *Philosophical Studies* 151: 479–91.

Whiting, Daniel: 2007, "Inferentialism, Representationalism and Derogatory Words", *International Journal of Philosophical Studies* 15: 191–205.

Whiting, Daniel: 2008, "Conservatives and Racists: Inferential Role Semantics and Pejoratives", *Philosophia* 36: 375–88.

Whiting, Daniel: 2013, "It's Not What You Said, It's the Way That You Said It: Slurs and Conventional Implicatures", *Analytic Philosophy* 54: 364–77.

Wiggins, David: 1987, "A Sensible Subjectivism?", in *Needs, Values, Truth*, Basil Blackwell, Oxford, pp. 185–214.

Williams, Bernard: 1981, *Moral Luck*, Cambridge University Press, Cambridge.

Williams, Bernard: 1985, *Ethics and the Limits of Philosophy*, Harvard University Press, Cambridge, Massachusetts.

Williams, J.R.G.: 2007, "Eligibility and Inscrutability", *Philosophical Review* 116: 361–99.

Williams, J.R.G.: forthcoming, "Normative Reference Magnets".

Williamson, Timothy: 2003, "Understanding and Inference", *Proceedings of the Aristotelian Society*, suppl. vol. 77: 249–93.

Williamson, Timothy: 2006, "Conceptual Truth", *Proceedings of the Aristotelian Society*, suppl. vol. 80: 1–41.

Williamson, Timothy: 2007, *The Philosophy of Philosophy*, Blackwell, Oxford.

Williamson, Timothy: 2009, "Reference, Inference, and the Semantics of Pejoratives", in Joseph Almog and Paolo Leonardi (eds.), *The Philosophy of David Kaplan*, Oxford University Press, Oxford, pp. 137–59.

Williamson, Timothy: forthcoming, "Gibbard on Meaning and Normativity", *Inquiry*.

Wittgenstein, Ludwig: 1929/65, "A Lecture on Ethics", *Philosophical Review* 74: 3–12. Posthumous publication of a lecture given in 1929.

Wolf, Susan: 1982, "Moral Saints", *Journal of Philosophy* 79: 419–39.

Wood, Allen W.: 1979, "Marx on Right and Justice: A Reply to Husami", *Philosophy and Public Affairs* 8: 267–95.

Wright, Crispin: 1992, *Truth and Objectivity*, Harvard University Press, Cambridge, Massachusetts.

Yablo, Stephen: 2000, "Red, Bitter, Best", *Philosophical Books* 41: 13–23.

Index

.

Ingram Content Group UK Ltd.
Milton Keynes UK
UKHW021807160723
425189UK00005B/88

9 780198 717829